4/04

49.95

This book was donated
to honor
the birthday of

Neil Segel

by

Meryl + Ronald Segel

2003

DATE

ENCYCLOPEDIA
OF MODERN
EVERYDAY INVENTIONS

ENCYCLOPEDIA OF MODERN EVERYDAY INVENTIONS

David J. Cole, Eve Browning,
and Fred E.H. Schroeder

GREENWOOD PRESS
Westport, Connecticut • London

Library of Congress Cataloging-in-Publication Data

Cole, David John, 1948–
    Encyclopedia of modern everyday inventions / David J. Cole, Eve Browning, and Fred
E.H.Schroeder.
        p.   cm.
    Includes bibliographical references and index.
    ISBN 0–313–31345–8 (alk. paper)
        1. Inventions—History—20th century.   I. Cole, Eve Browning, 1952–   II. Schroeder,
Fred E.H., 1932–   III. Title.
    T20.C56   2003
    609′.04—dc21   2002069620

British Library Cataloguing in Publication Data is available.

Copyright © 2003 by David J. Cole, Eve Browning, and Fred E.H. Schroeder

Library of Congress Catalog Card Number: 2002069620
ISBN 0–313–31345–8

First published in 2003

Greenwood Press, 88 Post Road West, Westport, CT 06881
An imprint of Greenwood Publishing Group, Inc.
www.greenwood.com

Printed in the United States of America

The paper used in this book complies with the
Permanent Paper Standard issued by the National
Information Standards Organization (Z39.48–1984).

10 9 8 7 6 5 4 3 2 1

Contents

Introduction

HOW THIS BOOK IS ORGANIZED

The scope of the *Encyclopedia of Modern Everyday Inventions* is implied in the title, but obviously it cannot cover everything that has been commonly found in homes, schools, shops, markets, offices, garages, yards, and playgrounds. The original plan was to limit the scope to fifty inventions, especially appliances. As the authors started research, they found that many inventions overlapped and that it would be better to cluster some of these under a general heading of a type of purpose or function. Thus fluorescent lamps and halogen lamps are included under **"Electric Lights,"** Scotch tape and Band-Aids under **"Adhesives Tapes,"** and razors and hair dryers under **"Hair Care Products."** On the other hand, some categories proved to be far too broad, like **"Sound Technologies,"** so separate articles were made for the now-obsolete record-playing **"Phonographs,"** their commercial application in **"Jukeboxes,"** magnetic technologies in **"Audio Recording"** and digital technologies in **"Compact Discs."** The result is that the alphabetized articles contain many more than fifty inventions. The index and cross-references will lead readers to the specific devices that interest them, while the full articles place each invention into a larger historical, technological, and cultural picture.

The basic methodology of the articles is historical. Precursors of inventions are mentioned where appropriate. Some inventions have been well chronicled in company histories, while for other inventions the authors have had to piece together the history from magazine articles, museum exhibits, consumer guides, and websites of antique collectors. Explanations of how things work and their underlying scientific principles are provided with a minimum of technical language. The human aspects of inventions are emphasized, both in the challenges faced by inventors and in people's responses to new products. Finally, each article speculates upon trends for the future. This has always been a chancy activity; unforeseen technologies can wipe out the entire direction of development. For example, at mid-century in 1950 no one predicted that typewriters, phonograph records, cash registers, and pinball machines would disappear except as collectible antiques (see the articles on **Digital Telecommunications, Phonographs, Calculators and Cash Registers,** and **Video Games and Computer Games,** respectively, for the stories of these). On the other hand, many prophets of 1950 assumed that personal helicopters would be in our garages in just a few years!

HUMAN INVENTIVENESS

Many of us tend to believe that inventors are very special people, almost god-like in their creativity. The ancient Greeks had several myths that comment on this. One is of Prometheus, a man who stole the "secret technology" of fire from the gods. Possessing control over fire divided humanity from all the other creatures, and opened the way to control nature by providing heat and light, and to refashion nature into new forms by cooking, ceramics, and metallurgy. In the myth the gods punish Prometheus with eternal torture for his audacity in making humans like the gods. Fire is the technological part of the story. But the name Prometheus in Greek means "forethinker," and Prometheus represents the uniquely human ability to think ahead and envision how things might be different. Another myth, that of Pandora (this name means "all-gifted"), tells of a woman who has been endowed by the gods with all good things such as grace and beauty, but who also has the very human characteristic of curiosity, which, like Prometheus' daring, has double-edged consequences, releasing all the evils that plague humanity, such as illness, aging, and death.

The point is that while there is something "god-like" about great inventors and inventions, essentially these are characteristics that are common to most human beings. Curiosity—I wonder if, I wonder why, I wonder how—and forethought—how could I change things from the way they are—are aspects of inventiveness. And so is a bit of audacity—why not try to do something about it? Invention has even become a part of the curriculum in many elementary schools. Children think about some sort of problem, such as how to feed your pet when you are away, or how to turn pages on a music stand when both your hands are busy, and then they devise some way to solve the problem, building models of their inventions. The authors have seen invention fairs where over a hundred fourth and fifth graders display and demonstrate their inventions. But for many everyday people, there are little everyday problems that people solve alone, such as how to end the clutter in the kitchen drawer, or how to pick up pet hair from furniture, or how not to misplace your remote, or how to unmold a gelatin dessert, or how to store recyclables more easily, or how to hold a camera steady. Usually the solutions stay at home. Sometimes they are shared over a soda or cup of coffee. Sometimes the solutions show up in "how-to" features in newspapers, magazines, chat rooms. Sometimes they are patented. Sometimes they go commercial. And sometimes they make millionaires.

There are several stages in the life of any invention that eventually came to affect our daily lives. As a result, there may be several different individuals or groups who might lay claim to being the inventor. Someone first had the idea, and may or may not have gone on and published or developed the idea. Someone attempted to build the first device; someone else may have perfected it and made it practical. Another person or firm may have introduced the first commercial model, a version actually placed on the market. Yet another may have been lucky enough, perhaps through marketing or other factors, to produce not the first but the first commercially successful product of this type. Still others may have modified the product to the form that led it to a successful maturity. In this book, we have tried to identify figures and firms that bring inventions from the dawn of the idea on one unique day through the stages that lead to the invention becoming a familiar presence in homes every day.

INVENTION IN THE TWENTIETH CENTURY

One characteristic of twentieth-century invention is the accelerated pace of change and sheer number of inventions. This acceleration began for the modern world in the period of European history known as the Renaissance (ca. 1400–ca. 1650) with such famous inventors as Leonardo da Vinci (firearm and lock mechanisms), Johannes Gutenberg (movable type printing), and Galileo Galilei (thermometer and improved telescope). This period also introduced the idea of patenting inventions, that is, granting to inventors the exclusive right for a number of years to manufacture and market their inventions. Each century from the 1400s on saw an increase in the number of patents, to the point where in the late 1800s an official with the U.S. Patent Office stated that his agency would soon have to close, because almost everything possible had been invented!

Another characteristic of twentieth-century invention is globalization. Although there had been great periods of inventive activity all over the world in ancient times, in modern history up to the twentieth century the centers of invention were in Western Europe, and later, in the United States. Some nations (for example, China, Japan, India, and Islamic countries) actually discouraged change for different reasons, such as fear that any change might jeopardize the secure social and political structure, or simply that tampering with divine will was sinful. Other nations were held back by the forces of illiteracy and repressive colonialism.

Very important agents for change and invention were certain universities where professors and students were actively encouraged to question, research, experiment, discover, and invent. These were especially vital in Great Britain, Germany, the Low Countries, and Scandinavia. Hand in hand with the free inquiry in universities was active encouragement from governments. National rivalries figured in as well. The adage "build a better mousetrap and the world will beat a path to your door" encapsulates the rivalries of nineteenth-century nations: for instance, if England had a better way of producing steel or cloth than Germany or France, the economic rewards and power went to the nation with the best methods and patents. And then the other nations would try to top those with other inventions.

With the twentieth century these influences spread, at first to Japan and the Soviet Union, later to such nations as China and India. Along with universities and national rivalry, profit-oriented research and development laboratories were created by industries specifically to find marketable new products and processes. Increasingly, they learned that discoveries in "pure science" might have the potential for later practical (and profitable) application.

The tremendous growth of invention in the twentieth century has affected all areas of human activity. Our focus is on the home, domestic technology that we encounter on a day-to-day basis. Military devices, many of which provided basic research and technologies for domestic and business uses, are not here, because they are not "everyday." Advances in medicine and surgery have touched our lives and culture, but they are not "everyday" in the sense that radios and frozen dinners are. Some other health-related things that are indeed "everyday," such as aspirin, vitamin supplements, and cold remedies, have also been bypassed here. A very large group of everyday items was omitted because they probably merit books of their own: sporting goods, dolls, board games, and mechanical toys. Very likely the most important omission is the automobile, arguably one of the most influential forces in twentieth-century culture worldwide. This omission was easily made: First, there are many, many books on the development of automobiles. Second, the subject is vast, as automobiles are not single inventions, but a system of many inventions, such as the internal combustion engine, pneumatic rubber tires, automatic shifts, emission controls, body design, and so on, as well as the many variants on the family car that are also everyday things, such as trucks, buses, recreational vehicles, and motorcycles.

Nevertheless, the automobile can serve as an example whose history resembles that of quite a number of the sections in *Encyclopedia of Modern Everyday Inventions.* The automobile's roots are in the last part of the nineteenth century. It does not become everyday until vital improvements were made in the twentieth century. Its early history is marked by individual inventors, some of whom achieved heroic reputations, like Henry Ford. Most of the automobile's subsequent history is not about individual inventions, but results from teams of engineers working in sophisticated corporate research laboratories. Its popularity depends upon mass production, mass marketing and expenditures of huge sums of money. Inventions of the first half of the twentieth century tend to be like this; in the latter half, when transistors, microchips, lasers, and other totally new developments became available, the main sources for inventions are big research laboratories. But the individual inventors are there too.

ENABLING TECHNOLOGIES FOR TWENTIETH-CENTURY INVENTIONS

Looking at the invention of things that became popular as everyday items, one can see four periods in the twentieth century that set it apart from the previous century. First was the spread of electric power into homes and businesses. This was started by Thomas Edison in the 1880s, and when its potential was demonstrated dramatically at the World's Columbian Exposition (the "Chicago World's Fair") in 1892 where all buildings and walkways were supplied with electric lights powered from a single dynamo—electrification was set to spread throughout the world. It was a gradual process, and in the United States many rural areas did not receive the benefits of electric lights and appliances until 1940, when federal projects such as the Tennessee Valley Authority's dams and hydroelectric plants provided electrical power. Even in cities and towns up to about 1920 electricity was supplied only during the daytime and early evening. Many electric appliances were invented in these early years, but their use was hardly convenient, as there were no plugs or receptacles. Irons for pressing clothes were the first popular appliance, although they had to be screwed into a lighting socket. Several inventors developed small motors that made possible electrified sewing machines, kitchen appliances, and vacuum cleaners. These first two decades were also the period of perfecting reliable internal combustion engines for automobiles. These also effected a slow revolution on farms, though horses, windmills, and steam threshers did not lose their importance for powering agriculture until the 1930s.

A second period of enabling inventions saw the development of radio communication and the commercial availability of synthetic materials, especially plastics of various kinds. The basic chemistry for creating polymers (artificially engineered long molecular chains) was partly established in the nineteenth century, and one successful invention at that time was to have a profound effect on popular culture. This was celluloid, originally developed as a substitute for ivory in billiard balls. But when George Eastman (1854–1932) used its flexibility and transparency to make roll-films in his Kodak cameras in 1889, the stage was set for billions of snapshots and thousands of movies. In 1909, Leo Hendrik Baekeland patented Bakelite, a hard plastic still used as an insulating material in electric and electronic products. The year 1912 saw Jacques E. Brandenburger's invention of cellophane, recognized immediately as a transparent food wrap, good for enhancing displays, for preservation, and for cleanliness, as well as for eventually leading to the invention of "Scotch" tapes. In 1928 the E.I. DuPont company, which manufactured various chemical products such as explosives, dyes, and paints using other inventors' patents, decided to establish a research laboratory, headed by Wallace H. Corothers (1896–1937). From this came such products as Lucite (1937), Nylon (1938, the first stockings), Orlon (1942), and many other synthetics. Other important plastics included PVC (polyvinyl chloride), introduced commercially by B.F. Goodrich in 1927 and used for water pipes, floor tiling, garden hoses, and phonograph records among many other applications, and Plexiglas, invented by Otto Rohm and Otto Haas in 1935. The effects on everyday products of these and many later synthetics seem endless: bottles, toys, wash-and-wear clothing, housings for telephones, cameras, computers; pill capsules, eyeglasses, contact lenses, grocery bags, audio and video tapes, sports equipment, automobile bodies, etc. As seen above, some date back to the previous century, such as celluloid and rayon fiber (both highly inflammable, and later reworked for safety), but most important early breakthroughs were in the 1930s and 1940s.

The third period is that of the late 1940s to the 1960s when transistors, printed circuits, microchips, and improved electric batteries contributed to making all sorts of devices more portable. The first electronic computers required entire rooms to hold them and depended upon radio vacuum tubes, which generated wasteful heat and required constant maintenance. In 1967, Texas Instruments introduced a "pocket calculator" capable of doing mathematical and scientific functions more rapidly than the giant machines of the 1940s. As calculators became smaller and cheaper, they became part of the world's everyday culture, and the technology was extended to radios, cameras, toys and games, and kitchen appliances, making things lighter, more durable, and portable.

The fourth period of enabling technologies is that of digital electronics and lasers. At first designed for uses in science and industry, they burst into the world of popular culture in 1980 with the marketing of compact discs, surprising the entertainment industry by quickly rendering LP records obsolete. Soon after, digital cameras were introduced, threatening to put an end to the century-old "celluloid" negatives, slides, and movies. At the very end of the twentieth century, the inventions that had revolutionized everyday lives in its early years appeared to be doomed. Digital messages relayed from satellites via laser beams and electromagnetic waves promised to render household electric wiring obsolete, while the commercial reintroduction of battery-powered cars indicated that the days of the internal combustion engine were numbered.

Inventions in the twentieth century radically changed everyday life. The drudgery of household washing, the incredible isolation of rural life, the accessibility of information—all these aspects of life were transformed in this tumultuous century. Behind those changes are the stories of inventors and opportunities, bright and dim ideas, cooperative activity and battles for invention credit (see **Television** for examples of all of these). Some products were born, grew to become essential, and disappeared entirely within the century (see, for example, Phonographs, and the discussion of photoflash bulbs in **Electric Lights**). There were problems searching for solutions (see **Compact Discs**), and solutions searching for problems (see Post-its in **Glues and Adhesives**). And there are, of course, many problems still searching for better solutions (see **Batteries**). We expect the next century of everyday inventions will be just as exciting as the last.

REFERENCES

Bronowski, Jacob. *The Ascent of Man.* Boston: Little, Brown, 1973.

Buechner, Maryanne, Lev Grossman, and Anita Hamilton. "Coolest Inventions 2002," *Time* 160:21 (November 18, 2002), 73–121.

Burke, James. *Connections.* Boston: Little, Brown, 1978.

Discover. Twentieth Anniversary Issue. October 2000.

McGrath, Kimberly, ed. *World of Invention,* 2nd ed. Detroit: Gale, 1999.

Petroski, Henry. *The Evolution of Useful Things.* New York: Knopf, 1992.

Scientific American. End-of-the-Millennium Special Issue: What Science Will Know in 2050. December 1999.

Timeline of Inventions

PRECURSORS TO TWENTIETH-CENTURY INVENTIONS

1623   First mechanical calculator, the "Calculating Clock" by Wilhelm Schickard (1592–1635)

1642   Blaise Pascal (1623–1662) builds "Pascaline" calculator at age 19

1684   In Royal Society lecture, "On Showing a Way How to Communicate One's Mind at Great Distances," Robert Hooke (1635–1703) describes a system of telecommunications using the recently developed telescope and a signaling device mounted high on poles

Early 1800s   Claude Chappé (1755–1805) and his brothers develop a semaphore telegraph system that was built throughout France under Napoleon

1800   Alessandro Volta (1745–1819) invents voltaic cell, which is the basic unit of electric batteries

1800   M. Biggin invents coffee percolator

1805   Oliver Evans (1755–1819) conceives design for a refrigeration machine

1806   Ralph Wedgwood invents carbon paper

1830s and 1840s   Electrical telegraphy developed by Samuel Morse (1791–1872) and others

1831   Friedrich Wilhelm Froebel's (1782–1852) educational building blocks

1842   First facsimile machine invented by Alexander Bain (1811–1877), a Scot

1846   Nancy Johnson invents home ice-cream maker

1848   In London, Frederick Bakewell invents a machine that could transmit a signature or other line drawing on metal foil wrapped around a rotating cylinder

1860s   Louis du Hauron describes idea for making color photographic film

1860–1889   Gaston Planté (1834–1889) invents and advances "wet cell" storage batteries

1865   John Alexander patents hand-operated dishwashing machine

1866   Hiram Maxim (1849–1916) invents hair-curling iron (heated externally)

1866   George Leclanché invents prototype of flashlight battery

1873   First practical typewriter ("Remington") produced by Christopher Latham Sholes (1819–1890) and Carlos Gliddens

1875   Thomas Alva Edison (1847–1931) invents mimeograph duplicator

1877   Eadweard Muybridge (1830–1904) produces first "moving pictures" of galloping horse

1877   Thomas Alva Edison invents the phonograph

1878   Oberlin Smith (1840–1926) applies for a patent caveat for magnetic recording

1879   First cash register is invented by James J. Ritty, a saloon keeper in Dayton, Ohio

1880s   Joseph Swan (1828–1914) and Thomas Alva Edison (1847–1931) develop incandescent lamp

1881   Englishman Shelford Bidwell demonstrates a device (precursor of television) that could reproduce a picture using a selenium photocell in a scanner

1882   Etienne-Jules Marey (1830–1904) invents "photographic gun," first motion picture camera

1883   Paul Nipkow (1860–1940) receives a German patent for a mechanical "electric telescope," precursor of television

1886   Josephine Cochrane builds dishwasher consisting of a wheel mounted inside a copper boiler

1887   Emile Berliner (1851–1929) patents the Gramophone and develops discs rather than cylinders for recording

1887   Heinrich Hertz (1857–1894) sends a wireless electric impulse across his laboratory, identifying the Hertzian wave as traveling at the speed of light

1888   Thomas Adams, Jr., installs vending machines for Tutti-Frutti chewing gum

1889   Prototype of jukebox appears in San Francisco with four listening tubes attached to an Edison phonograph

1889   George Eastman (1854–1932) introduces photographic film

1890s Guglielmo Marconi (1874–1932) experiments with sending Morse code messages via Hertzian waves

1892–1893   World's Columbian Exposition (Chicago World's Fair) is illuminated by electricity and introduces many appliances that became common in the following century

1894   Edison introduces the Kinetoscope, peepshow motion pictures

1894   First motion picture copyrighted in the U.S.: "Edison Kinescopic Record of a Sneeze"

1896   "Vitascope" motion picture projector introduced, based on work by Thomas Armat (1866–1948) and Edison

1897 Karl Ferdinand Braun (1850–1918) invents the cathode ray tube, basis of television receivers

THE TWENTIETH CENTURY

1900 Valdemar Poulsen (1869–1942) demonstrates the first commercial magnetic recorder: his Telegraphone records on piano wire

1901 Guglielmo Marconi (1874–1937) succeeds in receiving a transatlantic radio message

1901 H.S. Miller's peanut-vending machine introduced to public

1901 Herbert C. Booth patents a vacuum cleaner powered by a gasoline engine

1901 Frank Hornby's Meccano construction sets

1901 King Camp Gillette (1855–1932) invents disposable safety razor blade

1904 Dr. Arthur Korn (1870–1945) transmits a photo (wireless in 1905)

1904 John Ambrose Fleming (1849–1945) patents the oscillation valve, laying the groundwork for the vacuum tube

1905 H.W. Hillman's all-electric house in Schenectady, New York, demonstrates the viability of many electric appliances, although none are portable

1905 Albert Marsh invents nichrome wire for long-lasting electric heating elements

1905 Sarah Breedlove Walker (Madame C.J. Walker) (1867–1919) invents a heat and chemical process for straightening hair

1906 Charles L. Nessler invents "permanent wave" process

1906 John Gabel introduces a coin-operated machine allowing a choice of twenty-four phonograph discs

1906 Reginald Aubrey Fessenden (1866–1932) makes the first real radio sound broadcast

1906 Englishmen Charles Urban and G. Albert Smith patent a two-color "Kinemacolor" movie process

1906 Charles Franklin Kettering (1876–1958) adds an electric motor to the cash register

1906 Alva J. Fisher adds an electric motor to the washing machine, and receives the first electric washer patent on August 9, 1910

1907 Introduction of the tungsten filament for bright long-life incandescent lights

1907 Lee De Forest (1873–1961) invents the triode vacuum tube, making it possible to amplify a radio signal

1907–1908 David O. Kenney's patent for a vacuum cleaner system (wall-mounted); Corinne Dufour's portable upright invented about the same time; William Hoover manufactures Murray Spangler's version

1908   Melitta Bentz invents filter coffee maker

1908   Coin-operated Peerless Player Piano and later automatic musical instruments cause the end of coin-operated record-players for almost twenty years

c. 1908   Chester Beach perfects a small motor that operates on both AC and DC current

1908   Acetate safety movie film introduced

1908   Disposable paper cups introduced for soda-pop vending machines.

1909   Leo Hendrik Baekeland (1863–1944) patents Bakelite

1909–1910   Neon light developed by Georges Claude

1911   Charles Franklin Kettering's (1876–1958) electric starter introduced in Cadillac automobiles

1912   First feature-length film shown in the United States: *Queen Elizabeth,* featuring Sarah Bernhardt

1912   Italian film *Quo Vadis?* is longest early film, at almost two hours

1912   Jacques E. Brandenburger invents cellophane

1912   Hamilton-Beach produces a small lightweight motor that facilitates electrifying old-style sewing machines and many other tasks

1913   A.C. Gilbert's (1884–1961) Erector construction toys

1914   Alonzo Decker (1884–1959) and S.D. Black apply for patent for portable electric drill

1914 (1915)   Charles Pajeau's Tinkertoy construction sets

1914–1918   World War I. The United States enters the war in 1917; the actual Peace Treaty signed in 1919

1915   General Electric's Guardian refrigerator appears

1917   Gideon Sundback (1880–1956) patents zipper, originally used for rubber boots

1918   John Lloyd Wright's Lincoln Log construction toys

1919   Charles Nelson invents ice-cream bar

1919   Frigidaire refrigerator

1920s   First credit cards issued by American oil companies

1920s   Teletypewriters

1920s   First modern tampon, the Fax, sold

1920s   Clarence Birdseye (1886–1956) perfects methods of freezing fish and vegetables with a total of 168 patents

1920   Regularly scheduled radio broadcasts begin with Westinghouse's KDKA; by 1923 there are over 500 U.S. stations

1920   Kitchen Aid mixer for cake batters and other cooking needs

1920 24-year-old Russian Leon Theremin (Lev Termin) invents an all-electronic musical instrument

1920 Kotex disposable sanitary napkin introduced; worn with an elastic belt

1921 Earle Dickson's Band-Aid adhesive strips first marketed by Johnson & Johnson; the process was mechanized in 1924

1922 Stephen Poplawski patents the food blender, not marketed until the 1930s as the Osterizer

1922 First Technicolor film (two-color process)

1923 Lee De Forest (1873–1961) exhibits "Phonofilms"—talkies with sound recorded on the film

1923 Vladimir Kosma Zworykin (1899–1982) applies for patent on television camera tube

1923 Ditto (hektograph) duplicator invented in Germany

1923 Self-winding wristwatch patented

1924 Edmond Michel introduces Skilsaw, a hand-held portable circular saw

1924 Frank Epperson patents the Popsicle

1925 John Logie Baird (1888–1946) demonstrates electromechanical television system

1925 Richard Drew at 3M invents masking tape for auto painting

1925 Electrical amplification hastens the end of acoustic sound recording

1926 The Toastmaster pop-up bread toaster enters the domestic market, invented by Charles Strite in 1919 with improvements by Murray Ireland

1926 Richard Drew invents an adhesive paint-masking tape marketed by his 3M employer as Scotch brand

1927 PVC (polyvinyl chloride) introduced by B.F. Goodrich

1927 Justus Seeburg introduces first all-electric coin-operated phonograph

1927 Philo Taylor Farnsworth (1906–1971) invents working electronic television camera tube

1927 Film *The Jazz Singer*, starring Al Jolson, first feature-length talking motion picture

1927 Scottish inventor John Logie Baird (1888–1946) is the first to record a video signal

1928 Disney's *Steamboat Willie* is first sound cartoon

1928 Jacob Schick patents electric razor to be marketed in 1931

1928 Machine to slice whole loaf of bread at once

1928–1931 Experimental television broadcasts in Britain and the United States

1930s Pinball machines

1930s Latex rubber condoms introduced

1930s The Great Depression affects most of the world's economies

1930s U.S. federal dam projects (e.g., Tennessee Valley Authority) bring electric power to many rural areas

1930s Nickel-cadmium batteries perfected by German firm I.G. Farben

1930 Scotch transparent adhesive tape appears, originally as grocer's aid

1930 Richard Drew's 3M cellophane transparent tape enters the market

1930 Paul and Joseph Galvin's invention of a practical car radio marketed by Motorola (in 1937, they added push-button tuning)

1930 Presliced Wonder Bread

1932 Walt Disney is first to use a new three-color Technicolor process; first big color films not until 1939 (*Wizard of Oz* and *Gone with the Wind*)

1933 The first synthetic detergent in the United States, Dreft, introduced by Procter & Gamble

1933 and following German firms I.G. Farben and A.E.G. develop magnetic tape recorder, the Magnetophone

1934 First Laundromat, a "Washateria," opened in Fort Worth, Texas

1934 Tabletop electric broiler

1934 Edwin Howard Armstrong (1890–1954) demonstrates the superiority of frequency modulation

1935 General Electric's Disposall garbage disposer, developed by J.H. Powers

1935 Charles Darrow of Philadelphia patents Monopoly board game

1935 Otto Rohm and Otto Haas invent Plexiglas

1937 Men's clothing designers begin to experiment with zippers in trousers

1937 Bendix introduces the first automatic washer at the Louisiana State Fair

1937 Wallace Hume Carothers (1896–1937) of DuPont invents Nylon

1937 Lucite produced by DuPont Laboratories

1938 First commercial interior fluorescent lamps introduced by GE

1938 Nylon synthetic from DuPont Laboratories used for "silk" stockings

1938 Chester Floyd Carlson (1906–1968) invents basic process for Xerox copying

1938 Allen Dumont introduces first commercial television set in America

1939 Sir John Randall and Dr. Harry A. Boot at Birmingham University in England invent magnetron to produce high-energy microwaves

1939 DuPont chemist Roy J. Plunkett invents Teflon

1939 John Atanasoff (1903–1995) and Clifford Berry build electronic computer in Iowa

1939–1945 World War II; the United States enters the war in late 1941 after the Japanese attack on Pearl Harbor December 7; the war effort accelerates many inventions

1940s Les Paul is making recordings with his electric guitar, "The Log"

1940s Refrigeration and heating incorporated into drink-dispensing vending machines

1940 First multitrack stereo movie, Disney animated musical film *Fantasia*

1940 Frederick McKinley Jones (1893–1961) patents a reliable refrigeration machine for truckers

1943 Laszlo Biro files patent for ballpoint pen, developed in the 1930s with his brother

1945 Eugene Schneller of L'Oreal invents a cold permanent wave process

1945 William L. Maxson invents frozen dinners for Pan American Airlines

1945 Percy L. Spencer at Raytheon files patent for microwave cooking

1946 Black & Decker introduces first low-priced electric drills for do-it-yourselfers

1946? First heavy-duty synthetic laundry detergent, Procter & Gamble's Tide

1946 Earl Tupper introduces Tupperware

1947 Borden's introduces Cascorex, later renamed Elmer's Glue-All

1947 Home permanent wave kits introduced by Toni

1948 Peter Carl Goldmark's (1906–1977) inventions of the microgroove long-playing phonograph record incorporated in Columbia's LP system of 33⅓ revolutions per minute

1948 Bing Crosby has first pretaped radio show, using Ampex model 200 recorder

1948 Edwin Herbert Land (1901–1991) invents Polaroid Land instant photography

1948 Continental Can tests canned Pepsi-Cola

1948 Transistor invented at Bell Labs

1949 Kitchenaid introduces first home dishwasher machine

1949 Forerunner of Lego building blocks introduced in Denmark by inventor Ole Kirk Christiansen

1949 Norman Woodland and Bernard Silver invent barcodes, patented 1952

1950s GE develops halogen lamps

1950s Fast food franchise chains develop rapidly: Kentucky Fried Chicken in 1952, Burger King in 1954, McDonald's in 1955, Pizza Hut in 1958

1950s Carl Miller's Thermofax dry copier introduced by 3M

1950 Xerox 914 is first commercial office photocopier

1950 Diners' Club brings out first "universal" credit card acceptable worldwide for travel and entertainment

1950 Marion Donovan makes a prototype disposable diaper by cutting up a shower curtain and stuffing it with absorbent material; Pampers appear soon after

1950   Remington Rand Univac is first commercial computer

1950–1953   Electric dryers introduced by major manufacturers

1950   Zenith "Lazy Bones" wired remote control

1951   Eastman Kodak researchers Harry Coover and Fred Joyner rediscover cyanoacrylate, naming it Eastman Kodak #910; later brands include Crazy Glue and Super Glue

1951   R. Buckminster Fuller (1895–1983) submits patent for geodesic dome

1951   Crosby Enterprises demonstrates an experimental video tape recorder with 12 heads

1951   Velcro invented by Swiss inventor George de Mestral; patented 1955

1951   Franklin National Bank issues first bank credit card featuring revolving credit

1951   Oral contraceptives—"the pill"—developed

1952   Fred Waller introduces widescreen Cinerama

1952   Movies in 3D—the low-budget *Bwana Devil*

1953   Saran Wrap introduced

1953   CinemaScope system premiered with *The Robe*, developed by Fox using special lens system invented in 1920s by French professor Henri Chrétien

1953–1954   Sunbeam automatic frying pan has variable heat control, followed by H.K. Foster's detachable probe for S.W. Farber

1954   Clarke and Gilbert Swanson introduce the "TV Dinner" frozen meal

1954   First national color television broadcast, the New Year's Tournament of Roses on NBC; affiliated with RCA, which is producing color sets

1954   Musician inventor Les Paul works with Ampex in producing a three-track machine for studio recording

1955   Zenith light-operated wireless television remote control—the Flash-Matic

1955   Ohio stove manufacturer Tappan introduces first home microwave oven priced at $1,200

1956   General Electric's Toast-R-Oven combines toaster, oven, and broiler

1956   Ampex introduces very successful first spinning-head video recorder

1956   Zenith Space Command 400 is first successful ultrasonic television remote

1958   Jack Kilby (1923–), at Texas Instruments, and Robert Noyce (1927–1990), at Fairchild, create the first simple integrated circuits

1958   William A. Higinbotham uses oscilloscope and analog circuits to make "Tennis for Two" video game

1958   Lego plastic building-block toy patented

1960s   First mag stripes, on London Underground tickets

1960   Remington's "Lectronic" is first cordless electric razor

1961 Black & Decker's first cordless drill, powered by nickel-cadmium battery

1962 Launch of Telstar, the first communications satellite

1962 MIT students Steve Russell and friends create Spacewar, a space battle game

1962–1964 Dutch firm Philips introduces the compact tape cassette

1963 First all-transistor calculator, the Friden 130

1964 IBM and American Airlines create the largest civilian computing project to date, Sabre, a computerized airline reservation system

1964 Lava-Lamp invented

1964 Following FCC mandate, all televisions sold in the United States must be capable of receiving 82 channels, including 70 in new UHF band

1964 approx. Robert Moog and Don Buchla introduce first modular electronic music synthesizers to market

Mid-1960s Max Mathews at MIT develops Music V system for computer-based digital music synthesis

1965 Pull-tab for aluminum beverage can invented

1967 First handheld digital calculator—the Texas Instruments' "Cal-Tech"

1967 Douglas Englehart invents computer "mouse"

1967 Bull's-eye type barcode system installed in a Kroger grocery store in Cincinnati

1967 Amana introduces the first home countertop microwave oven, the Amana RadarRange

1968 Ralph Baer and associates file for the first videogame patent

1969 U.S. Defense Department establishes ancestor of Internet: ARPANET (Advanced Research Projects Agency NETwork), linking computers at four research sites

1969 Start of project to build first microprocessor, the Intel 4004

1969 Charles Hall invents waterbed (there had been earlier models)

1969 Sony introduced its first video cassette recorder, the U-Matic

1969 Sony introduces Trinitron one-gun picture tube

1970 Imax surround movie system premiered at Expo '70 in Osaka, Japan

1970 Magnetic stripe standards enacted; mag stripes appear on credit cards

1971 First home video game system, Magnavox Odyssey, developed

1972 Philips demonstrates a video laserdisc system

1972 Home Box Office introduces premium movie channel

1972 Pong video game

1972 Smartcards invented in France

1973 Carl Sontheimer's Cuisinart food processor

1973   UPC barcode adopted

1973   Snowboard patent by Robert Weber

1974   Transmission control protocol (TCP) developed to let quite different computers and networks exchange data

1975   Marcel Bich introduces Bic disposable razor

1975   Sony introduces $2,295 Betamax consumer VCR

1975   Yamaha introduces music synthesizers based on FM synthesis, discovered by John M. Chowning working at Stanford University

1975   Erno Rubik of Hungary invents Rubik's Cube

1976   JVC introduces VHS, a rival format to Betamax, for under $1,000

1976   Fairchild Camera and Instrument Company releases the first home game machine to put the games on removable cartridges, the Fairchild F system

1977   Highly successful Atari Video Computer System (later Atari 2600) cartridge-based video game system introduced

1978   Philips introduces the model 8000 LaserVision videodisc player

1978   First video rental store franchises

1978   X-10 home automation and remote control system

1979   First cellular phones appear in Japan

1980   Post-it removable adhesive notepaper introduced by 3M, the invention of Art Fry and Spencer Silver (patent had been applied for in 1970)

1980   Sony introduces the first consumer video camcorder

1981   RCA introduces its CED 100 SelectaVision video disc player

1981   IBM PC introduced

1981   Donkey Kong video game produced by Nintendo

1982   Philips and Sony jointly introduce compact disc with prerecorded digital audio

1983–1984   Home video game market collapses; many companies go out of business

1983   Nintendo introduces "FamCom" videogame system

1983   PacMan a hit arcade video game

1985   Sony introduces compact camcorders using 8-mm-wide tape

1985   CD-ROM standards adopted and drives introduced

1985   First soundcards for IBM PC computer

1987   Shin Ojima's programmable bread machine introduced in Japan

1987   Digital audio tape (DAT) recorders introduced

1990   Casio introduces first all-digital Phonemate telephone-answering machine

1991 Tim Berners-Lee develops standards at CERN in Europe for the World Wide Web (WWW)

1992 MiniDisc digital audio recording system introduced by Sony

1995 Nintendo introduces short-lived VirtualBoy 3D game system

1996 First DVD player appears in Japan, and United States the next year

1998 Lego Mindstorms integrate robotics with building-block toys

1998 Nintendo Gameboy gets a color screen

1999 Solar cell–powered radios introduced for consumers

Adhesive Tapes

String and sealing wax were early methods of holding things together. Gauze bandages were held in place by tied strips of cloth. In the twentieth century, these methods were augmented or replaced by tape products that use pressure-sensitive adhesives: Band-Aids, masking tapes, transparent tapes, and Duck Tape. The pressure-sensitive adhesives that made these possible are so named because they do not require heat, liquids, or mixing glues to be activated. Although there are hundreds of these products for many applications in industry and commerce, a few have become essentials of everyday living in much of the world.

BAND-AIDS

The earliest beginnings were cosmetic. In eighteenth-century England it became fashionable for ladies of the royal court to wear little decorative patches as "beauty spots" to draw attention to their choicest features such as a smooth brow, a graceful cheekbone, a curvaceous bosom. The spots were cut from silk and fastened with an adhesive composed of isinglass (a fish by-product) and glycerin. These court plasters (one meaning of plaster was a medical lotion that dried on the skin) would stick firmly but peel off easily. Court plasters were found to be useful for covering wounds, but other sticking plasters were developed using various natural adhesives like resins and waxes smeared on cloth tapes and dressings.

In 1845 Horace H. Day patented a surgical plaster composed of natural rubber and resin coated on cloth. Throughout the nineteenth century various tapes using natural (uncured) rubber were devised. It should be borne in mind that none of these were aseptic or antiseptic, as the germ theory of the English physician Joseph Lister (1827–1912) was new and most surgeons were slow to adopt Lister's antiseptic approach to washing hands and spraying operating theaters with carbolic acid. An American, Robert Wood Johnson (1845–1910), heard Lister speak in 1876 and thought of preparing a commercial line of germ-free surgical dressings. Nine years later he formed a partnership with his two brothers and began manufacturing in New Brunswick, New Jersey, incorporating as Johnson & Johnson in 1887. Johnson worked at finding methods to sterilize cotton dressings and, among other inventions, patented an adhesive compound of glue, glycerin, and sulfoleic acid in 1889. Many other inventions and surgical products were to come out of the Johnson & Johnson research laboratories. Band-Aids did not.

A cotton buyer for the company, Earle Dickson, was newly married in 1920. His bride was unaccustomed to kitchen work and had almost daily accidents with knives. Mr. Dickson would come home from work to find dinner ready and his bride with fresh cuts, scrapes, and burns, which he dressed in the usual manner, cutting a piece of gauze and applying this with adhesive tape. His breakthrough was to prepare ahead of time a strip of tape with squares of gauze at intervals, each covered with crinoline. Henceforth, when Josephine Dickson had her kitchen accidents, she simply cut off a ready-made bandage and applied it herself. Dickson's employers liked the idea and in 1921 began marketing handmade Band-Aids. By 1924 a machine had been developed to mass produce the home bandages. Various improvements and spin-offs have been made since: plastic strips, foam strips, dots, knuckle bandages, etc., but as an echo of the first court plasters in 1956 Band-Aids offered bright decorative patterns, perhaps not as beauty spots, but as youthful badges of valor.

MASKING TAPE

The Minnesota Mining and Manufacturing Company (3M) got into the business of adhesives with their original product, sandpaper, which required applying glue to paper or cloth and then sprinkling mineral grit such as silica, quartz, garnet, or aluminum oxide onto the tacky surface (see **Glues and Adhesives**). Their first big commercial success was a "wet or dry" abrasive, made possible by the invention of a waterproof glue by Francis G. Okie of Philadelphia. In 1921 3M bought Okie's patent and hired him to continue experimenting with adhesives. The main advantage of wet sanding cloth was health: most paints were lead-based, so dry sanding produced a dangerous amount of poisonous dust. This was especially severe in the auto industry, where several coats of paint had to be sanded smooth.

Richard Drew (1899?–1980), a young 3M research engineer, took some experimental sandpaper to demonstrate at an auto-paint shop in St. Paul in 1926. 3M had a policy of soliciting complaints and suggestions from factory workers who used 3M products, but the complaints Drew heard were not about abrasives. Two-color car bodies had become popular, but the workers were frustrated by the problem of masking one color while they sprayed on the second color. If they glued butcher paper to the body, the paper often had to be scraped off, injuring the finish. If they used surgical cloth tape to fasten newspaper masking, the paint bled through. Either way the job had to redone and costs rose. Drew decided to see if any of Okie's sticky blends might work on paper tape. After months of trying various materials, Drew found that a mixture of wood-glue and glycerin ap-

When 3M Corporation introduced "Pop-up" Scotch tape strips in the late 1990s, this advertisement reviewed the history of rolled tapes. It doesn't include the more specialized rolls of two-sided tapes and removable tapes, or the many types of nonroll "Post-its." (Courtesy 3M Corporation)

plied to smooth kraft paper (like grocery bag paper) would stick on and peel off without leaving any adhesive or lifting any paint. There still were problems that were finally solved by putting an improved adhesive on crepe kraft paper such as paper hand towels were made of. The goo wouldn't stick to the back of this paper, it had some stretchability for taping on curved surfaces, and it could be produced in handy rolls.

3M named this Scotch brand masking tape and marketed it with a plaid design. Consumers soon found that this pressure-sensitive paper tape had other uses than masking paint. It could be used to put posters on walls, to seal packages, to label objects, and to pick up lint from clothing.

SCOTCH CELLOPHANE TAPE

The even more versatile clear cellophane Scotch tape was also invented by Richard Drew in response to a specific industrial need. DuPont had introduced cellophane in the early 1920s. Made as a wood by-product, impervious to air and water, unaffected by heat, and crystal clear, it was an ideal food wrap. But Drew's challenge was to develop a sealer for slabs of insulation. Masking tape didn't work. A lab technician had been thinking of packaging rolls of masking tape in cellophane, for, with all its virtues, masking tape aged fast from exposure to moisture and aridity. Drew looked at the cellophane and conceived of a transparent cellophane tape that would seal the insulation, and also seal cellophane packages transparently. Experimentation with various glues (the first ones were too dark) finally resulted in 1930 with the famous Scotch tape. The uses people found for it were endless: patching split fingernails, mending turkey eggs, repairing torn pages, attaching labels to home-canned food, mending rips in clothing, holding broken toys together, fastening notices to documents and walls.

There were problems. It was hard to cut off pieces of tape, and the transparent end stuck invisibly to the roll. This was solved not by one of the research staff, but by a sales manager, John Borden, who invented the familiar tape dispenser with the serrated cutting edge. A more serious problem was that libraries and art collectors found to their dismay that after a period of time Scotch tape was hopelessly ruinous to precious paper. Another problem was that the gummy residue messed walls and windows. As photocopying machines came into common use, users discovered that Scotch tape was not really transparent, leaving ugly rectangular shadows on their copies. 3M continued product improvement, introducing Scotch Magic Transparent Tape to address all these shortcomings.

DUCK TAPE

The invention of Duck Tape is obscure. According to *The Duct Tape Book,* a partly whimsical, partly factual collection of uses for this versatile cloth adhesive tape, the origin was in World War II. The military needed a strong, waterproof tape for quick repairs to equipment and as a seal for ammunition cases. Johnson & Johnson's Permacel Division was handed the problem and developed a rubber-based adhesive to be applied to a mesh cloth that could be ripped rather than cut.

After the war, the military repair tape was found to be an ideal sealer for the joints in heating and air conditioning duct work. Johnson & Johnson did not add this tape to their line of medical supplies, but apparently transferred it to the Melvin A. Anderson company of Cleveland, Ohio, in 1950. A sometime employee of Anderson, Jack Kahl, bought the firm in 1971, and renamed it Manco, Inc. The silver duct tape was only one of the Manco pressure-sensitive tapes in their line of paint and hardware products, but customers kept writing to Manco extolling the different uses they had discovered. This prompted a promotional campaign, giving the punning name "Duck Tape" and a logo with a duckling wearing various working garments such as a painter's cap or tool belt. Users developed a genuine affection for this versatile product, which could mend canoes, tents, car bodies, torn carpets, football and hockey gear, hoses, and tool handles. It could fasten power cords to arena floors, seal packages, and be applied to literally hundreds of other uses. Manco, like 3M and Johnson & Johnson, manufactures many different kinds of pressure-sensitive products for specialized uses, but Duck Tape joins Post-its and Band-Aids in holding a special place in international popular culture. In volume, however, commercial labeling and package sealing, industrial uses, and medical applications outweigh everyday consumer uses.

The future of pressure-sensitive products points to more specialized uses in business, industry, the military, and outer space. Curiously, the most popular and successful products were developed before there was a physical and chemical theoretical base. According to Istvan Benedek, basic research began in the late 1970s. The physical structure of pressure-sensitive adhesives is now understood to be tiny balls with spaces in between that act like suction cups. Practical improvements in resistance to aging and temperature extremes continue. Special applications, such as double-sided carpet tape, and labels for new media, such as computer diskettes, videotape cassettes, and recorded CDs, continue to be developed (see articles on **Home Video** and **Compact Discs**). For consumers, easier to clean up price and other product labels are needed. In this area, the industry has done more for the security needs of retailers than for the convenience of consumers. Fortunately, the rise of the use of **barcodes** has made price labels less common than they once were, and back at home consumers have benefited from the wide assortment of sticky tapes developed in the twentieth century.

REFERENCES

Benedek, Istvan. *Development and Manufacture of Pressure-Sensitive Products*. New York: Marcel Dekker, Inc., 1998.

Huck, Virginia. *Brand of the Tartan: The 3M Story*. New York: Appleton-Century-Crofts, 1955.

Johnson & Johnson. *A Brief History of Johnson & Johnson*. New Brunswick, NJ: Johnson & Johnson, 1997.

———. *The Band-Aid Brand Story*. New Brunswick, NJ: Johnson & Johnson, 1999.

Kunzig, Robert. "The Physics of . . . Tape." *Discover*. July 1999, 27–29.

Nyberg, Jim. *The Duct Tape Book II*. Duluth: Pfeifer: Hamilton, 1995.

Petroski, Henry. *The Evolution of Useful Things*. New York: Alfred A. Knopf, 1992.

Audio Recording

Audio tape recording allowed music lovers to bring their music with them, whether in their automobiles or while jogging. In addition, tape recording became an essential part of a recording technology developed earlier, phonographs. In the last quarter of the nineteenth century, Edison and Berliner developed a purely mechanical method for recording sound: the phonograph. The electronics revolution of the twentieth century greatly refined that technology (see **Phonographs** and **High-Fidelity**). Electronics also made possible two major alternative methods of recording sound and other information: magnetic recording and optical recording. (For the story of optical recording, see the articles on **Compact Discs** and **Motion Pictures.** See **Home Video** for the development of VCRs and home video recording.)

WIRE RECORDING

All forms of magnetic recording depend upon the two core enabling technologies of the electric motor (appearing at the end of the nineteenth century) and the electronic amplifier. Amplifiers were based first upon De Forest's 1907 triode, and later upon the transistor. The triode and the transistor are electronic valves in which a weak signal can precisely control the flow of a much larger current. As a result, the original signal is amplified.

There are three main breakthroughs in the development of magnetic audio recording in addition to those underlying enabling technologies: the very idea of magnetic recording itself, magnetic tape, and the bias signal. The basic idea of magnetic recording is simple enough: any magnet will magnetize iron, if the iron is moved near the magnet. Drawing this implication was the key: so an electromagnet, which can produce a magnetic field of varying strength, could variably magnetize a length of iron if the piece of iron were moved past the electromagnet as it was producing a varying magnetic field. A record of the varying magnetic field would then be left behind as local variations in the direction and strength of the magnetization along the length of the piece of iron.

A hard trick then is to get iron into a workable form for this basic principle to be put to practical work. An American engineer, Oberlin Smith, applied for a patent caveat (a preliminary claim to an invention) for magnetic recording in 1878, and published his ideas for magnetic recording in 1888. But he was not able to produce a workable machine.

At the Paris Exposition of 1900, Danish inventor Valdemar Poulsen (1869–1942) demonstrated the first commercial magnetic recorder, his Telegraphone, which recorded speech on steel piano wire (see also **Telephone Answering Machines**). Poulsen developed the machine while at the Copenhagen Telephone Company, and applied for a patent in 1898. Poulsen's machine could record 30 minutes of speech on a spool of wire, with the wire pulled past the recording head at a rate of 84 inches per second. A main application was intended to be the recording of telephone conversations. Some later recorders used thin steel tape. However, without means for amplifying the signal during either recording or playback, these low-fidelity machines were not a great success, even with AT&T working on magnetic recorders in the 1930s. Wire recorders had a long life, and were made into the 1950s. In 1948 several cartridge-based machines were introduced—long before Philips applied the same idea to enclosing tape in audio cassette tapes.

TAPE RECORDING

Modern tape recording is largely a German invention, partly a result of the prowess of the German chemical industry. I.G. Farben, the German chemical company, worked with electronics firm A.E.G. from 1933 through World War II developing a magnetic tape recorder, the Magnetophone. These machines were used by German radio for prerecorded broadcasts—and allied soldiers listening to German radio were puzzled hearing the Berlin Philharmonic at midnight. Magnetic tape depended upon high-quality backing materials upon which a thin layer of dark-orange iron oxide powder could be glued. Paper tape was tried initially, but plastics were developed—especially first acetate, and later mylar tape—that proved far superior. Plastic tape could be very thin, and soon 1,200 and more feet of tape could be wound on a 7-inch-diameter reel.

Fidelity of early tape recording was poor—magnetic tape recording suffered from poor signal-to-noise ratio (dynamic range) and poor frequency response. After World War II, German patents were seized and American and British companies began production (much of it based on "liberated" Magnetophones). One of the key incentives came from radio and motion picture singing star Bing Crosby (1903–1977). Crosby did not like having to appear at the radio studio for live broadcasts, and sought to exploit the German tape technology. By 1948 the Bing Crosby radio show was pretaped on an Ampex model 200 recorder. That same year the founders of the future Sony Corporation were examining an American military tape recorder derived from the German designs.

The key to improved fidelity was the introduction of a bias signal. Magnetic recording is nonlinear: the induced magnetism on the tape is not linearly proportional to the magnetic field produced by the recording head. A 10 percent increase in field might produce a 5 percent increase in induced magnetism on the tape, the next 10 percent increase at the head might produce a 20 percent increase at the tape, and the last 10 percent increase at the head might again produce only a 5 percent increase in induced magnetism. In the 1940s some models of the Magnetophon incorporated a high-frequency bias signal that improved fidelity. Addition of this bias signal (around 100,000 cycles per second, that is, 100 kilohertz [khz]) mixed with the audio signal produces a much more linear response of the tape, and finally permitted high-fidelity recording of music. Normally the bias signal is mixed with the audio signal and sent to the recording head, an enclosed electromagnet with a tiny gap that is pressed against the moving tape. However, in the 1960s Tandberg (Norway) and Akai (Japan) produced tape decks with additional separate "crossfield" bias heads, placed on the back side of the tape opposite the recording head. The fluctuating magnetic field in the recording head gap leaves a "track" of recorded signal as a narrow band of oxide magnetized to varying degrees on the long ribbon of tape.

Another limitation of magnetic recording is random noise ("tape hiss") produced by the variously oriented magnetic particles as they pass by the playback

A portable audio cassette recorder, a miniature version of large open reel magnetic tape recorders, made possible by transistors and the compact cassette audio tape format introduced by Philips in the early 1960s. (Courtesy of Corbis)

head. Improved tape formulations have helped, but the key breakthrough was variable-gain amplifiers using techniques pioneered by former Ampex employee Ray Dolby, at Dolby Laboratories in the 1960s. Originally expensive and used only in recording studios, a simplified "type B" Dolby noise reduction system helped make the narrow slow-moving tape used in audio cassette recorders acceptable as a medium for recorded music—and as a result compact cassette recorders soon displaced open-reel tape recorders in the home.

MULTITRACK RECORDING

Multitrack audio recording was developed by guitarist-inventor Les Paul (born 1916 in Waukesha, Wisconsin). Ampex had produced multitrack scientific data recorders; Paul talked Ampex into producing a three-track audio recorder in 1954. This permitted overdubbing: a performer could listen to the signal recorded on the first track, and play or sing along, adding his or her own contribution on the second track. Paul used this to become a one-man band, adding additional tracks to those recorded earlier by himself. No longer must all the musicians performing a piece be present at the same time, a convenience that made possible the recordings in the 1990s of Beatles songs long after the death of John Lennon, and release of duets sung by Frank Sinatra with people he never met.

COMPACT CASSETTE TAPES

Open-reel tape is bulky and difficult to load—the difficult to handle tape must be threaded through the transport, past the heads, and anchored on the inner hub of the take-up reel. Dutch electronics giant Philips introduced a compact tape cassette, and players for the cassettes, in 1962–1964. The Philips cassette held $\frac{1}{8}$-inch-wide tape on tiny supply and take-up hubs. Holes through the cassette were provided for the capstan and guide pins, and an opening at one side let the tape heads make contact with the tape. This compact self-contained format made prerecorded audio tapes popular, and soon tape players in automobiles became common, and small portable personal tape players (Sony Walkman and clones) accompanied joggers and others far from AC line power. Other cartridge tape formats were also developed in the 1960s, including eight-track and four-track tape; both were used in car tape players. In these cartridges, $\frac{1}{4}$-inch-wide tape was in a continuous loop, and so could not be rewound or easily fast-forwarded. By the 1980s they were displaced by Philips' smaller compact cassette format, enhanced with Dolby noise reduction and better tape oxides.

Magnetic audio recording is currently used for motion picture soundtracks, on a magnetic stripe on the side of the film, and was used in home movies as a fairly expensive option for adding sound before camcorders displaced film for

Integrated circuits and Dolby noise reduction circuitry made possible high quality portable stereo cassette tape players. The most famous was the Walkman, made by Sony. (Courtesy of Corbis)

home-movie making. Digital audio tape (DAT) was developed as part of the digital revolution of the last two decades of the twentieth century, but by the end of the century was primarily used by audio professionals, not consumers. Sony parted with long-time consumer innovation partner Philips, and adapted the floppy disc to home audio, producing the 6-cm MiniDisc in late 1992. In the United States, this remained a niche consumer item at the end of the century.

A tape recorder consists of three main parts: the electromechanical tape transport that moves the tape past the heads, the record/play heads themselves, and the recording and playback circuits that carry the signal. The transport must be capable of moving the tape at a constant precise speed past the heads. A tape speed of $7\frac{1}{2}$ inches per second was standard for home open-reel tape decks, with slower speeds often available; compact cassettes use a speed of $1\frac{7}{8}$ inches per second. Just beyond the heads, a rubber-coated pinch-roller holds the tape against the capstan, a shaft turned by the motor. Turning the capstan at a constant speed poses a delicate engineering problem; early tape recorders used heavy fly-wheels to provide a constant speed; since the advent of integrated circuits, electronic servo motors have made smaller and much lighter-weight tape transports possible since the 1970s. The tape transport must also ensure that the tape gets wound on the take-up reel. Tape transports almost always provide for high-speed rewind of tape, and usually fast forward. This requires moving the pinch-roller away from the capstan and also pulling the tape away from the heads, to reduce wear. Tape transports can be completely mechanical apart from the motor, or can use electrically operated solenoids to shift modes from play to stop to rewind and fast forward.

The heads are very small electromagnets, a coil of wire wrapped around a C-shaped metal core, with a tiny gap over which the tape moves. The coils are embedded in a plastic, and all but the front surface is surrounded by a metal case to shield them from picking up stray hum and other noise. A separate erase head is positioned ahead of the record head. A single head can be used for both playback and recording, or separate record and playback heads can be optimized for their tasks. For stereo and multitrack recording, heads are stacked one above the other. Home stereo recorders, whether open reel or cassette, provide for recording of "both sides" of the tape. This is not really recording on both sides of the tape (which has oxide on only one side). Instead, the tape is divided into four tracks and the two heads each record on only a quarter of the width of the tape, each constituting a "track." The first and third tracks are recorded to form a stereo recording on one direction. When the tape is flipped over, the other two quarters of the same surface of the tape are recorded (the heads are now opposite the fourth and second of the tracks on the tape). (Some tape recorders automatically reverse tape direction, and either mechanically move the heads, or use additional heads to record and play on the other two quarters of the tape.)

The electronics in the tape recorder must amplify the signal to be recorded and the tiny signal being reproduced during playback. These circuits must also provide any equalization used. Equalization provides extra amplification of high frequencies during recording, to overcome tape noise or "hiss," which is more audible at higher frequencies. A mirror-image equalization "curve" provides reduced gain of high frequencies during playback to restore the balance between high and low frequencies in the sound the user will hear. The equalization curve, or amount of amplification at each frequency, is standardized so that tapes recorded on one machine may be played back on another without distorting the frequency balance.

A bias oscillator generates the bias signal, which is usually mixed with the record signal and used only during recording. Tape recorder circuits followed the core electronics developments of the century: vacuum tubes until the 1960s, then transistors, yielding increasingly to integrated circuits in the 1970s and 1980s. The small size and low voltage requirements of solid-state electronics permitted two developments to flourish: portable audio cassette players (Sony Walkman), and cassette players in automobiles.

Magnetic recording has the problem of saturation—the tape suddenly becomes completely magnetized, and increased signal at the recording head cannot cause any increase in magnetization of the tape. This produces severe distortion of an audio signal that is recorded at high enough levels to approach the saturation limit of the tape—as a result, all magnetic tape recorders must have signal level meters or built-in limiting circuitry that allows the recording signal to get close to saturation without encountering it. (Too low a recorded signal level results in poor signal-to-noise level—the trick is to get the signal level just right!)

By the end of the twentieth century much magnetic recording was digital, and the majority was on hard drives inside computers. Digital signals can be compressed by digital circuits that eliminate redundancy and so result in smaller file sizes. One popular format at the end of the twentieth century was "MP3." Compressed digital audio can be stored in solid-state "flash memory" chips and carried around in tiny players with no moving parts. Diamond Multimedia introduced the first portable MP3 player, the Rio, in the 1990s.

Magnetic recording research focuses on increased data density, and, to a lesser extent, faster retrieval times, which is important for computer applications, but not for audio. The primary area of research on audio recording in the last two decades of the twentieth century was in digital audio recording. However, the main formats, digital audio tape (DAT) and the MiniDisc, have not been popular with consumers (lack of prerecorded material may be an important reason). For audio playback, consumers largely switched from magnetic tape to compact disc during the 1980s. For home audio recording, compact tape cassettes have been preferred, but are yielding to recordable discs: CD-R (see **Compact Discs**). So the battle between optical and magnetic recording media continues.

Many predicted the demise of magnetic recording before the end of the twentieth century, but manufacturers have increased data density and (with the help of intense competition) have brought costs down. Hard drives cost about $500 for a 10-megabyte capacity in the early 1980s, for a cost of $50 a megabyte. By the end of the century a 20-gigabyte drive was around $200, or 20 cents, a megabyte (and was much faster at retrieving data). In constant dollars, corrected for inflation, the decline is even more dramatic. VCRs (see **Home Video**) had undergone a less dramatic decline (the format fixed data density), but still showed a drop from near $1,000 ($1,400 for the first 1970s Betamax) to around $100 over the period. Meanwhile, optical recording also dropped dramatically in cost, with CD recorders dropping from over $10,000 in the 1980s to below $200 by the end of the century. DVD recorders remained too expensive for home use at the end of the century. Optical recording holds great promise, but magnetic recording continued to hold its own and indeed flourished throughout the last decades of the century.

However, the future is not bright for audio tape recording. Recordable optical discs (CDR and DVD-ROM) are replacing magnetic tape recording for audio. Philips introduced single- and dual-deck audio cd copiers in the late 1990s. In addition, solid-state playback devices for compressed digital audio were introduced in late 1998, after a court injunction was lifted (record companies had sought to prevent sale of the Rio MP3 player). Compressed audio in MP3 digital format can be downloaded from the Internet and played back on a computer, or in turn downloaded into a tiny portable playback device like the Rio. Decline of the price of the solid-state memory prices (flash RAM) used by solid-state players accelerated growth of this additional rival to magnetic recording. Audio tape, with its vulnerability to magnetic fields, tape breakage, difficulty of adapting to a changer, and lack of random access, will probably be seen as a technology that completed its life cycle largely in the second half of the twentieth century.

REFERENCES

Ampex Corporate Background. http://www.ampex.com/corporatebg/

Morton, David. "Chronology of Magnetic Recording." 1998. http://www.rci.rutgers.edu/dmorton/mrchrono.html

Morton, David. *Off the Record: The Technology and Culture of Sound Recording in America.* New Brunswick, NJ: Rutgers University Press, 2000.

Ballpoint Pen

For many centuries prior to the twentieth, writing by hand required an elaborate set of activities and tools: quill or pen, the ink bottle or well with which to fill the writing implement, a blotting substance (sand or paper) to get the ink started drying once applied, and various cleaning tools for the inevitable drips and splashes of excess ink.

In 1888, an American leather tanner named John Loud patented a roller-ball-tipped marking pen for the convenient marking of animal hides. Loud's invention was never manufactured, but he had quietly initiated the race for the successful ballpoint pen. In three subsequent decades, some 350 ballpoint pen designs were developed, but none reached the stage of commercial manufacture and sale. A significant design problem lay in the ink being used, rather than the pen design itself; if the ink was formulated to be too thin, it would leak out of the pen when not in use; if too thick, it would clog. So while inventors struggled for a design that would be smooth-writing, quick-drying, leak-proof, and long-lasting, the traditional ink pen with all its fusses and flaws remained the only viable permanent-writing implement.

In 1935, a Hungarian newspaper editor named Ladislas Biro became decisively frustrated with ink pens as featured in his work. In addition to their leaks, blots, and splashes, their points tended to puncture the surface of newsprint. But Biro noted that the ink that was being used to print newspapers had the desirable property of drying very quickly. Assisted by his brother George, Biro developed a design for a pen with a rolling ball at the tip. A newspaper-type ink would be drawn down toward the ball by gravity.

In a truly odd turn of events, the Biro brothers on their summer beach holiday met the president of Argentina, Augustine Justo, who invited them to move to his country and establish a ballpoint pen factory. As World War II commenced, the Biros did move to Argentina, where they secured financial backers for their enterprise. Manufacture began in 1943.

The original Biro pen was not a commercial success, however. Its gravity-fed design necessitated a more-or-less upright barrel during the writing process, which was awkward. And the ink too often emerged in blobs rather than a uniform line. An improved design incorporated what the Biros called "capillary action" to draw the ink down the pen's barrel. A textured ballpoint acted in a sponge-like manner on the tube of ink, pulling it down toward the writing surface. Though this design was superior, the pen still did not become a commercial success.

The pens did attract the interest of American military personnel who had become acquainted with them in Argentina during the war years. Especially for airmen, there was a need for pens that would not suffer from the main liability of traditional ink pens at high altitudes: the tendency to explode. The U.S. Department of State undertook to encourage pen technology development by sending desired specifications to several American manufacturers. The Eberhard Faber Company paid the Biro brothers $500,000 for the rights to U.S. manufacture of their capillary ballpoint. The design was still imperfect, however, and the rights were sold along to Eversharp without commercial success.

Meanwhile the original Biro patents were nearing expiration. An enterprising Chicago salesman named Milton Reynolds purchased Biro pens and analyzed and copied their design. His pen, christened the "Reynolds Rocket," was launched with a sensational sales campaign at Gimbel's Department Store touting the "fantastic miraculous fountain pen . . . guaranteed to write for two years without refilling." The Rocket was a high-priced item at $12.50, yet it sold quickly—testimony to consumer discontent with previous writing implements. Alas, the Reynolds pen proved less than miraculous in performance, with inherited tendency to blot, leak, clog, and dry out far short of its two-year projected utility period.

There followed a decade of feverish research and development for would-be ballpoint pen moguls. New designs with the virtues of writing upside down or underwater were marketed with creative advertising. The actress and athlete Esther Williams was hired to demonstrate underwater ballpoint writing.

A ballpoint pen with a retractable tip was developed by the Frawley Pen Company. This feature allowed the writing surface of the ball to be protected from the drying effect of air exposure and also reduced blotting accidents to users' clothing. Frawley developed an aggressive sales campaign called "Project Normandy," in which Frawley representatives would burst into the offices of buyers and write on their shirt fronts, then offer to replace the shirts with more costly garments if the ink did not wash out easily. The "Normandy" tactics were highly successful; the Frawley pen thus marketed was named "Papermate."

Meanwhile in postwar France, Marcel Bich (1914–1994) also saw the vast potential market for an inexpensive reliable ballpoint pen. Having purchased a bombed-out factory near Paris, he began the manufacture of a pen combining the best design features of all currently known prototypes. The "Bic" pen used the new advertising medium of television to present itself in 1952 as the one and only ballpoint that "Writes first time, every time!" This Bic pen was clear-barreled for ease of viewing ink supply, and used a brutally simple body design in order to be as inexpensive as possible.

American ball-point pen models continued to involve features that would keep prices somewhat higher. The Parker Pen Company's "Jotter," marketed in 1954, featured aesthetically pleasing barrel designs and colors. Parker also used a

Retractable ballpoint pen. (Courtesy of Corbis)

tungsten-carbide textured ball-bearing point in some of its up-market pens during the 1950s.

During the 1960s, the metal ball-pointed pen was joined by a porous-tipped pen that allowed for a very wide variety of stroke widths and ink colors. So-called felt-tip pens cross over between writing media and art applications. Most recently, gel-inks incorporating texture and glitter have become available and extremely popular with youthful consumers.

But the utilitarian pen of choice, the one available on desktops around the world, rummaged for in briefcases and purses, picked up by accident from friends' tabletops, and exchanged like currency for urgent writing tasks, is the basic ballpoint of the modest Bic style. Today the Bic Corporation dominates the international market for inexpensive ballpoint pens, selling an incredible 14 million daily.

Some technology prophets foresee the end of handwriting altogether, as typing replaces writing in daily life. But for as long as handwriting persists, the trusty ballpoint pen will likely be its handiest sidekick in the workaday world.

REFERENCE

Gostony, Henry, and Stuart Schneider. *The Incredible Ball-Point Pen: A Comprehensive History and Price Guide.* Atglen, PA: Schiffer Publishing Ltd., 1998.

Barcodes and Magnetic Stripes

As computers became available for business use in the 1950s and 1960s, it was soon realized that they would be useful for inventory control. The problem was to find ways that a computer could read information that identified things in the real world. Adding "vision" to a computer has proven to be a very difficult problem. Several alternative ways of allowing computers to detect the identity of objects (and persons) were developed in the latter twentieth century.

PUNCHED CARDS

One technique was to utilize the punched cards that were widely used for data entry into computers throughout the 1950s through 1970s. The standard $3\frac{1}{4}$ inch by $7\frac{3}{8}$ inch manila cards had 80 columns in which holes could be punched, and 10 main rows, one for each digit. A "5" could be represented in a column simply by punching a rectangular hole in the fifth row in that column. If letters of the alphabet needed to be represented, an additional hole could be punched in one of three unlabeled rows at the top. These cards could be placed in pockets on a product, such as the packing box of a television set, for inventory control. Pockets carrying the cards were also glued inside library books, to check books out to patrons.

In 1932 Wallace Flint wrote a master's thesis at the Harvard University School of Business in which he described a future supermarket in which customers punched cards to indicate their product selections. A card-reading machine at the front counter would activate machinery in the rear storeroom to dispense the requested merchandise and bring it by conveyor to the front of the store. The envisioned market was a giant vending machine. Of course, this expensive technique could not compete with the self-service supermarket retail store that became popular instead.

Scanning cards was cumbersome. Cards must be handled by someone, and as a result they often got damaged, switched, or lost (punched cards often carried the warning "Do not fold, spindle, or mutilate"). It clearly would be desirable to have information on an item that a machine could read directly off the item. The banking industry developed magnetic inks and special "optical" fonts for printing characters that could be read by both humans and machines. These were used to imprint information on the bottom of the bank checks used by their customers. Plastic credit cards carried by consumers were made with the card number printed in raised machine-readable letters. Using a small roller at the point of sale to press the credit card against a "charge slip" made of layers of thin paper and carbon paper would transfer the card number to the slips of paper. A copy of the charge slip would be sent to the credit card clearing company. The U.S. Postal Service spent millions of dollars trying to develop machines to read addresses on envelopes, and to develop human and machine-readable fonts for mass mailed items. Unfortunately, any damage to the information printed using an optical font may result in erroneous readings. Machine-readable fonts have to be very precisely positioned for scanning, so this technique worked best for things like bank checks that can be fed through a machine that controls positioning.

BARCODES

There was an alternative to optical fonts that came to have wider application. The basic idea was to continue to use an optical identifier, which could be cheaply printed, but to abandon the requirement that the identifier be a font readable by humans as well. Relatively inexpensive sensors and circuits can reliably read a series of printed dark lines, or bars, of variable width. Optical readers could also have the advantage that they would not have to be in direct contact with the item being read.

In 1948, two graduate students at Drexel Institute of Technology in Philadelphia, Bernard Silver and Norman J. Woodland, took the first steps to develop a machine-readable code of bars after overhearing a conversation between one of the deans and the president of a local grocery store chain. Woodland developed barcodes composed of lines and also of concentric rings—like an archery target. His design used ink that glowed under intense ultraviolet light. The advantage of using rings was that they could be scanned in any direction. Silver and Wood-

A barcode. This is a universal product code (UPC); there are many other barcodes in use as well, including book number codes and product serial number codes. The original UPC design envisioned circular "bull's-eye" codes as well. The bars vary in width and can be scanned by an optical pickup in either direction. The numerical equivalent of the code is printed below it—useful for manual entry, when the barcode fails to scan.

land received a patent for a "Classifying Apparatus and Method" in 1952.

One of the first large-scale attempts to use optical barcodes was by American railroads. Railroads needed to identify the location of their rolling stock. It would be very useful if the cars making up huge trains could be automatically identified as they rolled past, and especially as trains were made up in switching yards. The American Railway Association worked to develop a code and reading system starting in the 1960s. The railway system used a code of orange-and-blue stripes on the side of railway cards. Unfortunately, the equipment was very expensive, and since railroad cars lead a tough and dirty existence, the codes were often unreadable. The project was abandoned in the mid-1970s.

Printed optical barcodes were in use in the 1960s in manufacturing. However, in retail stores up until 1970, thousands of workers roamed the aisles, individually applying a price tag to each item in the store. A price change, or a weekly sale at a grocery store, meant applying new price tags over old. Checkout clerks read price labels and keyed them into cash registers—and errors were common (and price disputes caused delays in checkout). Inventory control had to be conducted by frequent surveys of the stock situation on the shelves of the store. As computing costs fell, grocers hoped that a system that would allow a scanner to read item numbers directly into a computer would save a great deal of labor, improve accuracy, allow pricing flexibility, and provide for computer inventory control

In 1967, a bull's-eye barcode system was installed in a Kroger grocery store in Cincinnati. The codes were on stickers, applied to each item for sale by store employees. The grocery industry realized a universal system, with the code preprinted on the product, was both needed and was now practical. The U.S. grocery industry began a competition for design of a uniform product code in about 1970. IBM was not in this market but seized this opportunity to enter, and assigned G.J. Laurer to design a workable entry. After some revisions, this code won the design competition in 1973. It has been extended several times since to become an international universal product code.

Each UPC code contains a five-digit manufacturer code, followed by a five-digit code for the particular product. The Uniform Code Council issues manufacturer codes; manufacturers create codes for their products. A check digit at the end of the code has a value that depends on the previous digits and is used to help detect scanning errors.

Scanners are of two main types: wands and laser. Wands are inexpensive, but must be positioned close to the barcode and dragged across it in order to read it. Although they are much more expensive, laser readers are much less particular about positioning, and can read a code at a distance, including the barcode wrapped around a jar of pickles. Grocery and other large self-service stores usually have a laser scanner under a glass window in the checkout aisle. Many libraries switched to using barcodes to identify books—and patrons too, with a barcode on library cards.

At the end of the twentieth century, wand scanner costs had dropped so much that Radio Shack stores planned a program to give away barcode scanners that customers could connect to personal computers. This "CueCat" could read a barcode on a product or a code in a catalog and use the Internet to display information about a product.

MAGNETIC STRIPES

A different technology of machine-readable identification was developed along side optical codes. Sometimes it was desirable to have revisable information. A thin magnetic stripe, like a short segment of magnetic recording tape, could be affixed to a card. This revisable information could be used for tickets in a mass transit system—the balance on the card and the station at which a rider entered the system could be recorded on the card at the gate where the rider entered the system, and then the card could be debited as the rider exited. When the rider entered the system, the ticket was passed through an entrance gate that recorded the station name on the magnetic stripe (see **Audio Recording** for the development of magnetic recording technology). When the rider exited the system, the ticket was passed through the exit gate, the fare was automatically calculated and subtracted from the previous value of the ticket, and the new value of the ticket was magnetically recorded on the stripe. These features were incorporated in the first use of magnetic stripes on tickets for the London Underground subway system, in the early 1960s. They were then used later in the 1960s for the new San Francisco Bay Area Rapid Transit system (BART). By the late 1960s, such cards were also being used in college dining halls to keep track of use of meal plans.

In 1970, international standardization of stripe types and data led to the use of stripes on the back of plastic credit cards. Magnetic stripes were also used on airline tickets. Credit cards and transit tickets have been the major applications of magnetic stripe technology.

Smart cards were first patented in France in 1974, and their first use was in France in 1982. Smart cards include an integrated circuit chip. These can be "dumb," including only memory, or also including a microprocessor. The latter allows much-improved security; the microprocessor and its program can control access to the data on the card. High telecommunications costs in Europe led to wider use there than in the United States, where credit card authorization often takes place over phone lines. However, it is expected that smart cards will be widely used throughout the world because of their security features, and because they can store large amounts of data and act as an "electronic purse."

Wearable computing devices are also possible. Short-range digital radio technology, such as "Blue Tooth," developed at the end of the twentieth century, is designed to let embedded digital circuits in appliances communicate with each other and with users. It is expected that short-range digital radio communication will be widely used in the twenty-first century. And it is reasonable to expect that at some point in the twenty-first century, machines will finally learn to reliably read ordinary printed labels.

REFERENCES

Bar Code 1. Bar Code History Page. *http://www.adams1.com/pub/russadam/history.html*

Lauer, George. "Development of the U.P.C. Symbol." *http://members.aol.com/productupc/upc_work.html*

Seideman, Tony. "Bar Codes Sweep the World." *American Heritage of Invention and Technology,* vol. 8, no. 3. 56–63.

Batteries

Batteries are self-contained power sources that produce a direct current of electricity from chemical reactions. The basic scientific discoveries and inventions were all made in the nineteenth century, but batteries did not become common in everyday life until the first decades of the twentieth century with the use of batteries for flashlights, for automobile ignition and lighting systems, and for powering radio receivers. Major developments of the twentieth century were accelerated by World War II (1940–1945), by the space race of the Cold War between the United States and the Soviet Union, and by the environmental movements of the latter decades of the century. These later technologies made batteries smaller and more long-lived, whether for powering a heart pacemaker, a camera, or an automobile.

DRY AND WET CELLS

What is popularly known as a battery is actually an individual voltaic cell, named in 1800 after its inventor, Alessandro Volta (1745–1827). An actual battery combines two or more cells in series as when you put several cells into a flashlight or radio (the term "battery" comes from sixteenth-century warfare for an array of cannons "battering" an enemy together). A cell is composed of two electrodes, a negatively charged cathode and a positively charged anode, immersed in an ion-conducting chemical medium, the electrolyte. The electrodes dissociate into ions in the electrolyte by the process of oxidation/reduction. When the anode and cathode are connected by a conductor (for example, a wire passing through a light bulb), free ions migrate through the electrolyte from anode to cathode, producing an electric current. Thus, in a flashlight, when you move the switch "on," the current flows, and "off," the circuit is broken.

There are many possible materials usable for electrodes and electrolytes, but throughout most of the twentieth century the most familiar batteries were the carbon-zinc flashlight cell and the lead-acid car battery. The prototype for the flashlight cell was invented by French physicist Georges Leclanché in 1866. As it later developed, it had a zinc body containing an electrolyte in the form of a paste of zinc chloride. A carbon rod inserted into the electrolyte is insulated from direct contact with the zinc. For many years, the zinc cup was enclosed in cardboard

Flashlight batteries come in several sizes, such as this size "D." (Courtesy of Corbis)

and eventually the chemical reactions would swell the electrolyte, bursting the cup and often ruining the flashlight. Around 1940 some manufacturers encased the cup in a steel jacket to prevent leakage. This is now the general practice. There are two descriptive terms for this kind of cell: it is called a dry cell, even though the electrolyte is a damp paste, and it is called a primary battery, meaning that when exhausted, it cannot be reused.

The familiar car battery is made of wet cells—the usual electrolyte is a weak liquid solution of sulfuric acid. As a secondary battery it can be recharged by passing a direct current through its lead and lead oxide electrodes. The most important work on lead-acid batteries was by the French chemist Gaston Planté (1834–1889?). From 1860 to the end of his life he pursued the goal of a practical, simple secondary battery, or "storage" battery, especially for electric-powered street rail cars. (Horse cars were slow and dirty.) Although there were successes, the batteries were extremely heavy, weighing as much as two tons, requiring frequent recharging, and rarely lasting more than six months. In 1883, American inventor Thomas Edison (1847–1931) spoke of storage batteries as "a mechanism for swindling the public." Even so, batteries were used to augment his own great invention, **electric lights.** The current to homes and businesses from generators was very uneven, causing flickering and "brownouts," so batteries were used for "load-leveling" the direct current. By 1900 batteries for street railways were on the way out, having never caught on, but battery-operated automobiles briefly rivaled the new gasoline-powered autos. They had many advantages: quiet, clean, odorless, few moving parts, easy to start, and not requiring skillful gear shifting. Oddly, what killed popular interest in electric passenger cars for the next seventy or eighty years was the battery-powered electric self-starter for gasoline cars. Charles Franklin Kettering (1876–1958) in 1911 delivered his first electric car starter to the Cadillac Motor Company in Detroit; in two or three years almost all cars were free of the laborious and often dangerous method of starting with a hand crank. Kettering's company, Delco, continued to be a standard brand name through the century. (See also **Calculators** and **Cash Registers** for more on Kettering.) The kind of battery needed now was not a huge, heavy unit that needed to be recharged for daily use, but an SLI—starting, lighting, ignition— that needed only short bursts of power to start the car. Once going, a small generator turned by the car engine could recharge the SLI battery.

The actual design and components of batteries were much more complicated than described above, as electrodes were often made of special alloys (especially with antimony) or compound coatings, while electrolytes were mixtures of several compounds. To maximize the surface contact between electrodes and electrolytes, electrodes were made very thin, pierced to make a delicate grid, and separated by thin cardboard, rubber, or other sheet material. Various inventions from Europe and America were combined in 1900 in the Electric Storage Battery Company of Philadelphia's Exide, which was to become one of the important brand names of the century.

In addition to the problem of increasing the contact surfaces, engineers have had to deal with "polarization," which is a buildup of by-products around electrodes, among them, in some batteries, highly explosive hydrogen gas. The search for electrode material that is not subject to dissolving in the electrolyte continued for decades, often facing problems of cost. Thomas Edison searched through all the metallic elements for suitable electrodes to immerse in an alkaline rather than acid electrolyte, but had to reject silver and platinum as too costly, and didymium and yltria as too rare. Many substances that otherwise might be suitable such as antimony, cobalt, and mercury, are very toxic, although they have been used. The most economical compromise has been lead (also toxic), but this made the challenge of reducing battery weight a problem. Lead is cheap, but heavy. Electric forklift vehicles can turn this to an advantage, as they need a counterweight anyway, but for aircraft and spacecraft weight is a key issue. For everyday consumers, the main concerns have been such matters as long-life charges, fast recharging, quick recovery after a surge of output (as with flash cameras), and cost. Addressing these various needs and problems has produced a variety of batteries, most popular of which are alkaline, lithium, silver oxide, and "nicad."

NICKEL-CADMIUM RECHARGEABLE BATTERIES

Nickel-cadmium rechargeable batteries have become essential to the development of portable tools such as electric drills, saws, and screwdrivers as well as

lawn mowers, hedge trimmers, and other applications. Their history begins early
in the century as the Swedish chemist Waldemar Jungner and Thomas A. Edison
raced to develop a commercial alkaline cell. Edison's contempt for storage batteries was twofold: the earlier ones did not perform well, and the patents for lead
zinc were pretty well sewed up by other manufacturers. Initially Edison wanted
to invent a battery that he could sell to buyers of his phonographs, but by the
dawn of the twentieth century he was interested in electric automobiles. His research was devoted to alkaline electrolytes, but he experimented with electrodes
of copper, zinc, magnesium, cobalt, bismuth, cadmium, nickel, and iron. Nickel
was chosen as being insoluble in alkaline electrolytes and readily available. Many
nineteenth- and early twentieth-century products were nickel-plated for its
durable silvery finish. Cadmium was rejected as too expensive—thirty times
more expensive than lead—so Edison settled on nickel-iron alkaline batteries.
They became the chief rival to Exide for electric cars. However, Jungner had in
1901 taken out a European patent for nickel and iron or cadmium. Edison challenged the iron patent, winning in 1906, so from that point on, commercial development of nickel-cadmium was European. American interest in nicad was not
rekindled until after World War II. Nonetheless, Edison had pioneered a means
of making the nickel electrodes much lighter and more efficient. It was a complicated and costly process by which microscopically thin flakes of metallic nickel
were alternated with nickel hydroxide into a thin tube of nickel.

In 1929 the German manufacturing giant I.G. Farben improved on Edison's
process, perfecting a way of sintering flakes together (sintering is a metallurgical
method of fusing particles by pressure and heat without melting them). Not much
more was done until Adolf Hitler's second four-year plan of 1936. Hitler wanted
Germany to become independent of foreign raw materials used in military machines. The lead and rubber used in lead-acid batteries were vital imports. I.G. Farben agreed to build up an industry of improved nickel-cadmium batteries, which
were much lighter and operated well at lower temperatures. Although they did
not work as expected in warplanes, they were used in the new jet planes and rockets. The sintered electrodes were called Durac, and after the war the whole German plant was shipped to England. Modern nicads are "sealed" and have nickel
hydroxide cathodes and cadmium anodes in a small amount of potassium hydroxide electrolyte. They include features that permit gases to escape safely
into the environment. They hold a charge for relatively long periods and are
rechargeable for years.

Of the many types of batteries that were invented, at the outset of the twentieth century the most common primary batteries in use were zinc-manganese
(flashlights, toys, etc.), mercuric oxide–zinc (hearing aids, watches), silver
oxide–zinc (watches, cameras), and lithium (cameras, pagers, heart pacemakers).
For secondary rechargeables, the lead-acid car battery continued (with strict laws
for safe disposal and recycling), while nicads and lithium are favored for tools
and appliances. Nickel-metal-hydride (NiMH) rechargeables were gradually replacing nicads in some applications, such as digital cameras, lap top computers,
and cell phones.

The more distant future appears to belong to solar cells and fuel cells—not strictly batteries because they are not self-contained. Solar cell-powered radios became available to consumers in 1999. Both resulted from the need for electric power in spacecraft, although fuel cells were actually a *rediscovery* of Sir William Grove's 1839 invention of the process. The fuel can be any hydrogen-containing substance, including pure hydrogen, propane, methanol, etc. The fuel passes over a positive electrode where hydrogen ions and electrons are released into the electrolyte and migrate toward an oxygen electrode, producing electric current and water as by-product. Indications are that fuel cells will provide power to cars, homes, and industry.

REFERENCES

Schallenberg, Richard H. *Bottled Energy: Electrical Engineering and the Evolution of Chemical Energy Storage*. Philadelphia: American Philosophical Society, 1982.
"Who Sells the Best Cells?" *Consumer Reports*, December 1999, 51–53.

Bread Machines

Bread machines combine a food mixer with a minioven. Unlike other kitchen appliances, the bread machine came into being after the development of microprocessors, and so from its beginning, it could be programmed to perform a timed sequence of different actions. Making bread manually is a complex process with critical timing and temperatures for chemical reactions. Basically, the chemistry is the interaction of yeast (an active fungus) with flour, salt, and sometimes sugar. In the presence of lukewarm water and the carbohydrates (flour, sugar), the yeast multiplies quickly (fermentation), producing carbon dioxide gas. It is the gas bubbles that make bread "light." Most breads require three periods of fermentation before being baked.

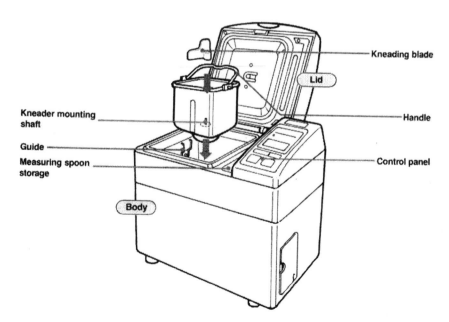

The "brains" of a Panasonic Bread Bakery are all concealed from the cook. Within the pan, all the complex actions and chemistry of traditional bread making are performed automatically. (Courtesy Matsushita Electric Corporation of America)

JAPANESE BREAD MACHINES

The story of the invention of bread machines as told by food expert Tom Lacalamita is an interesting tale of cross-cultural influences. The Japanese had never been a bread-eating culture, rice being the staple source of carbohydrates. After Japan was opened to Western trade in 1854 by the U.S. Navy under Commodore Matthew Perry, the Japanese military found that Western bread could be prepared in bakeries and taken into the field as food rations, while rice had to be prepared on site. But bread was not generally popular, even being opposed as a non-Japanese "invasion." Many years later, after the end of World War II in 1945, Japan suffered a severe food shortage. The American occupying forces under General Douglas MacArthur reintroduced wheat bread to feed schoolchildren, and this time the Japanese loved it. By the 1970s, young Japanese patronized bakeries for fresh-baked breads and rolls for breakfast. As they insisted on fresh-baked goods, women had to go out early every morning for bread.

An electrical engineer, Shin Ojima, invented the programmable bread machine to end this daily inconvenience. Although he had difficulty finding a manufacturer, at last in 1987 the first automatic bread machines were introduced in Japan. Over one million machines were sold in the first year, but their popularity ended soon. They were expensive, noisy, and took up a lot of space in the typically small Japanese dwellings. So in 1988 the manufacturers introduced the machines to the United States. At a price of over $400, in the first year 15,000 units were sold.

Five years later, the sales had increased a hundredfold and other manufacturers had entered the market. Various improvements were made, such as making the products look more like bread from a loaf pan. In the 1990s prices dropped as low as $90, supermarkets stocked premeasured flour packages for multigrain, herbal, bran, and other breads, and many cookbooks were available with recipes for baking all sorts of breads. Using the bread machines only through the "dough-making" cycle, recipes appeared for homemade pizzas, pitas, focaccias, and fancy ethnic rolls and buns. The future appears secure for bread machines. As with many other appliances, though, they take up scarce space on kitchen countertops. Fermentation cannot be rushed, and it does take forethought to have the ingredients ready for when one wants to bake the bread, so for many would-be bakers, "store-bought" bread loaves will remain the greatest convenience.

THE BREAD MACHINE CYCLE

Bread machines consist of an outer case with a closing lid and a removable inner bread pan. The bread pan typically is surrounded by a loop of heating element. The bread pan has one or two small openings at the bottom for one or two motor-driven shafts. A rubber seal prevent the contents of the bread pan from leaking out around the shaft. The shafts are fitted with simple paddles that act as dough hooks to mix the ingredients and to knead the dough.

The "brain" of the bread machine is a digital timer that runs the machine through a cycle. The ingredients—flour, water, yeast, and small amounts of additives such as salt and sugar—are carefully measured and placed in the pan. Some machines have special yeast dispensers; most just require that the yeast be added in a way that keeps it away from the wet ingredients until the initial mixing cycle. The operator presses some buttons to select a cycle (a higher heat will be used for crustier bread, and so forth).

The cycle typically consists of an initial mixing of the ingredients. This is followed by a resting period, warmed by the heater, while the yeast, now activated by the moisture and sugars, grows. Then the motor is turned on and the dough is kneaded. Kneading is followed by a main rising of the dough, with the heater maintaining the proper temperature. A secondary kneading and rising may follow. The heater is then turned on for the bake. At the end, a beep—and the smell of fresh bread—notifies the user that the cycle is finished. The pan is removed from the machine, and the baked bread is turned out. On many machines, the kneading paddles are removed by hand from the finished bread. A variety of cycle options are available to allow for different types of bread, baking in a separate pan, adding ingredients midway through the cycle, and especially for delayed bake, where the machine can be set up before going to bed and the user will be greeted the next morning with fresh-baked bread.

REFERENCE

Lacalamita, Tom. *The Ultimate Bread Machine Cookbook.* New York: Simon & Schuster, 1993.

Calculators and Cash Registers

The digital microelectronics revolution first made its way into many homes, offices, and stores in the form of electronic calculators and cash registers. These products seemed amazing at the time they were introduced. The cash register was revolutionized by digital integrated circuits and solid-state display technologies. These same technologies brought capable calculators into the home and school locker.

CASH REGISTERS

As retail establishments grew larger than single-proprietor stores, there came to be a problem of guarding against dishonest clerks. One solution, used well into the twentieth century, was for a department store to have no money at the various points of sale in the store. Instead, the money paid by the customer and the bill of sale were enclosed in a small cylinder and were sent by a pneumatic tube to a central cash room. There the money was kept and all accounting was done manually. A receipt and any change owed the customer were sent back via the pneumatic tube to the clerk on the sales floor to hand over to the customer. No money was kept on the sales floor.

The first cash register was invented in 1879 by James Ritty (1837–1918), a saloon keeper in Dayton, Ohio. As a saloon owner, Ritty knew the need for a machine to total sales and to record them. Ritty got the idea for his invention from seeing a device that recorded propeller rotations on transatlantic steamships. Ritty's register displayed totals using hands that moved on a large clock-like face. John H. Patterson (1842–1922) operated a nearby store in Ohio with his brother, selling miners' supplies. Knowing he was losing money from unrecorded sales, he bought two of "Ritty's Incorruptible Cashier" machines. He was so impressed with the results that he bought the rights to Ritty's machine, made improvements (recording the transactions on a paper tape), and founded the National Cash Register Company in 1884. One early advertising motto was "Stop the forgotten charge, use a National Cash Register." In 1906, Charles Kettering added an electric motor to the cash register (Kettering kept adding motors to things, and is most famous as the inventor a few years later of the electric starter that first appeared on Cadillac automobiles).

These early registers were impressive engraved brass machines—but the shortage of brass needed for shells during World War I caused brass to be replaced by much plainer painted steel. Patterson had a genius for marketing and organization, and quickly built a large and successful company during the early years of the twentieth century. Many people learned their managing skills at NCR: Patterson hired and later fired a former piano salesman named Thomas Watson, and Watson went on to build IBM.

In the early 1960s, as computers became available, some cash registers added the ability to record their transactions on punched paper tape. This information could then be fed to a central computer to keep track of and reconcile accounts. These innovations helped make larger self-service "discount" retail stores possible. The development of integrated circuits made possible "point-of-sale terminals"—cash registers that were connected directly to central computers. Soon these were joined by Universal Product Code scanners (see **Barcodes and Magnetic Stripes**), and by the end of the twentieth century cash registers were extensions of a computer system that not only read UPC codes and recorded sales, but also tracked inventory, made change, took credit card information, and tracked buying habits.

CALCULATORS

The early history of calculators is connected with famous geniuses. French mathematician and philosopher Blaise Pascal (1623–1662) is often credited with inventing the first mechanical calculator in 1642, at age nineteen. Pascal's machine, which he called the "Pascaline," still exists. Reportedly, Pascal invented the machine to assist his father, who was a French tax collector. Pascal built many versions and sold some of the machines. Turning metal wheels on the machine allowed one to do addition and subtraction. However, it is now known that credit for the first mechanical calculator should go to Wilhelm Schickard (1592–1635), a German professor and protégé of astronomer Johannes Kepler, for the 1623 "Calculating Clock."

A later calculator with more capabilities than either of these was invented by philosopher-mathematician Gottfried Wilhelm von Leibniz (1646–1716). Leibniz is perhaps best known as a coinventor (with Isaac Newton) of calculus and as an advocate of a relativistic theory of space as part of a general metaphysics that made minds the fundamental constituents of all reality. Frustrated by the complexity of building a decimal calculator, Leibniz envisioned the design of a calculator using balls to represent binary digits—anticipating the basic concept that governs computer arithmetic today.

Mechanical calculators continued to be developed in the nineteenth century. Power for the machines came from the operator. One important advance was to

Two ways of crunching numbers: a Burroughs mechanical adding machine from the early twentieth century, and a Casio electronic scientific graphing calculator from the end of the twentieth century. The Burroughs is operated by hand. It has 10 keys for each column; it prints (using type bars and an inked ribbon) when the handle is pulled down. The many keys of this type of machine were replaced by electric "10-key" adding machines in the middle of the century. The electronic pocket calculator was made possible by the development of digital integrated circuits in the 1970s. (Courtesy of David Hicks)

add keys for the entry of numbers, replacing the dials of the first calculators. Manually powered adding machines used well into the twentieth century often had keyboards with 80 or more keys arranged in columns, with a separate key for each of the 10 digits in each column. The operator would punch in the number, and as each key was depressed it would stay down. Inspection of the keyboard provided a check on whether the number had been entered correctly or not. Then a large lever on the right side of the machine was pulled, and the entered number was added to that displayed on dials in the windows at the top of the machine, and the keys popped back up awaiting the next entry.

The twentieth century brought electric power and much more complex mechanical calculators. Complex calculators that could do division often had a moving carriage at the top of the machine. Entering a problem would result in a long and complicated series of mechanical operations, with the carriage shifting one place at a time as the display wheels and their internal driving wheels were spun by the motor. By the 1960s, mechanical calculators were widely used in business and universities, but not in many homes. The machines were expensive, and moderately capable ones were the size of large typewriters. Some of the leading adding machine and calculator makers were Monroe, Burroughs, Marchant, Friden, and Olivetti.

ELECTRONIC CALCULATORS

Practical electronic calculators required a hardware revolution: solid-state electronics and new display technologies. They also required a conceptual shift, to the binary arithmetic envisioned by Leibniz. Since digital electronic control and arithmetic units require very complex circuits with large numbers of transistors, the first electronic calculators made with discrete transistors were still large and extremely expensive. To make these devices common required integrated circuits.

Texas Instruments was an early manufacturer of transistors and electronic instrumentation. It was also a pioneer in the creation of integrated circuits. Discrete circuits, with many separate transistors and components, require large amounts of space for the separate components, their insulation and packaging, and their sockets and mountings. Discrete circuits are also expensive to assemble. An integrated circuit (IC), by contrast, places more than one transistor junction on a single silicon "chip." Other electronic components (resistors, capacitors) can be created on the same piece of silicon, along with the connections between them. Entire circuits that would require millions of discrete components to be assembled can be created in the area of a square centimeter on a single thin slice of silicon. In 1958, a single silicon transistor cost around $10; in the year 2000, an integrated memory circuit containing 100 million transistors was about the same size and cost about the same price. Thus integrated circuits made possible enormous savings of space and cost, and allowed much more complex circuits to be incorporated in household products than would be possible with discrete components mounted on circuit boards.

In 1958 Jack Kilby (1923–), at Texas Instruments (TI), and Robert Noyce (1927–1990), at Fairchild, created the first simple integrated circuits (Noyce went on to be cofounder of Intel Corporation ten years later; Kilby was awarded the Nobel prize in physics in 2000). For a time, calculators continued to use discrete components, including tubes and relays. The first all-transistor calculator, the Friden 130, did not appear until 1963. Japanese manufacturers, including Canon, Casio, Sony, Sharp, and Oi, were also developing electronic calculators. By 1965, integrated circuit complexity had evolved enough that Jack Kilby led a team at

Texas Instruments to develop the integrated circuits for a miniature handheld calculator—the "Cal-Tech," with a prototype ready by early 1967.

In 1969, Japanese manufacturer Busicom approached the newly founded Intel Corporation to develop a competing calculator integrated circuit. Intel responded by proposing that a general-purpose computing IC be developed. This became the first microprocessor, the Intel 4004, and the basis for the personal computer revolution in the decades to follow. Meanwhile, by the early 1970s TI was not only supplying ICs, but also had entered the retail market with its own pocket calculator, the Datamath (TI's other main line of consumer ICs were voice synthesis chips used in SpeakNSpell educational toys). In the early 1970s Mostek, another new company also located in Texas, was also producing calculator ICs, and Hewlett Packard entered the market with the 1972 introduction of the HP-35 scientific calculator, an instant success despite a $395 price tag.

For the calculator consumer, the 1970s were a decade of great innovation, as prices fell and performance increased. By 1975 hundreds of manufacturers were making portable calculators with LED displays. At this time, the manufacture of slide rules ceased. Silicon electronics had replaced sliding wood and ivory.

ELECTRONIC NUMERICAL DISPLAYS

Mechanical calculators and other devices can display digits by moving wheels or cylinders that have numerals painted on them. Mechanical cash registers originally displayed prices and totals by pushed-up tabs on which numerals were printed. Electronic numerical devices need alternative forms of display. Several types of electronic digital displays were developed in the twentieth century. One of these was the Nixie tube, developed by Burroughs. A Nixie tube was cylindrical glass, in various sizes. The end of the cylinder formed a circular window through which the electrodes inside could be seen. Essentially a neon light, the Nixie had 10 cathodes lined up inside, each in the form of a numeral. When 90–200 volts were applied to a cathode, it emitted an orange glow in the shape of a numeral. Other related tubes had electrodes inside that displayed not whole digits, but the segments making up digits (and some characters of the Roman alphabet). Such tube-type displays were somewhat expensive, and the high voltages required made them not well suited for low-voltage microelectronics.

Another form of display used a stack of 10 rectangular pieces of acrylic plastic. A pattern of holes drilled in each piece formed the outline of one of the 10 digits. Tiny "grain of wheat" light bulbs at the edge of each piece of drilled acrylic could illuminate the edge of the pieces one at a time. The pattern of holes in the piece of plastic whose edge was being illuminated would light up and be visible from the front of the stack. This form of display had lower voltage requirements than Nixie tube displays, and could be made in large sizes. But it was also cumbersome and expensive, and characters were not displayed with equal brightness, as light had to pass through all the sheets in front of the one being illuminated.

The solution to these shortcomings was the development of solid-state electronic displays. The first type to appear was a solid-state light source—the light-emitting diode (LED). The second was the liquid crystal display (LCD). Fluorescent displays have also been also used. Dot matrix printing technology allowed for inexpensive printing calculators.

Calculators have been built into digital watches. More expensive pocket calculators will graph equations on larger, sometimes color, displays. Software calculators are included with home computer operating systems, such as Windows. However, it is not surprising that for many purposes, handheld calculators are most handy. Handheld calculators compete with small handheld computers, "personal digital assistants." These PDAs have more capabilities and often have larger displays, though they often lack a keyboard. It appears that a portable do-all device will evolve, a combination PDA, calculator, wireless phone, and e-mail reader. Cash registers are likely to remain specialized computer terminals. But as the use of electronic funds increases, the cash drawer may disappear.

REFERENCES

Ball, Guy, and Bruce Flamm. *Collector's Guide to Pocket Calculators.* Tustin, CA: Wilson/Barnett Publishing, 1997.

Crandall, Richard L. *The Incorruptible Cashier: The Formation of an Industry, 1876–1890.* Lanham, MD: Madison Books, Inc., 1990.

———. *The Incorruptible Cashier. Volume 2: The Brass Era, 1888–1915.* Lanham, MD: Madison Books, Inc., 1996.

Marcosson, Issac F. *Wherever Men Trade: The Romance of the Cash Register.* New York: Arno Press, 1972.

The Old Calculator Web Museum. "Calculator History Timeline." *http://www.geocities.com/ SiliconValley/Lab/7510/timeline.html*

Redin, James. "The Calculator Wars." *http://www.dotpoint.com/xnumber/wars.htm*

Yesterday's Office. Articles, links, and discussion. Joplin, MO: Asay Publishing Service. *http://www.yesterdaysoffice.com*

Cameras

Cameras have become such a common feature of daily life that it is hard to imagine a time when photography was largely confined to professionals in portrait studios, when photographs were rare and costly, or when the average person lived and died without ever having seen a picture of himself or herself.

PHOTOGRAPHIC FILM

The proliferation of cameras is largely a function of developments in film (see also **motion pictures**). From the invention of photography on through the late nineteenth century, photographs were made by the exposure of glass plates covered with light-sensitive liquids. Wet-plate photo technology had obvious expenses, inconveniences, and limitations.

George Eastman (1854–1932) was one of the pioneer developers of dry-plate photography, in which sheets of glass were coated with a dusting of light-sensitive chemicals. And in 1885 Eastman produced the first transparent photographic "film." Photographic film has two components: a base and a coating. The base of most photographic film is a processed wood product called cellulose acetate, with a plastic-like consistency. The coating is a light-sensitive emulsion of silver salts.

Once this lightweight film was made available, camera technology began a rapid process of development as smaller, simpler, and lighter, thus less costly, types of cameras were designed and manufactured.

KODAK BOX CAMERAS

In 1888, Eastman marketed a simple camera called Kodak, with the advertising slogan, "You push a button, we do the rest." The Eastman-Kodak Company quickly achieved prominence in its mission of making the camera an indispensable possession for everyone. Ever-more convenient features appeared, such as daylight loading (1891), roll film with an exposure-counter window (1895), affordable color film (1935), automatic exposure control (1938), fully automatic film processing (1948), and disposable flash bulb units and cartridge-loading film (1963).

The technology behind the common flash bulb has a long and complex history (see also **electric lights**). Early flash pictures were taken using a rather dangerous technique of combustible powder explosions. The electronic flash is largely the invention of the American engineer Harold Eugene Edgerton (1903–1990), who began taking out patents for his flash devices in the 1930s. One of the early commercially available flash units was the Wabash Electroflash Portable Battery Model, which weighed in at 11 pounds. Edgerton received contracts for designing aerial reconnaissance flash photo equipment during World War II, after convincing skeptical critics by producing beautiful aerial photographs of Stonehenge taken at midnight. Flash bulbs were miniaturized largely thanks to transistors, which enabled the electronic circuitry to be greatly reduced in size and weight.

In the early years of the twentieth century, specialty cameras achieved enormous popularity; thus the Kodak Brownie was designed for children and sold for $1.00, taking film that cost 15 cents a roll. The Brownie first appeared in 1900 and continued in production for many years. The child-friendly camera was a brilliant market strategy, since child photographers could be relied upon to grow up and both continue taking photos and invest in more elaborate cameras. But the Brownie was also the camera of choice for many adults who appreciated its economy and simplicity.

The "Pocket Instamatic," an economical box-camera from Kodak. (Courtesy of Corbis)

The Kodak Coquette was a camera designed to appeal to women; small in size, it came with a matching lipstick holder and compact. The Coquette lasted only two years (1930–1932), however.

POLAROID INSTANT CAMERAS

The instant camera was invented by Edwin Herbert Land (1909–1991) and marketed as the Polaroid Land camera in the 1940s. Land was a plastics engineer and had been doing work with plastics that polarized light, blocking out some of the vibrations of light rays. Polarizing plastics found immediate applications in sunglasses, and in other products that utilized their light-filtering capacities. Land conceived the camera application while on vacation in New Mexico in 1943, when one of his children asked why they had to wait so long for pictures to get developed. Land immediately set to work developing a camera film that would develop its image within a few seconds of exposure.

The first instant cameras produced sepia-toned images. Successful and sharp black-and-white image cameras appeared in 1950, and color Polaroid cameras hit the market in 1963. The instant camera was an enormous success, and it is estimated that by the late 1960s, half the households in America owned a Polaroid camera.

Cameras today range from the inexpensive disposable to the bells-and-whistles high-tech imports of Nikon and Leica. And the still photograph became an indispensable witness and record of everyday life in the twentieth century.

The Polaroid Land camera, with automatic focus and built-in flash. (Courtesy of Corbis)

REFERENCES

Kodak Corporation. *http://www.kodak.com*

McPartland, Scott. *Edwin Land: Photographic Pioneer* (Masters of Invention series). Vero Beach, FL: Rourke Enterprises, 1993.

Nikon Corporation. *http://www.nikon.co.jp*

Wade, John. *A Short History of the Camera.* Watford, England: Fountain Press, 1979.

Wallace, Joseph. *The Camera (Turning Point Inventions).* New York: Atheneum Press, 2000.

Weinsberg, Peter. *Land's Polaroid: A Company and the Man Who Invented It.* Boston: Houghton Mifflin, 1987.

West, Nancy. *Kodak and the Lens of Nostalgia (Cultural Frames, Framing Culture).* Charlottesville: University Press of Virginia, 2000.

Cleaning Products

The twentieth century witnessed a growing fascination with cleanliness, both personal and domestic. The word "hygiene" comes from an ancient Greek term for "health," and belief in a correlation between physical soundness and clean bodies and environments took root in the American mind in the early 1900s. Developing knowledge of the connection between bacteria and infection fueled interest in killing germs, on hands, on clothing, and on household surfaces. Consumer interest in seemingly endless varieties of specialized cleaning products remains strong, although concern about environmental impacts has also become a market-shaping force. Many of the new cleaning products developed in conjunction with a new piece of cleaning technology; thus, for example, the **washing machine** encouraged the development of specialized soaps and detergents, and the household clothes **dryer** invited dryer products such as softeners and antistatic sheets.

LAUNDRY

Soaps and detergents clean fabrics by reducing the surface tension of water with surface action agents or "surfactants." This causes the water to become more receptive to soil particles. Surfactants also work to loosen, emulsify (disperse in water), and hold soil in suspension.

Soap making dates back to at least 2800 B.C., but in the nineteenth century the mass production of soaps for markets produced lively competition among soap makers. An American product that achieved tremendous popularity was the soap named Ivory, produced by Procter & Gamble from the 1880s on into the present day. Ivory was touted for its purity, long-lasting quality, smooth texture, and lightness ("It floats!").

The first soap designed explicitly for washing machines was also a Procter & Gamble product: Chipso was essentially a chopped-up version of a standard soap formula with enhanced solubility.

The real technical breakthrough in laundry products came with the chemical synthesis of detergents. In a detergent, the surfactant is an organic compound molecule with differing properties at its "ends." One end of the detergent's

Specialized household cleaning products and tools. (Courtesy of www.comstock.com)

surfactant molecule is called "hydrophobic" ("water-hating"). This end is attracted to soil particles in the fabric. The other end is "hydrophilic" ("water-loving") and is attracted to the wash water. Thus, the surfactant grabs up soil particles and drags them out into solution with the water. This dirt-nabbing drama is played out at the molecular level in washing machines worldwide.

Different types of detergent surfactants have been developed to meet the challenges of differing water hardness or softness, different types of soils, the range of wash water temperatures appropriate for types of fabrics, and so forth. In addition to surfactants, detergents today contain molecules known as builders, which produce a water-softening effect, antiredeposition agents to keep the soil particles in suspension, corrosion inhibitors for the good of the machine's parts, fluorescent whitening agents, colors, fragrances, pacifiers, enzymes, and suds control agents. As such, detergents present a fascinating study in chemistry.

In 1933, Procter & Gamble produced Dreft, its first mass-marketed synthetic detergent. The company used radio advertising intensively to educate the public about Dreft's advantages, funding entire radio dramas, which came to be known somewhat incorrectly as "soap operas," with detergent commercials interspersed. One year later a sister product, Drene, was the first detergent-based shampoo. In 1946 Tide was announced by the same company as "a washing miracle," and its popularity was astounding.

For more stubborn soiling, or for large job locations such as hospitals and hotels, something stronger was required in addition to the now-standard detergents.
In 1913 a method of making sodium hypochlorite bleach from natural brine
through electrolysis was discovered, and Clorox appeared. Its name is derived
from chlorine and sodium hydroxide, the two substances that combine to form
the active ingredient. Clorox was an unfamiliar product and had to create its market; this was done with extensive distribution of free samples. In its early years,
the Clorox Company instructed retailers to give away three out of four bottles.
Eventually the product attained a high regard for its cleansing and sanitizing or
germ-killing properties.

In 1972, scientists at Procter & Gamble developed a way of impregnating light
fabric sheets with fabric softeners, and Bounce dryer sheets were born. The heat of
the drying cycle releases the softeners upon contact with clothing. Now entire suburban neighborhoods are at times suffused with the well-known fragrance of dryer
sheets, so widely are they used as a final touch in the laundering process.

ALL-PURPOSE CLEANING PRODUCTS

Synthetic detergents found their way into hundreds of new household cleaning
products, many of them specialized for one type of surface such as glass, wood, or
tile; others are "multipurpose" or "all-purpose." An enduring example of the latter type of product is Procter & Gamble's Mr. Clean. Its trademark image of a burly
smiling bald man with one gold earring was introduced in 1958 through radio and
television ads; the jingle "Mr. Clean will clean your whole house, and everything
that's in it!" promised universal applicability for the bright-golden liquid.

Aerosol cans propelled dusting aids such as Pledge and oven-cleaning products of great strength and toxicity. A subsidiary market of sponges, mops, applicators, scrub pads, and brushes made of various plastics developed alongside the
cleanser arsenal that gradually took up residence under the sink in most American homes.

HAND AND BODY CLEANSERS

The first perfumed beauty soap to be successfully marketed was Procter &
Gamble's Camay in 1926, and it quickly found competitors that offered mildness,
moisturizing qualities, youth-preserving attributes, and more.

Deodorant soaps also claimed a healthy market share. In the 1980s, liquid hand
soaps and shower soaps appeared, in a bewildering array of scents and colors.
Today, keeping America clean is, in short, a multimillion-dollar project.

REFERENCES

Silvulka, Juliann. *Soap, Sex and Cigarettes: A Cultural History of American Advertising*. Belmont, CA: Wadsworth Publishing Co., 1997.

Stone, A. Harrison. *Chemistry of Soap*. Englewood Cliffs, NJ: Prentice-Hall, 1968.

Compact Discs

The compact disc revolutionized home audio when it was introduced in 1982. CDs, as they were immediately known, rapidly replaced the phonograph record as the primary medium for home-recorded audio (see **Audio Recording**). The compact disc now takes many forms, including the familiar digital audio compact disc, "CD-DA"; CD-ROM for computers; CDR and CD-RW (the recordable forms); and DVD, or digital versatile disc, a higher-capacity disc used for both video (prerecorded movies) and computer data. There are many other less common formats for compact discs as well, including photo-CD, CD-I interactive discs, and karaoke discs. All of these are just variations in the way data is formatted on the disc.

All types of compact disc are based upon several core-enabling technologies: laser, solid-state laser, digital integrated circuits (ICs) for digital-to-analog conversion and servomotor control technology; plastics (polycarbonate); error correction coding schemes and their implementation in ICs; and signaling modulation schemes. These many technologies came together in the early 1980s to make possible the digital compact disc.

VIDEO DISCS

The compact disc evolved from the video disc. The video disc in turn had the phonograph record as a predecessor. In the 1980s there were format battles as the world's major consumer electronics manufacturers provided competing formats and technologies in the effort to provide recorded video in the home. The challenge posed by the enormous data densities required by video led to many solutions: some were mechanical, some used capacitance pickups (RCA Spectra Vision). The discs were large, typically 12 inches in diameter, and often had to be flipped over in playback as both sides were needed to hold a movie. Philips developed a successful video disc that used lasers to read the recorded signal. This LaserVision Disc system had two advantages: the laser could read a very high-density signal, and the laser did not physically touch the disc, so there was no wear from repeated playback. However, all these disc systems had to compete with older magnetic tape technology, repackaged in convenient form as the home video cassette recorder (VCR). The several advantages of the discs were thinness, ease of reproduction, and very rapid ac-

An optical disc. Information is recorded as a spiral track of tiny pits in a plastic disc, coated with a reflective material. The data is read by a narrow laser beam moved slowly across the rapidly spinning disc. The intensity of the reflected laser beam fluctuates between high and low as the pits spin by, producing the varying digital output signal. (Courtesy of Corbis)

cess to information no matter where it was on the surface of the disc (just remove the pickup). Despite the advantages that discs have, the VCR had one very important advantage: it was both player and recorder, a feature consumers valued highly.

MUSIC CDs

Philips' LaserVision system was analog—although it used lasers, the signal varied with the brightness of the image. In the late 1970s, Philips used its experience with the video disc to develop and propose a digital audio recording format. Of the Japanese companies approached with a prototype, Sony had the most interest and brought their experience with digital encoding and error correction techniques. So Philips and Sony jointly developed the modern compact disc system. A principal inventor for Philips was Johannes P. "Joop" Sinjou, and for Sony, Toshitada Doi. Sony released is first CD player in October 1982. The first CD was a Billy Joel recording. The very first CD players were quite expensive, and the audiophiles argued about the accuracy of the sound. But prices fell rapidly and the CD very quickly eliminated the vinyl LP record from store shelves. Thus ended nearly a century of the reign of the phonograph.

As personal computers became popular in the 1980s, the manufacturers turned their attention to computer applications and the compact disc read-only-memory

(CD-ROM) standard was set out in the "yellow book" of 1985. The first successful CD-ROMs were encyclopedias and national telephone directories. In the 1980s most commercial computer software and games were distributed on floppy diskettes; now almost all distribution of software is on CD-ROM.

DVDs

Finally, in 1997 the "digital versatile disc," or DVD, was introduced, after a standards battle and considerable worry from the movie studios about copying. The DVD uses a shorter-wavelength laser and can be recorded in two layers and on two sides—as a result it can hold at least 7 times more data than an audio CD. Most important from a commercial standpoint: a DVD can hold a two-hour movie. Indeed, the name DVD originally stood for digital video disc. Of course, like any digital media such as CD-ROM, DVD can hold more than just video data, and so the name was made more generic.

CD technology is a complete system that includes the disc itself, the format of the information recorded on the disc, the disc player, and the disc-manufacturing process. These are all interwoven—the disc was not possible without a format for getting large amounts of information on so small a disc, nor without a means of mass-producing discs—and, of course, there must be players to retrieve the information encoded on the discs.

Let us begin with the disc itself. A compact disc is 12 centimeters ($4\frac{3}{4}$ inches) in diameter. It consists of three layers: A base of polycarbonate plastic is stamped or molded to create tiny pits in its surface. This surface is transparent, not reflective, and on this embossed plastic base an extremely thin layer of shiny aluminum is deposited in a vacuum chamber. Finally, a layer of protective transparent acrylic plastic lacquer is applied to the disc and spun so that it spreads to form a thin even layer. It is then hardened by exposure to ultraviolet light.

The original digital audio recording is made on magnetic tape. This original signal is used to power a laser that is focused on a photosensitive layer on a smooth glass master disc. The master is chemically developed—the places where the light from the pulsed laser hit the master disc are dissolved away, leaving pits. The now-pitted glass master is electroplated to produce a nickel metal master. This master is used to produce a "mother"; the mother is in turn copied to produce son "stampers." These are used as molds to produce the actual compact discs. The stampers gradually wear out and are replaced during a long production run.

The information-carrying pits are in a stream that spirals out from near the center hole of the disc. In a full disc, this spiral is a four-mile-long string of binary data, ones and zeros represented by pits and the absence of a pit. About 60 widths of this spiral of digital data fit in the width needed by a single groove on a phonograph record.

The compact disc player contains the following mechanical and optical components: a variable speed motor to spin the disc, a servomotor to position the reading assembly over the desired part of the spiral data track on the disc, a laser and optics system to focus a beam of coherent light on the surface of the disc, and finally a solid-state light sensor to detect the fluctuating light reflected from the spinning disc. In addition, there are the electronic components: the player requires control circuitry to spin the disc and position the read assembly at various points on the disc, and to display information to the user. A digital-to-analog converter circuit takes the digital signal from the photodetector and produces the analog audio signal that can be amplified and heard using headphones or speakers.

A semiconductor laser and a lens assembly precisely focus the infrared beam (wavelength 780 nanometers) on the reflective aluminum layer in the disc. Since the beam is focused on the aluminized layer beneath the surface of the disc, the system tolerates some surface dirt and scratches on the surface of the disc. If the light beam hits the smooth, unpitted reflective surface on the disc, it is reflected back through the optics and detected by a photodiode. On the other hand, if the laser beam shines on a pit in the reflective surface, the reflected light will be greatly reduced and the photodiode will fall below a threshold. And so the data stream from the pickup is digital. This signal must then be converted to an analog audio signal. This conversion also involves error correction. The playback circuits may also include antiskip memory. A CD player subjected to jolts will have the read assembly knocked off its intended position on the data stream. Antiskip circuits include a "buffer" or temporary data store that allows the player to read the disc ahead of the data currently being played. When the player is jolted and the disc cannot be read, data can still be sent to the user, drawing on the data in the temporary memory buffer. When the disc can be read again, the player catches up by reading faster and filling up the buffer once again. In addition to these digital circuits, a CD player typically has a small amplifier for the audio signal.

Manufacturers of digital electronics continually improve their performance. The main thrust of digital disc development is greater data densities and increased fidelity to the original (especially in resolution).

The data density in an optical storage device such as a compact disc depends on the wavelength of the light used to make and read the disc. The first available solid-state lasers were infrared, and these are used in compact discs. Then red-visible light lasers were developed, and these are used by DVD. Currently, there is intense work on the commercial development of blue lasers, which will permit much higher amounts of data to be recorded on the same size surface. Alternatively, small CDs could be used. Although DVD-ROM has been available for computers for several years, it has not been nearly as successful as movies on video DVD. Computer users have not seen much use for the enormous amounts of data DVD can store. Titles have been limited to multimedia encyclopedias, the entire library of back issues of *National Geographic,* or a few national phone directory and other databases. Game players have by and large been content to play games distributed on up to a half-dozen or so CD-ROMs. But the announcement by Sony that the successor to the Playstation videogame system, the Playstation 2, would have a DVD drive indicated that the game development will proceed in the direction of higher data.

Some have predicted that the advent of blue lasers will mean that DVD will have a short life and will be quickly replaced by higher-density systems. The typical audio compact disc may then become smaller in diameter, more portable, and easier to carry. Techniques for compressing audio signals (for example, MP3 format) and the development of solid-state electronic storage (flash RAM) has made possible portable audio players that store music on digital memory chips and have no moving parts. As the price for this technology falls, it may partially replace the compact disc for audio reproduction. But in the foreseeable future, there is no technology that can match the high-quality, inexpensive reproduction, and ease of use that the compact disc provides.

REFERENCES

Lenk, John D. *Complete Guide to Compact Disc Player Troubleshooting and Repair.* Englewood Cliffs, NJ: Prentice-Hall, 1986.

Pohlmann, Ken C. *Principles of Digital Audio.* Englewood Cliffs, NJ: Sams/Prentice-Hall Computer Publishing, 1989.

Poor, Alfred. "Optical Disc Technology: An A–Z on Laser Light Storage," June 27, 2001. *http://www.extremetech.com/article/0,3396,s=1039&a=5803,00.asp*

Sony Disc Manufacturing (division of Sony Corporation). "Compact Disc," 1998. *http:// sdm.sony.com/media/cd.html*

University of Washington. *http://www.ee.washington.edu/class/ConsElec/Chapter1.html*

Construction Toys

Construction toys, such as Lego bricks, are designed to encourage young people in creative activities while developing fine-muscle motor skills.

ALPHABET BLOCKS AND FROEBEL'S GIFTS

The first person to propose such toys was the English philosopher John Locke (1632–1704); some of Locke's alphabet blocks were produced following his 1693 *Some Thoughts Concerning Education*. These ideas were extended by the German philosopher Friedrich Wilhelm Froebel (1782–1852), and his "gifts," as he called the blocks, not only influenced major figures of the twentieth century, but also were still available in 2000. Froebel, who invented the idea of kindergartens ("children's gardens"), promoted the ideas that manual training would unite the child's hand and brain and that play was useful as an aid to personal expression. In 1831 he introduced the gifts as wood objects in three geometric shapes: cube, cylinder, and sphere, but later added more complex shapes. These came to America in 1872, manufactured by Milton Bradley as "Kinder-Garten Alphabet and Building Blocks." One disciple of Froebel who was educating her children at home, Anna Lloyd Wright, saw the blocks in a toy exhibit at the 1876 Centennial Exposition in Philadelphia and bought a set for her son Frank, who later, as a world-famous architect, recalled the Froebel blocks as a major influence on his creative development. Not only Frank Lloyd Wright (1867–1959), but also the genius inventor of the geodesic dome, Buckminster Fuller (1895–1983), and the Russian abstract painter Wassily Kandinsky (1866–1944) grew up with Froebel blocks. The Milton Bradley company went on to become one of the major toy manufacturers of the twentieth century, while the simple cubical blocks continue to serve as an introduction to construction skills for infants. Possibly the main drawback in block sets is their vulnerability to be knocked over, ruining the child's structure.

MECCANO AND ERECTOR SETS

Frank Hornby of Liverpool, England, patented "Mechanics Made Easy" in 1901. This is a system of perforated metal strips of different shapes and sizes that

The 1927 Sears, Roebuck catalog included two of the longest-lived twentieth-century construction kits, Erector Sets and Tinkertoys. The Bilt-E-Z kit wasn't so successful, but notice that it addresses both boy builders and "Girls! Think of the thrill of building your own doll house to order, with as many stories, rooms and porches as you want." (Courtesy of Sears Roebuck and Co.)

can be assembled in myriad arrangements with nuts and bolts. The company grew rapidly, and in 1908 Hornby bought out his partner and changed the name of the company and the construction sets to Meccano. More variety was offered, such as gears and bright colors, and Meccano sets were sold throughout the British Commonwealth. Branch factories were established in Spain, France, and Argentina, and annual competitions were held for the best and most creative structures. There were many imitators of Meccano worldwide. Although the English company went bankrupt in 1980, its former subsidiaries in France and Argentina continued to produce Meccano sets throughout the century.

For a short time there was a Meccano factory in New Jersey, but the competition of the American Erector Sets was too fierce. They were the brainchild of one of the more prolific inventors and flamboyant marketers of the century, Alfred Carlton Gilbert (1884–1961). An accomplished athlete who won over a hundred medals in various sports in college, and the Olympic Gold in pole vault (for which he held the world's record in 1908), A.C. Gilbert also was a talented magician. This hobby he turned into a business while in his senior year at Yale, naming it the Mysto Manufacturing Company. After completing his degree in medicine, he expanded Mysto. But in 1911, inspired by watching girder construction of skyscrapers, he began working on a construction toy set. In 1913 the Mysto Erector was introduced, and over the next half century, the A.C. Gilbert company offered increasingly larger and more sophisticated Erector Sets, capable of building a 6-foot-high motorized parachute jump, motorized cars and trucks, carousels, Ferris wheels—and anything else "his boys" could conceive of. Gilbert continued to invent, holding over 180 patents for motors, gearboxes, appliances, and electric model trains. He also expanded into manufacturing chemistry sets, which were as influential on budding scientists as the Erector Sets were for young engineers. As with Meccano, competitions and prizes were offered, and newsletters went out to loyal fans, with tips and plans. The A.C. Gilbert Company folded in 1967, and as a final irony, the French Meccano Company later purchased the right to call their product Erector, although these are actually Meccanos.

TINKERTOYS AND LINCOLN LOGS

Shortly after Erector Sets came out, wooden Tinkertoys were introduced. The inventor was Charles Pajeau, a tombstone cutter from Evanston, Illinois. Pajeau had noticed a baby playing delightedly with wooden spools (such as sewing thread is wound on). His invention had flat spools with a hole drilled through the middle and identically sized holes around the circumference. Sticks, thinly notched at each end, could be inserted firmly into the holes, thereby making it possible to interconnect spools in all directions. Pajeau also provided cardboard vanes that could be gripped in the notches on the sticks. With sticks in all the circumference holes, and vanes at the end of each stick, an eight-vaned propeller could be constructed. To demonstrate the versatility of the Tinkertoy set, Pajeau persuaded a drugstore in Grand Central (railroad) Station in New York City to put a Tinkertoy windmill in the store window. Pajeau hid an electric fan to the side, and the windmill spun about. He also hired men to sit in the window, demonstrating how the spools and sticks worked. Police had to disperse crowds, but Tinkertoys were off and running. By the end of 1914 (or 1915—there is confusion about which was the product's first year), close to a million sets had been sold. The sales of the first sixty years exceeded 100,000,000 sets. By the 1980s, with Tinkertoys now a product of the giant Hasbro company, the wood had largely been replaced by plastic. Wood had always been problematic as being susceptible to swelling and shrinking with changing humidity. Around 1960 Tinkertoy brought architectural construction up to date with metal "Curtain Wall" skyscraper sets. Although Tinkertoys were mainly designed for small children, as recently as 1992 Tinkertoys were being used by physics teachers for three-dimensional demonstrations of atoms and molecules.

The other popular wood construction set of the century was Lincoln Logs. These were invented by John Lloyd Wright (1892–1972). Like his famous father, he grew up playing with Froebel blocks, but he claimed that his inspiration for the invention was from accompanying Frank Lloyd Wright to Japan in 1917 where his father's Imperial Hotel was being built in Tokyo. Drawing on traditional Japanese techniques, some of the hotel was constructed of intersecting wood beams. John Lloyd Wright (himself a distinguished architect) introduced his invention in 1918. There are many systems of notching and connecting log structures in different folk cultures, but the Lincoln Logs method is not too far from what Abraham Lincoln would have known in old Kentucky and Illinois. Like Tinkertoys, Lincoln Logs were an instant success. And like Tinkertoys and the metal construction sets, they were superior to play blocks because the parts interlocked. In 1943, the company was sold to Playskool. In some years, a million sets were sold, and in 2000, Lincoln Logs were still going strong. One disclaimer should be noted about John Wright's and A.C. Gilbert's accounts of their inventions: some critics suggest that Gilbert was copying Hornby's Meccano and that Wright copied an 1866 toy log set invented by Joel Ellis. The construction sets here discussed had the greatest sales and longevity in production, but there were many other kinds of sets, including large block and log sets in wood, plastic, and cardboard designed especially for group play in kindergartens and nursery schools.

LEGOS

Without any question, by the end of the twentieth century the popularity of the earlier inventions had been surpassed worldwide by Lego sets. The word "Lego" was coined by the Danish master carpenter and joiner Ole Kirk Christiansen (?–1958) from the Danish words for "play well"—LEg GOdt. Later it was brought to the attention of the company that in Latin, *lego* can mean "I study, I put together." Christiansen started making wooden toys in 1932 in Billund, Denmark, but the famous construction sets were not yet among them. The forerunner of these were "Automatic Binding Bricks" introduced in 1949 and sold only in Denmark. In 1953, these were renamed Lego bricks, but the design of studs and tubes was not patented until 1958. However, by then the company had already launched the "Lego System of Play" with 28 sets and eight vehicles, and had expanded sales beyond Denmark into Germany. Partly as a result of a fire in the wood factory, production changed over to all plastic, at first cellulose acetate, then ABS (acrylonitrile butadiene strene). In 1968 Legoland Billund, a Lego theme park, was opened; in 1996 they welcomed their 25 millionth visitor, and soon opened other Legolands in England and California. Undoubtedly the basic reason for Lego's success has been the versatility of the bricks: it is said that the possible combinations of bricks run into astronomical figures. Furthermore, children could integrate their other toys such as dolls, soldiers, and cars into their Lego creations. However, the company has continuously expanded the line, introducing special sets for trains, doll houses, circuses, castles, floating and diving boats, as well as motors. In 1998, Lego Mindstorms came out, integrating robotic technology with the building system. Like Meccano and Erector before them, Lego sponsors contests. In 1998 records were broken for the tallest tower buildings in Australia, Russia, and Estonia, all over 24 meters (about 27 feet) high. By the end of the century, there were Lego factories in Denmark, Switzerland, the United States and South Korea, and the many options available dominated the construction toy industry.

The future development of construction toys is clearly indicated by computer programs of the 1990s. At first allowing "building" and viewing in a single program, by 2000 the builders could build virtual structures into which characters from other game programs could be introduced to move within a unique and original environment. On-line, widely separated builders and players can bring collaborative "visitors" to interact within the newly created environments. Holographic constructions are certainly indicated, which could allow the builders themselves to interact with their creations.

There are trade-offs with all this technical versatility: parents appreciate not having a clutter of components around the house, as well as not stepping barefoot on sharp bricks in the dark or rushing puppies to the veterinarian with ingested plastics. On the other hand, the world of a computer screen or even a holographic room does not convey acquaintance with a genuine world of tactile reality that Froebel intended to unite hand and brain. For that, blocks and bricks and snap-together parts will continue.

REFERENCES

Cho, Erin. "Lincoln Logs: Toying with the Frontier Myth." *History Today.* April 1993, 3–34.
Coffman, Barbara, and Arlan Coffman. "Building by the 'Little Folks': Early Architectural Construction Toys in America." *Home Sweet Home: American Domestic Vernacular Architecture,* ed. Charles W. Moore, Kathryn Smith, and Peter Becker. New York: Rizzoli, 1983.
O'Brien, Richard. *The Story of American Toys.* New York: Abbeville Press, 1990.
Watson, Bruce. "'Hello Boys!' Become an Erector Master Engineer!" *Smithsonian,* May 1999, 120–134.

Convertible Furniture

Furniture that folds up for ease of storage and portability has been with us for over two millennia. Beyond the roll-up beds and mobile kitchens that shepherds and nomads carried on their backs or on the backs of their pack animals, sophisticated folding stools and chairs are pictured in ancient Greek vase paintings of the sixth century B.C. But the twentieth century witnessed a flowering of designs for changeable or "motion furniture" and their production for mass markets in which such home furnishings create a home aesthetic and encourage the development of a definite lifestyle.

THE MURPHY BED

Pioneering in the field of motion furniture was William L. Murphy, who in 1900 secured the patent for the famous Murphy bed. Murphy was born in Stockton, California, in the late 1870s, and moved to a one-room apartment in San Francisco as a young man. He wished to be able to entertain guests in this apartment, but had no space. Noting that a significant amount of his available floor space was taken up by his bed, Murphy began work on prototypes for a bed that would fold away when not in use. The successful model was a door bed, with a spring-operated counterbalancing design to prevent unintended folding of sleepers into walls. This was christened the Murphy door bed, and a company by that same name was created shortly thereafter. It was followed in 1918 by the Murphy pivot bed, which pivoted on the doorjamb of a dressing closet, then lowered into sleep position.

Although the Murphy bed enjoyed great success among crowded apartment dwellers, it also gave rise to many scenarios in comedy, as dramatic malfunctions of door beds were pictured causing havoc in small quarters. Many Murphy pivot beds are still in use today, in hotels, dormitories, and fire departments.

The Murphy Door Bed Company diversified into kitchen applications of convertible furniture with the Cabrinette in 1928, a compact kitchen with many devices capable of being folded away when not in use.

Since the market niche for Murphy bed is one in which living space is limited, demand for such foldaway domestic products waned in the years following World

The Murphy bed saves living space by folding away when not in use. (Courtesy of Murphy Beds Direct)

War II, when more spacious single-family homes with low-cost mortgages funded by the Veterans Administration became widely available. Murphy beds experienced a resurgence of popularity with the economic recession of the 1970s, and once again during the prosperous 1990s when home "media centers" created the need for a convenient napping place for media-blitzed suburbanites.

RECLINING CHAIRS

Recliners got their start as porch furniture made entirely of wood. And they had their origins in novelty and comfort-seeking rather than need. In the 1920s, two Michigan cousins named Edward Knabush and Edwin Shoemaker began tinkering with designs for unusual combination furniture. Knabush was a farmer who was disenchanted with the rural subsistence life; Shoemaker had a day job as a desk maker but tinkered in a wood shop in the evenings. One of their first marketable products was "The Gossiper," a chair and table combination designed to accommodate a telephone and a telephone user.

But the product that really fired their mutual enterprise was a wood-slatted reclinable porch chair billed as "Nature's Way of Relaxing." Its mechanism, which would prove hard to improve upon, involved slots along which its back, seat, and the supports for a rising foot platform could slide. This chair was patented in 1928.

It was quickly followed by an upholstered model for indoor use. Shoemaker and Knabush held a contest to name the new chair; the winning name was "La-Z-Boy." Their company, now named Floral City Furniture, pioneered the traveling furniture show, which was modeled on the circus and also used large tents for display of the new products. Refreshments were served and the owners' families were pressed into service for entertainment. These shows allowed many potential customers to try out the reclining chairs, and greatly fired enthusiasm for their comfort and adaptability.

Platform rockers were introduced in the years following the World War II and a built-in ottoman, or "Otto-matic," was added to these. The "Tranquillator," a vibrating mechanism, could be added for an additional cost.

As its name indicated, the La-Z-Boy was originally and principally a man's chair. It symbolized the relaxation and well-earned rest of the man of the house, and its aesthetic values were designedly masculine: it tended toward largeness, heaviness, and solidity. In the mid-1950s, a recliner with an adjustable back was marketed; the "Hi-Lo Matic" would accommodate the supposedly lower shoulders and smaller torsos of women. In the 1960s recliners specifically designed for women appeared at last. Advertised as offering "the most comfortable part of HER day," these chairs were smaller and had a generally softer appearance, both in design and in upholstering options. A dual recliner in love-seat form also appeared at this time.

During the 1990s the reclining chair, love seat, or couch has taken on additional functions. Foldout arms to accommodate beverages and food have been added. Most recently, these mega-chairs have incorporated storage units, massage and heat functions, built-in phones, laptop computer modem hookups, and drink-cooling refrigeration units. They thus greatly facilitate the lifestyle of that twentieth-century denizen, the couch potato. Indeed it could plausibly be argued that the development of the recliner and the increase in television viewing hours per capita are linked social phenomena.

SOFA BEDS AND FUTONS

The sofa bed has its origin in the years of the Great Depression following the stock market crash of 1929. Many Americans lost their homes and farms during this time, and the combining of households that ensued produced a need for more sleeping space than could be contained within bedrooms as such.

In 1930 the Simmons Company marketed a studio couch from which a bed frame and relatively slim mattress could be unfolded. In 1931 competitor Bernard Castro developed the Castro Classic sofa-sleeper mechanism, in which springs interconnect metal bands stretched across a frame. From the beginning, the central design problem for sofa beds was balancing ease and convenience of un-folding the bed with comfort of sleeping surface. A thinner mattress and lighter-weight frame fold away more easily, while a heavier mattress and sturdier frame accommodate the sleeper more comfortably.

A different approach to the sofa sleeper is the futon bed or couch. "Futon," which comes from a Japanese word meaning "place of rest," entered the American vocabulary in the years following World War II. The original or Japanese futon mattress is unrolled on the floor for sleeping purposes, and its original American offspring followed suit. However, a supporting convertible couch frame was shortly developed and it could accommodate a heavier mattress. In the futon couch, the couch itself just consists of the sleeping mattress in a folded position. This eliminates the need for an outer wood and upholstered frame to conceal the sleeping surface when the couch is in "day" mode. Futons enjoyed a burst of enor-mous popularity during the counter-cultural movement of the 1970s, when dis-content with American politics and traditions caused many to look to Eastern alternatives in modes of thought and ways of living; the futon became not just a place to sit or sleep, but a philosophical statement about living lightly and spir-itually.

Futon frame design has passed through several developmental phases. Early futons used a mattress that folded along its width, sometimes twice, to create the sitting or sofa form. In 1985 Canadian Ron Massey developed a futon frame that hinged along the length of the mattress, a significant addition to both conversion ease and sleeping comfort. With the addition of the slider feature, the futon in its couch phase can now rest flush against the living room wall, converting to bed form by extending itself outward into the living space and not requiring any shifting of the frame's legs.

Convertible furniture in the twentieth century thus reflects both changing historical and economic circumstances, and the enduring American fascination with gadgetry. In turn, such furniture shapes our lives, enabling us to combine the uses of our domestic spaces in creative ways.

REFERENCES

Fiell, Charlotte, and Peter. *Industrial Design A–Z*. New York: Taschen, 2000.
Futon Life Magazine. Archived at *http://www.futonlife.com*
La-Z-Boy, Inc. *www.lazboy.com*
The Murphy Bed Company. *www.murphybedcompany.com*

Copiers and Duplicators

When Xerox and computers equipped with printers and scanners became available to offices and homes, the two processes of copying (making a facsimile of an original document) and duplicating (making multiple copies of a document) came together. Previously copying and duplication required separate devices. Before the development of photography in the mid-nineteenth century, making copies of books, plans, maps, and artwork was a job for skilled manual labor, exemplified by the copyists of medieval monasteries and scriveners in law offices laboriously copying contracts and correspondence in "a big round hand." Making multiple copies was also hand labor until the Renaissance, when engraving, woodcuts, and etching were developed for duplicating pictures and maps and when, after 1450, movable-type printing made the mass production of books possible. The histories of these technologies before the twentieth century are easily available.

CARBON PAPER AND MIMEOGRAPH

For ordinary office work, the first breakthrough was the invention of carbon paper by Ralph Wedgwood of London in 1806. Carbon paper requires considerable pressure, which quill pens of the day could not supply, so its practical use was probably confined to receipts where the original could be written in pencil. With the development of a practical production-model typewriter in 1873 (Christopher Latham Sholes and Carlos Glidden's "Remington"), clear carbon copies of correspondence became routine, though legibility deteriorated with more than three sheets. Only two years later, in 1875, Thomas Alva Edison invented the mimeograph, which was a mainstay in office and school duplicating for the next century. The key to mimeos was a stencil (originally a paraffin-coated paper). When the typebar of the typewriter struck the stencil, the shape of the letter would be cut through the coating. The cut stencil was then removed from the typewriter and fitted to an ink-filled drum in the mimeograph machine. The stencil was rotated as sheets of paper were fed and the ink squeezed from inside the drum through the cut letters in the stencil. The mimeograph process could deliver as many as several thousand copies.

HECTOGRAPHS AND SPIRIT DUPLICATORS

In 1923 a simpler process for smaller numbers of copies was invented in Germany. Called the hectograph (in America the trade name Ditto became the popular term), the original process used a gelatin tray or pad. A special water-soluble pencil image (any color) or a typewritten master sheet produced from a "carbon" backing similar to the pencil "lead" was pressed onto the gelatin. The written image was absorbed into the surface of the gelatin. Sheets of paper then could be pressed against the gelatin and the images were pulled from the gelatin. The gelatin method allowed for gelatin pads to be attached to a drum as in a mimeograph machine. The second hectograph method was liquid or spirit duplication. As with the gelatin process, the ink was in the master (i.e., there was no supply of ink as the mimeograph had). As the drum rotated, a volatile liquid (especially denatured alcohol, or "spirits") moistened the ink to allow transfer of a small quantity of the ink on the master to sheets of paper, producing as many as 200 or 300 copies (copies becoming fainter toward the end of the run). For small operations, the mimeo and ditto machines were hand-operated with a crank to turn the drum, but electrified machines were more practical for large output.

BLUEPRINTS AND WHITEPRINTS

Specialized duplication methods are used for architectural and engineering drawings that are much larger than the letter-sized carbons, mimeos, and dittos. Blueprints require a rather complex chemical process. Drawings are made on translucent drafting paper or cloth. The drawing is placed in contact with paper treated with ferric ammonium citrate and potassium ferricyanide. When exposed to light, the areas not having drawn lines turn blue. A blueprint is thus a negative drawing. Another method, called diazotype, was introduced later with a similar exposure to light, but using other chemicals. It produces a positive or whiteprint.

XEROGRAPHY

Except for carbon copying, which has a very limited output, the preceding methods are all liquid processes.

The search for a dry-copy method began in the late 1930s. There were two approaches, each based on very simple principles of physics. The first, photocopying, was based on the principle that, unlike static, electric charges attract. The second, thermography, was based on the principle that radiant heat is more readily absorbed by darker objects. The actual development of each approach into reliable commercial products took a decade. The first successful experiment with

For long, clean runs . .
Sears Mimeographs give you up to
20,000 copies per stencil

Electric Self-inking Mimeo

Feeds and runs automatically
. . your hands never touch ink

$**149**95 cash $11.50 monthly

Prints up to 60 copies a minute! Extra large self-inking drum feeds itself right amount of ink from inside. Floating impression roller keeps printing uniform at any paper thickness. Automatic reset counter counts to 9,999. Receiving tray. Static eliminator for single sheet pick up.

Takes post card up to legal-size sheets (8½x14 in.). Charcoal gray metal. 33¾x15x13½ in. high. 110–120-volts, 60-cycle AC only. With 6 stencils, stylus, correction fluid, signature plate, dust cover and 2 pounds black ink.

3A5931N–Shipping weight 39 pounds.............. $149.95

Mimeograph Supplies

The mimeograph machine, invented in the 1870s by Thomas Edison, and the spirit duplicator (e.g., Ditto) were standard office fixtures for business, government agencies, schools, and churches throughout most of the twentieth century. The mimeograph stencils (items 1 and 2) could be saved and rerun. After a year or so, mimeo paper tended to age and crumble; Ditto copies faded quickly. These models were in the 1969 Sears Roebuck mail order catalog: a decade later they would be destined for the junk pile. (Courtesy of Sears Roebuck and Co.)

Chester Carlson invented the electrostatic process for Xerox in 1938, but it would be ten years before a machine such as the one shown here was perfected, and not until 1950 that the first automatic office model was marketed. (Courtesy Xerox Corporation)

xerography (*xero* is from the Greek for *dry*) is easily dated, for the first message that physicist Chester Carlson (1906–1968) copied was the date of his invention: 10–22–38 (October 22, 1938). Carlson was at that time in the patents department of a large electronics company in New York. His invention was an electrostatically charged plate that would attract a fine powder to a projected image of the original text. Perfecting this process was the task of Roland M. Schaffert, a physicist with the Battelle Memorial Institute of Columbus, Ohio. He began work in 1944 and in 1948 the photocopier was ready. The first office model was the "Xerox 914," introduced in 1950. It is a very complex and precise machine.

First, there is an optical system composed of a bright light that shines on the original document and lenses and mirrors to project the image onto a drum coated with a light-sensitive material. The drum is given a negative electrical charge. Where the projected light falls on the drum, the charge is neutralized; where the projected image blocks the light, the surface of the drum remains negatively charged. A positive charged powder ("toner") composed of carbon and plastic is attracted to the negatively charged areas of the image on the drum. A sheet of copy paper is given a negative charge, pressed against the rotating drum, and the powder is electrostatically transferred to the paper. A heater warms the plastic in the powder, which thereupon partly melts and impregnates the paper fibers with black carbon (or colors), sealing the image. The drum is then given a new all-over negative charge, and the process is ready to repeat for the same document (if multiple copies are wanted) or for a new document. Thus photocopying (single copies) and dry duplication (multiple copies) are possible with one machine.

As can be seen, extreme mechanical precision is needed to coordinate all these optical, electrical, and motion processes. The early Xerox machines were marvels for being able to copy letters, contracts, and even pages from books and periodicals. Later models became increasingly versatile, being able to do two-sided copying, gathering and collating pages, stapling, and binding, with special settings for copying photographs or enlarging/reducing the image, and eventually copying in high-quality color. The optical system has been dubbed "analog" to distinguish it from the system of digital scanners adapted from computer technology. However, the electrostatic concept of Chester Carlson remained basic for photocopiers.

THERMOFAX

Thermographic copying was the brainchild of Dr. Carl Miller of 3M Corporation. His inspiration was looking at a leaf on a snowbank on a sunny day. The brown leaf absorbed the radiant heat from the sun, the snow reflected the rays. The leaf therefore melted a duplicate image into the snow. Miller experimented with heat-sensitive paper. As 3M's *Innovation Chronicles* states, Miller "took the cellophane wrap from a box of candy . . . , coated it with a heat-sensitive, mercury-based salt and then stretched the coated cellophane over an image. When this image was placed under infrared light [infrared is the radiant heat wave of the light spectrum] the darker portions of the underlying image were registered onto the coated cellophane." This was in the early 1940s; in the early 1950s, after a million dollars of 3M research and development, Thermo-Fax was introduced as the first "convenient" dry-copying office machine. 3M also takes pride in having developed the first dry-color-copying machine in 1968. It worked effectively but was not a commercial success as most businesses and educational institutions were satisfied with black-and-white copiers. As other kinds of color copiers were introduced around 1990, the market changed, and with digital color printing from personal computers, color has become a standard in copying and duplication. At the century's end, the old methods of duplication and copying, including thermography, were obsolete, almost nothing remaining except the abbreviation "cc" on e-mail messages, for "carbon copy." The printing industry too has discarded the technologies that gave us the novels of Jane Austen and Ernest Hemingway, and even copying and duplication by means of cameras and film has given way to digital reproduction of images. Indeed, the photocopier is declining rapidly as a duplicator, because in many schools and businesses the distribution of "handouts" has been replaced entirely by computer "printouts" or simply reading the message on a screen. At the same time, digital technology has been applied to the mimeograph to produce easy to use copiers (e.g., Risograph) that combine these two twentieth-century technologies.

REFERENCES

Better Buys for Business: The Mid-Volume Copier Guide. Malvern, PA: Progressive Business Publications, 1999.

McGrath, Kimberly, ed. *World of Invention.* 2nd ed. Detroit: Gale, 1999.

3M Corporation. *www.3m.com/about3m/pioneer/miller.html*

Credit Cards

Credit cards are a twentieth-century economic invention designed for the mutual benefit of consumers and businesses. The technology evolved from a simple paper system to worldwide digital automation of "plastic money."

Extending credit, i.e., "charging" purchases, for retail goods was until 1900 local and personal. With a largely rural population in America, the village general store was obliged to provide goods on credit until crops were harvested and sold. In towns and cities, the corner grocery likewise offered this service to the neighborhood, usually on a monthly basis. The first major departure from this personal economic relationship was in 1900 when Richard Sears experimented with a "Send No Money!" campaign for goods from the Sears, Roebuck mail order catalog. This policy lasted only two years.

The next experiment with nonlocal credit was in the automobile industry. Until 1916 the policy was cash up front for car purchases. Henry Ford had made this easier by assembly line production of cheap Model T cars and he soon dominated the market. The more expensive cars countered with installment sales; you could drive your new car away and pay for it over a period of time. In 1919, General Motors set up their own financing (GMAC, the General Motors Acceptance Corporation), thereby ensuring profit on the actual sales and on the interest on loans.

At this time half of all car sales in the United States were on installments; by 1922 this had risen to 73 percent and dealers were lowering the customary 50 percent down payment and extending the customary 12-month payback. As with Sears, Roebuck's earlier experience with insecure credit risks, defaulted loans soon led to tighter controls.

RETAILER CREDIT CARDS

The first credit cards also came out of the automobile boom in the early 1920s. Oil companies such as Texaco issued credit cards for gasoline purchases. It was a convenience especially appreciated by traveling salesmen, and it was a means of assuring that they would be loyal to the credit card's gas stations. After World War II credit cards proliferated, especially for business travel and in department

Credit card being processed. (Courtesy of Corbis)

stores (which traditionally had approved installment payments for major purchases such as furniture, or, more often, "layaway" plans whereby the store kept the goods until the payments were complete). Except for department store installment payments, these were all 30-day charges without interest. Each card, however, was issued by an individual retail or service chain. Business travelers carried special wallets to hold an array of cards for oil companies, airlines, hotels, and restaurants.

In 1950 Diners' Club, which had a card accepted by various expensive eating places, launched a "universal" credit card for travel and entertainment. Eight years later, the Diners' Club card was accepted at 17,000 outlets in 76 nations. Card holders paid only five dollars annually for this service, but the Club got 7 percent on every charge. In 1958, American Express, which had long been in the business of serving international travel, started a "war" with Diners' Club, each trying to acquire or ally itself with other credit cards, such as Gourmet Guest Club, Sheraton and Hilton hotels, Avis and Hertz car rentals, Mobil and Amoco oil companies. Card holders gained the convenience of a single monthly bill, not to mention less crowded pocketbooks. Retailers won customers who watched for the credit card emblem, as well as freedom from having to bill individual customers. The credit card companies profited from every sale. Physically, the cards changed too, moving from cardboard, from which the customer's number had to be copied, to plastic, with raised numbers and letters that could be placed in a hand embosser that provided carbons of each transaction for customer, vendor and card company. The embossers also changed from a lever device to a roller that would imprint both the customer's and the vendor's identification.

BANK CREDIT CARDS

In 1951, the bank credit card had a modest introduction at the Franklin National Bank. The main difference from universal credit cards was that the bank offered "revolving" credit; the balance owed was not due in full each month. The card holder had the choice of full payment or making an installment payment on the balance for which the bank charged interest on this consumer loan (which in reality is what it is). The early problem faced by the banks was getting enough card holders so that the bank could assure potential retailers that there actually were customers who wanted to use these cards. The initial approach was ethically questionable and ultimately illegal: banks mailed unsolicited credit cards to addresses in their locality. This practice was reborn in the 1990s with banks offering immediate cash loans to those who would accept their card—and the equally immediate debt. A second problem with the early bank cards was that in most states banks were limited to their locality and therefore could hardly challenge the international scope of the travel-and-entertainment giants. One exception was California, which permitted branch banking. The Bank of America therefore could provide cards that were valid statewide. In 1966, they introduced the national BankAmericard (eventually Visa), which could be issued by other affiliated banks. In Great Britain, the Barclay Bank chain issued the BarclayCard identical in appearance with reciprocal international credit. The following year, eastern U.S. banks came together to issue the rival Master Charge (later Master-Card).

While the American Express and Diners' Club cards had emphasized upscale establishments and conservative economics (bills were payable in full monthly), the bank cards were essentially high-interest installment loans (the national average in 1997 was 18.8 percent) on all kinds of merchandise. Bank credit cards revolutionized consumer behavior. New card holders invariably fell into a "buy now, pay later" psychology and almost immediately purchased goods that they could not afford to pay for at the end of a month, and since they could add on purchases without careful forethought, unpaid balances rose. Runaway debt and personal bankruptcy became a pattern. In 1998, an estimated 60 million American households each owed over $7,000 on their "plastic," and rather than significantly reducing the principal, were paying banks over $1,000 each year in interest and added fees. The ease of simply providing one's Visa number spawned whole new marketing inventions, such as telemarketing and Internet "catalog" shopping. Ironically, by the century's end, consumer credit had gone full circle, as supermarkets came to sell staples on credit, just as the village grocer had done a hundred years before.

The credit card technology kept pace. Rather than physically embossing each charge slip, cards had a magnetic strip with full identification that was simply "swiped" through a scanner for instant digital communication of charges and instant authorization of valid credit status (see **Barcodes and Magnetic Stripes**). Physically signing the charge slip became little more than a quaint ceremony, as more reliable means of identification, such as voice printing or scanning of eyes, were in the works for the next century.

REFERENCES

Calder, Lendol. *Financing the American Dream: A Cultural History of Consumer Credit.* Princeton: Princeton University Press, 1999.

Friedman, John, and John Meehan. *House of Cards: The Troubled Empire of American Express.* New York: Putnam, 1992.

"On-the-Cuff Travel Speeds Up." *Business Week,* August 16, 1958.

Russell, Thomas. *The Economics of Bank Credit Cards.* New York: Praeger, 1976.

Digital Telecommunications

Telecommunications is communication at a distance: generally, any distance much greater than a person can shout. While books such as this one communicate, and at a distance, we shall focus on real-time two-way communication and in particular on the digital and electrical systems developed throughout the nineteenth and twentieth centuries.

The precursors of today's telecommunication networks were the optical communication systems developed before the electric telegraph. The early forms of such systems included signal fires and smoke signals, some with messages relayed from station to station over great distances. In his 1684 Royal Society lecture "On Showing a Way How to Communicate One's Mind at Great Distances," Robert Hooke (1635–1703) describes a system of telecommunications using the recently developed telescope and a signaling device mounted high on poles. The device used ropes to lift and display cutout letters. Hooke recognized the need for control codes, such as "resend" and "message received." He also attended to the need to encrypt messages to keep them private. Data security was a concern from the start.

In the first half of the nineteenth century, Claude Chappé and his brothers developed a semaphore system what was built throughout France under Napoleon, and was planned for extension into England to support a French invasion. The semaphores were a large pivoting crossbeam (like a see-saw), mounted on a tower, and with a wand at each end that could be moved to various positions by an operator below, using cables and pulleys. Stations were about 6 miles (10 kilometers) apart. Each semaphore station replicated the incoming semaphore's position; the sending station operator watched and would signal if the transmitted signal was not being correctly displayed by the receiver. There was also a collision control signal that a station could send if it received incoming signals from the stations in both directions. Many of these control features were to reappear in the most popular late-twentieth-century digital network, Ethernet.

Electrical telegraphy, developed by Samuel Morse (1791–1872) and others in the 1830s and 1840s, was one of the first practical applications of electricity. It soon replaced optical telegraphy, and linked cities around the world. Telegraph systems had a symbiotic relationship with another emerging technology, railroads. Telegraph systems used railroad rights-of-way and stations, and railroads used the telegraph to dispatch trains and communicate with switchmen.

Automatic printing telegraph machines were tried very early (indeed, Morse's first machines traced a line on paper). These evolved into teletypewriters in the 1920s. Teletype machines were large electric typewriters that could be operated remotely. A message typed into a machine at one location transmitted an encoded signal to the machine at the other end and the received message was printed just as it had been typed. In the mid-twentieth century, teletypes were a standard means for rapid communication of text for government, corporations, and newspapers. Teletype machines were also used as terminals on early computers. Many could punch-paper tape, recording the keystrokes in machine-readable form. These formed an early binary code, as the tape either does or does not have a hole at each position across its width. A message could be composed "off-line" on paper tape and later transmitted at higher speed, to reduce expensive long-distance rates.

FAX

The telegraph and its successors in effect digitally encode the alphabet as binary numbers. These are ideal for text. But there had long been an interest in the transmission of images as well. The basic method for doing this is fairly obvious—imagine a photo that is cut up into, say, 100 narrow strips. The strips are glued end to end, forming a long ribbon. Run the ribbon past a photocell, and an electrical signal will be produced that varies with the darkness of the strip. The original photo can be recreated at the receiving end by powering a spot of light with the incoming electrical signal, and moving the light back and forth across a piece of light-sensitive paper. So the basic idea is the same as that used in television: "scan" a two-dimensional image back and forth, effectively forming a sequential "one-dimensional" strip of light and dark. Then convert the light and dark into an electrical signal. Reverse this process at the receiving end. The transmitted electrical signal can be either analog (voltage varying with the brightness of the image) or digital (binary numbers representing different brightness levels). Early systems used analog signals; then, as the cost of digital electronics dropped, later systems used digital signals.

The first facsimile machine (from *factum simile*—Latin for "make it the same") was invented by Alexander Bain (1811–1877), a Scot, in 1842, about the same time as Morse's telegraph. Bain's device was ahead of its time, and could not compete with the simpler and practical Morse telegraph. Bain used a pendulum with a wire at the tip to scan a bed of metal type containing the message—the type bed was advanced slowly as the pendulum swung back and forth, scanning the message. Current flowed when the pendulum contacted the metal portions of the typeface. A synchronized pendulum at the receiving end recreated the message by swinging over sensitized paper that turned dark at the point under the pendulum tip whenever there was an electric current flowing. For sending text messages, it was simpler to tap out Morse code, but Bain's method held the seeds of sending images over great distances.

In 1848 in London, Frederick Bakewell invented a machine that could transmit a signature or other line drawing on metal foil wrapped around a rotating cylinder. But three more breakthroughs were needed for modern fax, which scans an ordinary visible image rather than an electrically conductive original: photography (to get non-text images on paper), a device to convert varying light intensity to varying electrical current, and methods of synchronizing the rotation of the transmitting and receiving cylinders. Photography developed throughout the nineteenth century. In 1873, it was discovered that the electrical resistance of the element selenium varied with the intensity of light that falls on it. In 1881 an Englishman named Shelford-Bidwell demonstrated a device that could reproduce a picture using a selenium photocell in a scanner. Dr. Arthur Korn (1870–1945), a German professor, developed this idea starting as a teenager in 1885, and after much work, he transmitted a photo in 1904, with a wireless transmission a year later.

In the 1920s, various companies developed (expensive) commercial fax equipment. Eventually, integrated circuits produced a revolution in fax as they did elsewhere, allowing small, inexpensive fax machines to appear on desktops throughout the world. The drum was dispensed with, and solid-state elements scanned a whole line as an original document was fed slowly through the machine. By the end of the twentieth century, many fax machines used xerographic or inkjet technologies to recreate the original image on "plain paper," replacing the special sensitized paper used in earlier machines. In addition, modems, used by computers to transmit and receive digital data over phone lines, typically added the capability to receive and transmit fax data as well. Thus a document could be created on a computer, and transmitted to a fax machine, another computer, over phone lines, with no original paper copy ever existing.

THE INTERNET

Originally, computers received data from non-real-time sources. Users prepared all their data in advance. Programs were run one after the other in batches, with data entering the computer on punch cards (see **Barcodes and Magnetic Stripes**) or magnetic tape (see **Audio Recording**). Time-sharing systems became available in the 1960s, with multiple users connected to a single computer, at remote "terminals." Soon it became apparent that a computer might connect not just to multiple users, but to other computers at remote sites as well. In addition, the July 10, 1962, launch by American Telephone and Telegraph (AT&T) of Telstar, the first communications satellite, began an era of dropping costs for long-distance communication of information.

In 1964, IBM and American Airlines created the largest civilian computing project to date, Sabre, a computerized airline reservation system linked to terminals in the offices of over 1,000 travel agents across the United States. Five years later, in 1969, the U.S. Defense Department established ARPANET

(Advanced Research Projects Agency NETwork), linking computers at four re-search sites. Over the next 10 years, this network grew to include over 100 sites. In 1986, the National Science Foundation (NSF) established a newer high-speed network for university sites, dropping the military connection. This network was wildly popular, fueled in part by the growing popularity of personal computers. NSF allowed the network to grow and become an independent service, including commercial and home users, with over 30 million computers networked by the end of the twentieth century.

The Internet is based on communication standards for sending packets of data that are prefaced by address information, and electronic routers that can route the addressed packets to their destinations. Transmission control protocol (TCP) is a standard developed in 1974 that lets quite different computers and networks exchange data. In the early years of the Internet, users used several small appli-cations to use data sent over the Internet. One of these was Telnet, which allowed a user to log in to a remote computer and run applications on the remote com-puter, just as if the user were local. Another standard, file transfer protocol (FTP), allowed whole files to be sent from one computer to another. Other applications allowed creating and reading short messages—e-mail. And Usenet was devel-oped, an electronic bulletin board system that allowed public viewing of mes-sages posted by users (unlike e-mail, which has controlled recipient lists).

As more and more documents came on-line, systems for organizing these and making them easier to access were needed. FTP was cryptic and cumbersome to use. One popular standard developed at the University of Minnesota was Gopher (named both for its function, fetching, and also for the University of Minnesota mascot). This system displayed text menus of numbered items. By typing the number of a menu item, the user would immediately be able to view a submenu or a document. This system was text based, and did not require any new appli-cations at the user's end.

At the same time, computer power was rapidly increasing. Graphics and mul-timedia had become common computer fare, and the mouse had become stan-dard as a way of interacting with displays on screen. In 1991, Tim Berners-Lee (born in London in 1955) was working at CERN, a research center in Europe. Berners-Lee developed standards for a hypertext system for linking users with information on remote computers connected to the Internet. Hypertext is text (or other media, such as maps) with embedded links to other documents, or even specific positions within a document. One can "click on" a link and be "taken to" another document. The CERN team developed standards for what they called the World Wide Web: hypertext transfer protocol (HTTP), hypertext markup language (HTML), and URL (universal resource locator). URLs are Internet addresses to specific files on remote computers (e.g., http:// www.d umn.edu/ index.html). HTTP is a standard for hypertext document transfer. HTML is a standard (or "language") for writing and displaying documents, allowing them to be attractively formatted, to have multiple fonts and hypertext links to other files, and to contain images, sounds, and other media forms.

Displaying HTML pages requires a special application, a Web browser. Popular browsers included Lynx (early browser running on Unix systems and providing only text, no images), Mosaic, Netscape, and Internet Explorer. The requirement that a user must have browser software was a hurdle in the way of using the World Wide Web, but the happy convergence of cheap and capable personal computers, the availability of free and low-cost browsers, and the opening of the Internet to home and commercial users led to tremendous growth of the Web in the 1990s. Thousands of new Web-based companies were born, and the Internet became a common way to access information, read news, browse libraries, play games, and communicate with friends and co-workers.

The Internet is likely to be around for a long time. The future holds improvements and extensions of this technology. Increased bandwidth is a certainty.

A microcomputer from the 1990s, in a "tower" case. This personal computer system includes an optical disc drive (CD-ROM, CD-R, or DVD), and a smaller floppy disc drive (in the lowest drive bay in the case). Personal computers were used for word processing, playing games, and to connect to the Internet for e-mail, Web browsing, and downloading music and images. (Courtesy of Corbis)

It is expected that the high-speed future Internet will eventually provide on-demand entertainment content, such as motion pictures, so viewers will not be confined to scheduled mass broadcasting times. There will be increased wireless access to the Internet. Users will have lifetime e-mail addresses. Convergence technology, where a formerly separate technology combines with Internet technology, was appearing by the end of the twentieth century and is likely to grow. An example is the set-top box, which puts an Internet browser onto the living room television screen. Another example is wireless phones that can access the Internet and display e-mail. Internet appliances have had mixed success—these are small computers that are primarily intended as Internet access devices, rather than as stand-alone computers.

People may wear Internet devices that signal their presence and communicate with devices in their current environment. Internet technology embedded in traditional appliances will link these to each other and users—you will be able to click a recipe on your browser screen and your microwave will be programmed to cook it, your dryer may blip your cell phone to let you know clothes are dry. Advertising will be increasingly targeted and customized, since advertisers can use the Internet to track who views their ads. User applications will scan news and other sources on the Internet, bringing back just the items that are likely to be of interest to a particular user. Libraries will be increasingly electronic data sources rather than book warehouses. Battles will continue to be fought to defend intellectual property against ever-easier ways of transferring data. People will socialize over the Internet, accidents of geography becoming less important to personal relationships. The long-term social effects of such fast and unlimited worldwide telecommunications are difficult to predict.

REFERENCES

Berners-Lee, Tim (with Mark Fishcetti). *Weaving the Web: The Original Design and Ultimate Destiny of the World Wide Web by Its Inventor.* New York: HarperCollins, 1999.

Moschovitis, C.J.P., Hilary Poole, Tami Schuyler, and Theresa Senft. *History of the Internet: A Chronology, 1843 to the Present.* Santa Barbara, Ca: ABC-CLIO Inc., 1999.

Winston, Brian. *Media Technology and Society: A History from the Telegraph to the Internet.* New York and London: Routledge, 1998.

Dishwashers

Wealthy families in the nineteenth century usually had a scullery maid who washed the pots and pans and utensils used in food preparation. Dishes and valuable silver might have been washed separately in a special copper or silver sink in a butler's pantry near the dining room—sinks made of soft metals to reduce dish breakage, and away from kitchen maids who might pocket the silverware. Less wealthy families washed pots, plates, and flatware together in the kitchen sink. Early kitchen sinks were deep and not part of counters. By the middle of the twentieth century, divided sinks were fairly standard, and sinks were set into a countertop work surface. On this countertop adjacent to the sink might be a dish-drying rack on a removable drainboard sloped into the sink. Mild synthetic liquid dishwashing detergents had been developed by this time. There were efficient at removing grease from cookware and dishes. In some households, dishwashing was done by two persons at a time, one washing, and the other drying with a dish towel.

Could an appliance aid in dishwashing? The techniques used for automatic clothes washing do not adapt well to washing dishes: dishes cannot be dropped into a tub nor can they be tumbled around in a tub of water to make them clean. Nevertheless, the basic needs are the same in both appliances: an enclosed chamber must contain the items to be cleaned, water must be admitted to the chamber and later pumped out, and the cleaned items must be at least partly dried. Hand dishwashing relies on mechanical scrubbing of the surfaces to be cleaned. Because of the many irregular surfaces of pots, pans, dishes, and silverware, this process is hard to automate. The solution, of course, is to change the process and find a suitable substitute for scrubbing.

The first approach to a dishwashing machine, illustrated in the patent by John Alexander in 1865, is to arrange dishes in a rack submerged in a tub of water, and use a hand crank to spin the rack in the water. This is little more than mechanical swishing of dishes in the sink, which everyone knows will not get dishes very clean. Furthermore, what does come off the dishes is likely to be redeposited back on them. The solution to building a machine that can get dishes clean turned out to involve several factors: substituting sprayed water for scrubbing, using extremely hot water; and using a detergent too caustic to be used in hand dishwashing.

The inventor of the first commercially successful dishwasher was Josephine Cochrane, a wealthy and determined woman living in Shelbyville, Illinois. One of

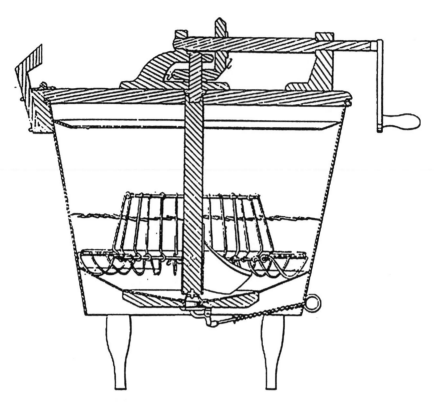

The patent diagram for the first mechanical dishwasher, by L.A. Alexander in 1865. The dishes sat in a rack submerged in water at the bottom of the tub. Josephine Cochrane's later design was the basis of the machines that found a place in kitchens in the second half of the twentieth century. The main operational change was to lower the water level below stationary racks of dishes and use a powerful electric-motor-driven pump to spray the dishes.

Mrs. Cochrane's goals was to reduce the breakage of dishes that so often occurred in hand washing. In 1886 Mrs. Cochrane built a dishwasher consisting of a wheel mounted inside a copper boiler. The wheel had wire compartments to hold her dishes, and it turned, moving the dishes through hot sudsy water. This Cochrane dishwasher was a prize winner at the 1893 Chicago World's Fair, and was then sold to restaurants and hotels. However, such machines were too large, and used too much hot water, to be successful in ordinary homes. Interestingly, Cochrane's company was eventually part of the Kitchenaid company, which introduced its first home dishwasher in 1949. Many appliance companies produced military goods instead of appliances during World War II; many new appliances came out after the war. The nation had recovered from the 1930s Great Depression, and there were millions of returning soldiers marrying and establishing new households.

The modern automatic dishwasher differs from the clothes washer in that the tub is never filled. Instead, inside the tub movable racks (usually two) hold the dishes in place, and the door is sealed with a gasket and special door latch. Then the tub is filled to a very shallow depth with much hotter water than could be used for hand washing. In most dishwashers, there is a heating element at the bottom of the tub that serves two purposes: heating the water used for washing and rinsing, and later providing heat to assist in drying the dishes.

The heart of the dishwasher is the pump. The pump sits below the tub, usually at the center of the bottom of the tub. In modern dishwashers, the pump is directly driven by an electrically reversible motor. Turned in one direction, it pumps water up into the washer tub, where rotating spray arms spray the dishes. When the motor is reversed, the now dirty water is pumped out of the tub into the sewer.

Thus the main components of a typical modern dishwasher are:

- A tub with a watertight door. In the United States, these are usually 24 inches wide and fit under a kitchen counter.
- A reversible pump and motor below the tub
- A spray arm that spins in the middle of the tub, spraying the dishes (up to three spray arms). The arm is turned by the water escaping from the spray holes.
- An electrically operated solenoid valve (a solenoid is an electromagnet) that lets water into the tub from the domestic hot water supply
- A fill switch (often a rubber diaphragm mounted in the bottom of the tub— the weight of the water eventually overcomes a spring and trips a switch, cutting off the solenoid valve that is admitting water to the tub)
- A detergent dispenser
- A heating element in the bottom of the tub
- A timer to control the solenoid valve, pump, detergent dispenser, and heater
- Racks for dishes (typically two levels, and a removable tray for flatware)
- Sound insulation covering at least part of the tub

An automatic dishwasher works by using a timer to repeat a simple three-part basic cycle:

1. turn on solenoid valve and admit hot water until tub has a couple of inches of water;
2. turn on pump and vigorously spray dishes;
3. reverse pump and pump out the dirty water.

Then do it again. And again and again. Usually some detergent is in an open cup in the door and so is dumped into the first cycle when the dishwasher door is closed. This might be followed by another rinse cycle, which is exactly the same as a wash cycle but without detergent. Then an electrically opened detergent dispenser introduces the remaining detergent into a long main wash cycle. This is then followed by a series of rinse cycles without detergent. Finally, the pump is kept off and the heater is turned on for a long optional heated dry cycle (the heater can be turned off to conserve energy). The dishwasher door must be carefully designed to prevent water from getting out during the wash and rinse cycles, while permitting water vapor to escape during the drying portion of the cycle. In addition, there is an "interlock" switch that will not permit the pump to operate if the door is not latched.

Dishwasher tubs were originally made of steel, like other major appliances. But steel rusts. So dishwasher tubs were then coated with porcelain enamel, or, later, plastic. Expensive dishwashers used stainless steel tubs. More recently, many dishwasher tubs are made entirely of plastic, eliminating the corrosion problem. Some early dishwashers did not pump the water out of the tub; rather they drained down into a drainpipe, with a solenoid valve controlling the drain. This restricted where such dishwashers could be installed. And some dishwashers used small fans to circulate the hot air, thereby speeding drying of the dishes. Dishwasher timers originally were electromechanical, with a geared-down motor, similar to those used in electric clocks, turning a shaft of cams very slowly (around 1 revolution per hour). The cams trip switches controlling the pump, detergent dispenser, inlet solenoid valve, and heater. At the end of the century, some models of dishwasher continued to use mechanical timers, while some used digital electronic timers.

Some dishwashers also have a dispenser, usually mounted on the inside of the door, for a wetting agent. Wetting agents added to rinse water help prevent water spots from forming during drying, which is a problem in areas where the water has a high mineral content. Since the temperature of the water is important for best cleaning, some models heat the water in the tub before starting the cycle.

On some expensive models at the end of the twentieth century, manufacturers included dirt sensors that could detect the amount of dirt in the wash water and modify the wash cycle to take account of the extra soil. These sensors typically work by shining infrared light through the water (similar dirt sensors were being used in some **vacuum cleaners**).

Dishwashers have been made both as built-in appliances and as "portables." Both types are now usually front-loading (the door is on the front and folds down, racks slide out to allow dishes to be loaded and unloaded), but top-loading dishwashers were also made. Built-in dishwashers are mounted beneath the countertop adjacent to the sink. They require three permanent connections: electrical, hot water, and drain. Portable dishwashers are on casters and may be top-loading. Portables are not permanently connected to electricity or plumbing—they plug into a wall socket and have combined intake and discharge hoses that temporarily attach to the kitchen faucet. The sink faucet is turned on (hot only) when the dishwasher is run; the dishwasher pumps its discharge into the kitchen sink.

Spraying and pumping are noisy, so dishwasher manufacturers continue to refine noise reduction techniques. The tub is hit by the spray, so the outside of the tub is usually fitted with a rubber or fiberglass noise insulation blanket. Water conservation has become an important issue in some areas, so manufacturers are faced with a trade-off of using less water and sacrificing cleaning ability. Conserving water also helps with energy conservation, since the main consumption of energy in dishwashing is to heat the water that is used.

Ultrasonic washers have been used in industry and laboratories since the middle of the twentieth century. These commercial cleaners are usually small, and are used for cleaning very small parts. An ultrasonic transducer converts the high-frequency electrical signal from an oscillator circuit into ultrasonic waves in the water or other cleaning solvent. The agitation spreads throughout the bath, loosening dirt from all around the parts. These cleaners are especially useful for hard-to-clean parts. Ultrasonic cleaning technology may have future applications in home dishwashing.

Another design that has been proposed is a dishwasher that is part of the dining table: after the meal, the tabletop flips over and the dishes are cleaned in the washer below. At the end, dry dishes appear all set in places as the tabletop flips back upright. Although mockups of such dishwashers were displayed in the Monsanto "House of Tomorrow" at Disneyland, they have remained in Fantasyland.

Robotics research continues, although the results are much slower than early fans of robots predicted. Still, household-cleaning robots may become a reality. If so, these might replace brute-force spray methods (which require hand loading and unloading of the washer) with good old-fashioned scrubbing, performed by a robotic arm.

Meanwhile, some homes at the end of the twentieth century included two standard dishwashers. Clean dishes are removed from one dishwasher, used, and then placed directly in the second dishwasher. Thus the dishwashers serve the function of cupboards, storing clean dishes until they are used. This arrangement eliminates the chore of unloading the dishwasher.

REFERENCES

Brooke, Sheena. *Hearth and Home; A Short History of Domestic Equipment.* London: Mills & Boon, 1973.

De Haan, David. *Antique Household Gadgets and Appliances, c. 1860 to 1930.* Poole, England: Blanford Press, 1977.

Rubin, Susan Goldman. *Toilets, Toasters, and Telephones: The How and Why of Everyday Objects.* Browndeer Press/Harcourt Brace, 1998.

Wood, Robert W. *All Thumbs Guide to Repairing Major Home Appliances.* Blue Ridge Summit, PA: Tab Books, 1992.

Wooldridge, Woody. *Repair Master for Kitchenaid Dishwashers.* West Jordan, UT: Master Publications, 1990.

Electric Power Tools

Since the earliest pioneers learned to build their own homes with the hand tools and materials at hand, a kind of versatile self-reliance has been a legendary American tradition. But in the early nineteenth century improved transportation by way of railroads made available factory-milled building materials. City dwellers lived in homes built by professional craftsmen, and while many farm people continued in the "self-reliant" tradition, their work was all manual, limited to what could be done with handsaw, auger, brace-and-bit, and other hand tools.

Electric drills and other portable hand tools became an important part of household kits in much of the industrialized world in the second half of the twentieth century. The basic invention was much earlier, by men whose names are associated with the world's preeminent manufacturer of power tools for domestic markets, Black & Decker.

POWER DRILLS AND SAWS

Alonzo Galloway Decker (1884–1959) and Samuel Duncan Black were in 1906 both employees of a firm that manufactured telegraphic printing apparatus. They collaborated on some engineering projects, and in 1910 set off on their own with the Black & Decker Manufacturing Company in Baltimore, Maryland. Black was president in charge of the business end, while Decker devoted his time to design and manufacturing. The portable electric drill he invented had a combination of features that were revolutionary. First, he perfected a "universal" small motor that could operate under alternating or direct current. Second, for ease of operation, he invented a "pistol grip" for holding the drill. Third, he invented a switch like a gun trigger that could switch both on and off with a single motion. Other electric switches required two switch elements. All three innovations were combined in a patent applied for in 1914 (granted in 1917), and, to a large degree, influenced the design of portable tools for the remainder of the century

As with all Black & Decker's early products, the drill was for industrial use. It weighed 21 pounds and cost $230 in 1916. But previously drilling had to be done with a hand-operated drill or on a stationary drill press, powered either by a heavy-duty electric motor or from belt connections from steam engines or water

1,245,860.

Patented Nov. 6, 1917.

Black & Decker's patent for an electric hand drill had several revolutionary features, but the drills were confined to industrial use until the late 1940s when lighter and cheaper models changed the way homeowners could "do-it-yourself."

mills. The concept of marketing portable tools for nonindustrial use would wait for another quarter-century. Another important forerunner for the domestic tool market was the Skilsaw, introduced in 1924 by the inventor Edmond Michel and his business partner, Joseph W. Sullivan. As with drill presses, saws with circular cutting blades were large stationary machines. Michel's invention made it possible to take a circular saw wherever electric power outlets were available.

Black & Decker anticipated a market of power tools for homeowners. They began to explore this possibility as early as 1942. After the close of World War II they introduced the world's first line of lower-priced tools, beginning in 1946 with quarter-inch and half-inch drills (the size is the maximum diameter drill bit that can fit into the chuck, which is the cylindrical clamp that holds the bit). They also produced bench stands that converted the portable drill to a small drill press, and various accessories that greatly expanded the versatility of a single electrically powered machine. This took off like a shot for many social and economic reasons. The war was over, the former military personnel and war industry workers had seen portable tools in action and had used them, and Congress passed the G.I. Bill of Rights, which, among other provisions, guaranteed low-interest home loans to veterans, resulting in a building boom for suburban homes (some, like the "Levittowns" of the eastern states, constructed with unfinished second stories).

By 1954, *Consumer Reports* was evaluating 27 quarter-inch drills from 15 different manufacturers. In the same year, a *Collier's* magazine article called the quarter-inch drill "America's most popular gadget," and among accessories mentioned sanding discs, emery wheels, lamb's wool polishers, cut-off saw blades, screw drivers, reciprocating saber saws, paint mixers and hole saws. However, an engineer with Black & Decker cautioned that the drills were designed only for drilling holes, and that any attachments compromised the effectiveness of their intended functions. He also cautioned about overloading, which could burn out the motor. The typical speed of 2,000 rpm was too fast for most polishing and too slow for clean sawing.

These problems were addressed in 1965 with the first variable-speed, reversing double-insulated (eliminating the three-prong grounded plug) drill. In 1982 Black & Decker introduced electronic drills with microprocessors built in. These keep the speed steady, automatically feeding more power to the motor as the load increases. However, for most home workshops, the lower-priced quarter-inch drills were supplemented with other specialized portable tools such as sanders, staple guns, sabre saws, and "skil"-type circular saws.

CORDLESS TOOLS

Complete portability was limited by having to plug into an electrical outlet. Builders often had to use a portable generator to operate tools. Homeowners who wanted to work on a roof or in an outbuilding had to string long extension cords, or resort to old-fashioned hand tools. Black & Decker introduced the first cordless drill in 1961, powered by a nickel cadmium battery. They also developed cordless space tools, including in 1968 an Apollo Lunar Surface Drill for getting core samples from the moon. By the end of the twentieth century cordless tools were supplanting most portable hand tools, not only for woodworking projects, but as lawn mowers, hedge trimmers, and other yard and garden chores. At that time, many were very heavy due to attached battery packs. Lighter, more powerful, and longer-lasting batteries will solve this problem, but otherwise, the quarter-inch drill and all its relations seem to be here to stay.

REFERENCES

Barrett, Jim. "Inside the Cordless Revolution." *Consumer Digest.* May/June 1997, 65–69.

"Decker, Alonzo Galloway." *National Cyclopædia of Biography.* New York: James T. White and Company, 1963. Vol 46: 156–157.

"Decker, Alonzo Galloway, Jr." *Ibid.* Clifton, NJ: James T. White and Company, 1978. Vol. M, 25–29.

"Electric Drills." *Consumer Reports,* November 1954, 517–521.

Hand, A.J. "Electronic Drills—Worth the Money?" *Popular Science,* July 1982, 116.

Stevens, Leonard A. "America's Most Popular Gadget." *Collier's.* July 9, 1954, 80–83.

Electric Lights

In the absence of artificial illumination, vehicles halt, factories close, and reading, close work, and games cease. Vision changes from the most informative to the least informative of our senses. Some theorists have speculated that one of the reasons we sleep is to keep us out of harm's way when our most important sense modality fails.

INCANDESCENT LAMPS

For most of human history, fire was the main form of artificial light. Torches and oil lamps have been used since ancient times. Not until the nineteenth century were there substantial improvements, including the introduction of gas lights. But by 1880, one of the most famous inventions of all time was achieved: the incandescent electric light. Thomas Alva Edison, at his laboratories in New Jersey, built on the work of others (especially the Englishman Joseph Swan) and in the course of thousands of trials perfected an electric lamp that gave a useful amount of light while lasting up to 600 hours.

When an electric current is passed through a resistance, heat is produced. Incandescent lamps use an electric current to heat a thin conducting strand, the "filament," to such a high temperature that it glows—"incandesces." Edison's incandescent lamp used a carbon filament. The filament is mounted in a glass bulb that is evacuated or contains inert gases, such as argon. The absence of oxygen prevents the filament from oxidizing (if the glass bulb is broken while the filament remains intact, the filament will oxidize—burn up—in a fraction of a second). Early light bulbs were blown glass and were relatively expensive, so they were recycled—the lower ends were cut off and the filaments were replaced (Sylvania started as a light bulb refurbisher).

The modern form of the incandescent lamp was a product of the twentieth century. The key development was the introduction of the tungsten filaments over the period 1907–1911. Tungsten is hard and brittle and so is a very difficult metal to form into a wire filament. Many obstacles had to be overcome before it could be the centerpiece of long-lived bulbs that cost only a few pennies each. Much work on making tungsten filaments was done in the first decade of the twentieth century, but the breakthrough came in 1909 when William D. Coolidge (1873–1975) succeeded in making ductile tungsten from tungsten powder, using a combination of heat and mechanical working of the metal. The main advantage of tungsten over carbon is efficiency brought on by higher filament temperatures. At higher temperatures, objects emit more visible light relative to heat. Tungsten filament lamps soon were ten times as bright as Edison's carbon filament lamps of equal wattage.

However, these brighter bulbs were harder to look at. So another twentieth century lighting development was the inside frosted bulb. The "soft white" form of the frosted bulb was introduced in 1949. The glass bulb is etched chemically to produce a very inexpensive built-in diffuser that softens the light from the thin intense line of light at the filament. At the end of the twentieth century, inside-frosted tungsten filament incandescent lamps were by far the dominant form of domestic artificial light.

Incandescent lamps can be dimmed merely by reducing the filament voltage. Originally, variable-voltage autotransformers were used, but in the home these bulky and expensive devices were replaced by solid-state dimmers using silicon-controlled rectifiers. These SCRs are rapid electronic switches that permit current to flow for only a part of each alternating-current cycle. They dim by rapidly turning the current on and off.

The most dramatic electric light of the twentieth century was the searchlight. Initially developed to spot aircraft at night, these huge lamps, with their intense beams focused by a large parabolic reflector, were used with dramatic effect at Nazi party rallies in the 1930s and to light the sky at Hollywood movie premiers. Yet some of the most interesting developments in electric lamps occurred at the other end of the scale, the low-intensity lights needed for indicators and instrumentation. Electric lights were developed for traffic control, replacing traffic cops stationed at corners, and signs moved by electric motors. These electric traffic signals had to be standardized, and laid out so as to accommodate the most common form of color blindness, red-green.

A specialized incandescent bulb that ran its entire life cycle from invention, widespread adoption, to obsolescence entirely in the middle of the twentieth century was the photoflash bulb. Interior photography outside a brightly lit studio required a fraction of a second of very bright light. This was provided until the 1930s by electrically igniting magnesium flash powder. Needless to say, this was dangerous (and smelly). The completely enclosed photoflash bulb was developed in Germany in the late 1920s. Photoflash bulbs had a thin glass or plastic enclosure, and contained a tangle of a thin wire or ribbon of combustible metal such as magnesium and aluminum in an oxygen-rich environment. Applying a very small voltage could ignite the metal ribbon, which then burned with a brilliant flash. By the middle of the century, the flash bulb was one of the major consumables used by amateur photographers. Various multibulb lamps with built-in reflectors were developed in the 1960s, including rotating four-bulb cubes and lamps in strips.

The expense of these one-time-use lamps encouraged the development of a reusable bright-flash lamp. Soon solid-state electronics made it possible to meet

An incandescent light bulb typical of the second half of the twentieth century. The glass bulb is frosted on the inside to provide diffused "soft white" light. The two ends of a tungsten filament connect to the metal threads and to the center contact on the base. Standard wattages of this type are 40, 60, 75 and 100 watts. Such bulbs last 750 to 1,000 hours and cost well under a dollar at the end of the twentieth century. (Courtesy of Corbis)

the high voltage requirements of the gas discharge xenon strobe lamp. This lamp emits a bright-white light, and as part of an electronic flash, it had become the standard for photography by the end of the century.

HALOGEN LAMPS

An additional development of the incandescent lamp toward the end of the twentieth century was the halogen lamp. Incandescent lamps face an intrinsic trade-off—higher currents and temperatures increase efficiency (more light, in lumens, per watt of electric current), but higher temperatures reduce filament life. The filament actually evaporates over time (and is redeposited, eventually appearing as a dark smudge on the inside of the glass bulb). For this reason, the bulb of a standard incandescent lamp must be relatively large.

In the 1950s General Electric discovered that instead of the usual inert gases in an incandescent lamp, adding a reactive halogen gas (such as iodine or bromine) inside the bulb greatly reduces the net loss of the tungsten filament, allowing halogen lamp filaments to be operated at higher temperatures, with increased efficiency, and with a smaller bulb and brighter, whiter light than ordinary (less expensive) inside-frosted incandescent lamps. The filament in a halogen lamp is

operated near the melting point of tungsten, 3,410° C, and is constantly evapo-
rating. As the evaporated tungsten nears the relatively cooler surface of the outer
bulb, the tungsten combines with the reactive halogen gas rather than depositing on the surface of the bulb. This tungsten halide gas then flows back near the
hot filament, where the intense heat decomposes it and the freed tungsten is redeposited (temporarily!) on the filament. Thus the tungsten is continuously recycled in a halogen lamp. Halogen lamps were originally used on aircraft, and by
the 1980s were available for domestic lighting.

NEON LIGHTS

The twentieth century also saw the invention of two main alternatives to incandescent electric light: gas and vapor electric discharge lamps and solid-state
lamps. These have become increasingly important, and the future of artificial
light likely largely belongs to them.

Gas discharge lighting involves passing an electric current through a gas or
metal vapor. The gas or vapor molecules emit light. Unlike incandescent light,
the light from gas discharge lamps consists of very specific wavelengths, not a
broad range of wavelengths. Different gases emit light at different very narrow
bands in the spectrum. The feature was exploited in 1909–1910 in France by
André Claude, using lamps filled with the inert gases, such as neon. These lamps
can be made in long thin tubes bent to form shapes, such as letters. When the
lamp is filled with neon, it emits a characteristic bright-orange light. These lamps
require very high voltage (thousands of volts for the long tube lamps used in
signs) and so are used with a high-voltage transformer. Neon light has advantages and disadvantages. Colored lighting is easy to achieve with direct gas discharge lighting, but high voltages are required and broad-spectrum lighting
approximating sunlight is impossible—without an additional invention. That invention is the fluorescent lamp.

FLUORESCENT LAMPS

A fluorescent lamp is a two-stage discharge lamp. The glass tube is filled with
argon and mercury vapor at low pressure. An electric current passed through the
vapor causes it to emit ultraviolet light (UV, or "black light"). The second stage
occurs at the wall of the tube, which is coated with a phosphorescent material.
This material absorbs UV light and reemits visible light. The idea was described
by Alesandre Becquerel in a paper published in 1859. But the commercial development took a long time and was largely the work of General Electric in the
United States in the mid-1930s. The first commercial interior fluorescent lamps
were introduced in 1938.

Despite the two stages of light production, fluorescent lights are much more efficient than incandescent lamps, and the lamps are longer-lived than incandescent bulbs. The disadvantages compared to incandescent lamps are electrical complexity, difficulty of dimming, noise, size, and light that in the most common (that is, inexpensive) lamps is bluish ("cool white"). In the last decades of the twentieth century, largely in response to increased energy costs, many smaller "compact fluorescent" lamps were developed that used standard screw-base incandescent fixtures. Compact fluorescents use smaller tubes, often folded, and many have solid-state electronic controls to replace the heavy, bulky ballast and starters of previous generations of fluorescent lights. However, compact fluorescent bulbs have an initial cost of 10–50 times the cost of an incandescent bulb. Yet because of its life cycle cost-effectiveness, fluorescent lighting was the standard lighting in commercial and institutional settings in the second half of the twentieth century. In the home, however, incandescent lighting was much more prevalent except in utility areas.

INDICATOR AND PILOT LIGHTS

In the home, there was increasing need for appliances to visibly communicate with users. Pilot lights were generally low-voltage incandescent bulbs (operating at the 6-volt or so filament voltage used in vacuum tube radios and televisions). Devices that did not have low voltage available often used small orange neon pilot lights. An especially interesting lamp was the "Magic Eye" tuning lamp developed in the 1930s for radios (it was also used for record level monitoring in some tape recorders). The Magic Eye was a triode with an added positively charged fluorescent target that glowed a characteristic green when struck by electrons coming from the cathode. The grid could vary the size of the fan-shaped glow at the center of the "eye."

Displaying digital information using lamps posed a special challenge (see **Calculators and Cash Registers**). The forms that became most common were solid-state lights developed in the 1970s and 1980s: electroluminescent and fluorescent panels and especially the light-emitting diode (LED). These devices are compound semiconductor diodes (instead of silicon, they are a compound of other elements, especially gallium and arsenic, or other combinations of elements from columns III and V of the periodic table). The diodes have phosphorescent materials at the junction. As the current flows through the diode and the positive and negative charges meet at the junction, these materials emit a characteristic color of light. LEDs are very long-lived and efficient; high-brightness versions were being used for signs and traffic signals by the end of the twentieth century. Their low current and voltage requirements (1–4 volts DC) made them ubiquitous as indicator lamps and display panels on electronic devices such as videocassette recorders, digital alarm clocks, and microwave ovens.

The future of solid-state lighting is bright indeed. Work progresses on solid-state lights for everything from flat televisions to general lighting. Greater brightness, higher manufacturing yields, and longer lives for new types such as organic light-emitting diodes all appear to be technical problems that may be largely solved in the early decades of the twenty-first century. Large flat light panels of such materials may replace ordinary light bulbs. In the meantime, as energy costs rise, compact fluorescent bulbs will continue to gain in popularity over incandescent bulbs.

REFERENCES

Adair, Gene. *Thomas Alva Edison: Inventing the Electric Age.* New York and Oxford: Oxford University Press, 1996.

Baldwin, Neil. *Edison: Inventing the Century.* New York: Hyperion Books, 1995.

Bowers, Brian. *Lengthening the Day: A History of Lighting Technology.* New York and Oxford: Oxford University Press, 1998.

Israel, Paul. *Edison: A Life of Invention.* New York: John Wiley and Sons, 1998.

Thomas, Jo Ann (ed.). *Early Twentieth Century Lighting Fixtures.* Collector Books, 2000.

Wallace, Joseph. *The Lightbulb.* Turning Point Inventions. New York: Atheneum, 1999.

Weiss, Richard J. *A Brief History of Light and Those Who Lit the Way.* Singapore: World Scientific Publishing Company, 1996.

Electronic Musical Instruments

From before recorded history, people have been making music using musical instruments. We can divide these traditional acoustic instruments into three broad families: percussion instruments, in which sound is produced by striking something (drum, xylophone); stringed instruments, in which sound is produced by plucking or bowing a stretched string (guitar, violin, harpsichord); and wind instruments, in which sound is produced by flowing air that creates oscillations (flute, clarinet, trumpet, pipe organ). Many of the instruments we know today reached their current form before 1800. But acoustic instruments are still being invented: Antoine Sax (1814–1894) invented many instruments, including the saxophone (patented 1846), and American composer/inventor Harry Partch (1901–1974) invented many percussion instruments and organs in the middle of the twentieth century.

Most musical instruments, whether acoustic or electric, have parts that serve three main functions:

An oscillator—the part that vibrates, originally producing the sound. In acoustic instruments, the oscillator may be a string, reed, or even the musician's lips (brass instruments). Not all oscillators produce the same sound continuously. A plucked string, for example, produces an initial loud complex sound (the "attack"), which then decays gradually in amplitude. The sound waves may have different shapes—reeds are similar to square waves, strings and flutes produce sine waves.

An amplifier or acoustic coupler—a part that enables the small vibrations of the oscillator to move large volumes of air. In acoustic instruments this couples the oscillator to the air around it. Examples include the body of a stringed instrument, and the soundboard of a piano. Without this part, the sound would be faint and thin.

A filter—a part that emphasizes some frequencies of sound over others. This helps give each instrument its characteristic timbre or sound quality—the same note sounds different on trumpet and French horn.

ELECTRIC GUITAR

The twentieth century was the century of electronics. Lee De Forest's 1906 invention of the triode vacuum tube permitted the creation of electronic oscillators and amplifiers. These made possible new musical instruments—and changed music itself.

The most straightforward application of electronics to musical instruments is to add an electronic amplifier to an existing acoustic instrument. The most widely used example of this type of instrument is the electric guitar. Musician-inventor Les Paul was an electric guitar pioneer. Les Paul, born Lester William Polfus in 1916 in Waukesha, Wisconsin, became a country music performer in Chicago. Paul's first experiment in the 1930s involved taking a phonograph pickup (the transducer that converted the moving grooves of the phonograph into an electric signal) and jamming the needle into the top of his wooden guitar. So began a series of experiments to perfect a pickup and to control feedback. By the 1940s, Paul was making recordings with "The Log," a hollow-body guitar that had been sawed in half and had a four-by-four piece of wood inserted. Solid-body electric guitars were introduced by Leo Fender (1909–1991), who had invented an improved pickup, and the Gibson guitar companies. The amplified acoustic guitar had evolved into an electronic instrument built around steel string oscillators.

Other electronic instruments with at least partly mechanical oscillators were introduced during this period. The best known is probably the Hammond organ. The oscillators in this organ are a bank of toothed wheels mounted on a motor-driven spinning shaft. Pickups are mounted near the edge of toothed wheels—as the teeth move by a pickup, an oscillating electric signal is produced. An organ keyboard controls which pickup signals get amplified. (Interestingly, a similar spinning wheel and pickup was later used in the distributor in electronic ignition systems in modem automobile engines.)

Paul went on to help invent the multitrack tape recorder, which impacted studio recording by allowing performers to record their contributions on separate tracks of a wide magnetic tape—or even allowing a single performer to play along with himself, as Paul and his wife, Mary Ford, often did. (See **Audio Recording.**)

ELECTRONIC MUSIC SYNTHESIZERS

One of the first inventors of an entirely electronic musical instrument was the Russian Leon Theremin (1896–1993). Then Don Buchla and Robert Moog (1934–) developed the analog electronic music synthesizer in the early 1960s. These were followed by digital synthesizers in the 1980s and 1990s. We will discuss these developments in turn.

In 1920, in St. Petersburg, Russia, 24-year-old Leon Theremin invented a revolutionary all-electronic musical instrument based on the discovery that the position of a human hand could change the pitch of an electronic oscillator.

Electronic keyboards imitate many traditional musical instruments by using digital synthesis. (Courtesy of Bob Jacobson/Corbis)

The theremin is a monotonic instrument—it produces a single note at a time (woodwinds are monotonic also, while almost all stringed instruments are polyphonic—they can produce more than one note at a time, as when a guitar player produces a chord). The most interesting feature of the theremin is that the player's hand is part of the oscillator. By moving her hand nearer or farther from the antenna, the player changes the pitch of the oscillator. The theremin does not produce fixed notes, but slides from pitch to pitch, like a trombone or pennywhistle. Theremins produce an eerie sound, and proved popular in Hollywood for use in the sound tracks of horror movies (and in the Beach Boys' song "Good Vibrations"). Part of the fun of theremins is watching the performer play them— waving hands in the air, the gliding sound being produced as if by a ghost instrument.

Electronic oscillators work on the same general principles as mechanical oscillators (such as a pendulum in a grandfather clock or a plucked string): a system moves repeatedly back and forth between two states, with the change between states taking a fixed amount of time. In an electronic oscillator, for example, a capacitor may alternately be charged (storing voltage) and discharged, over and over again.

In a theremin, the actual sound is produced by combining the outputs of two oscillators. One is a fixed oscillator, the other is a variable-frequency oscillator, with the antenna being one of its components. Both oscillators operate at ultrasonic frequencies, well above the range of hearing. When the variable oscillator departs in frequency just a little bit from the frequency of the fixed oscillator, audible "beat" frequencies are produced. For example, if the two oscillators are at 100 kilohertz and 101 kilohertz, respectively, the difference signal, 1,000 hertz, will be produced—well within the audible range. In addition, the Theremin has a second antenna, used to control the volume of the instrument. Finally, a foot switch is used to short out the speaker and thereby cut the sound completely off when silence is desired.

Theremins are still being made—by Robert Moog, one of the inventors of the electronic music synthesizer. Moog was an electrical engineer from Cornell University; Don Buchla was an engineer working in the San Francisco Bay area. By the early 1960s, the transistor was widely available and inexpensive circuits were being developed using transistors instead of vacuum tubes. Tubes and transistors were used in electronic organs. In these organs, fixed-pitch oscillators were turned on and off by the keyboard, and the amplifier gain was controlled using a foot pedal. Buchla and Moog realized that instead of using transistors in fixed circuits each permanently connected to a specific key on the keyboard, a modular electronic music instrument could be created if the oscillators were controlled by a voltage. In a modular instrument like this, the various parts of the instrument are connected to other parts by movable patch cables, like an old-time telephone switchboard. Indeed, a setup of a synthesizer came to be known as a "patch."

Buchla and Moogs' instruments are like a theremin in that the pitch of the oscillators could be continuously varied. But unlike the theremin, where the pitch is controlled by the distance of the player's hand from the antenna, these new voltage-controlled oscillators had their pitch controlled by a voltage. So anything that produced a voltage in the right range could be used to control the oscillators! One controller was a long sliding resistor, called a "ribbon controller," which was played by sliding a finger along a wire. Other controllers were traditional-looking keyboards and sequencers (which use automatic timers to produce a sequence of voltages). Other low-frequency oscillators could also be used to generate control voltages.

In the same time period, Max Mathews at Bell Labs was working on using digital computers to produce music. His complex program Music V turned a huge mainframe computer into a digital music synthesizer—provided the computer was connected to a digital-to-analog converter. Using Mathews's software, a single person could directly control a virtual orchestra of simulated instruments. Music V did not work in real time—digital sound production requires outputting numbers at a very fast pace (often 44,000 numbers per second), and in this period many computers were too slow to directly produce sound. Instead, the computer worked at its own pace and the stored output was later converted to sound.

These early systems could produce additive synthesis (adding simple waves to make more complex ones) and subtractive synthesis (using filters to selectively remove components of a signal). Another form of music synthesis was developed by John M. Chowning (1934–) at Stanford in the late 1960s. Frequency modulation (FM) synthesis uses 2, 4, 6, or more oscillators modulating each other and can produce a variety of interesting sounds. This technology was licensed to Yamaha in 1975 and was featured in their highly successful model DX-7 synthesizer and related models in the mid-1980s. Yamaha soon produced digital and single-IC versions of FM synthesizers, and these appeared as option cards for computers: first as the IBM Music Feature (circa 1985), then as the AdLib music card and, finally, on the highly successful Creative Labs Soundblaster card.

The 1980s saw a rapid move from analog to digital synthesizers. Integrated circuits brought the cost of digital electronics down and the speed up. Digital-to-analog converters also rapidly became more capable and less expensive. The move to digital was also helped by the adoption of the MIDI (musical instrument digital interface) standard. This standard specifies the electrical signal by which one device (a computer or a keyboard) can control another (e.g., a synthesizer, or even theater lights). MIDI signals are not sound signals; they are control signals determining which note is played, along with the volume, loudness, and optionally other parameters.

Increasingly inexpensive digital electronics also made possible a new form of synthesizer, sample playback (also widely known as digital wavetable synthesis). This form of synthesis is the most common type used commercially today. In a wavetable synthesizer, a brief digital recording of an acoustic instrument is stored in a computer memory chip. This sample is then manipulated by the synthesizer—shifted up and down in pitch, replayed ("looped") to make notes of longer duration, and so forth. There are many complications—the attack portion of the sample is not looped, and there are limits to how much a sample can be shifted in pitch before it starts to sound unnatural (a solution is to use multiple samples, recorded at different pitches in an instrument's range, but this requires more sample storage capacity). A pioneer of this form of synthesizer was Ray Kurzweil (1948–).

Leading synthesizer manufacturers at the close of the twentieth century included the Japanese companies Roland, Korg, and Yamaha (also known for its acoustic instruments), and in the United States Emu and Ensoniq, both of which were purchased by the Singapore computer peripherals company Creative Labs in the 1990s.

Electronic music synthesizers continue to evolve. Several other synthesis techniques have been developed but are no longer widely used, including phase distortion and hybrid techniques combining sample playback for the attack phase of a note and digital oscillators for the sustained portion. At the end of the twentieth century most music synthesizers were essentially computers. In the 1990s, entirely software-based synthesizers were developed, requiring no more hardware than a personal computer with a digital-to-analog converter—a return to the idea of Music V. In addition, new techniques of mathematical modeling of physical sound production enable computers to produce sounds based on mathematical descriptions of physical instruments. We might think of these as virtual acoustic musical instruments—they behave like real physical instruments, and their sound production is produced by similar internal relationships, but these processes are entirely simulated by a computer. For personal computers, main categories of software include music instruction software and sequencer software. The latter allows the computer using MIDI information to record, edit, and play a musical composition—much as word-processing software allows a writer to enter, edit, and print written works.

In the future, we can expect music synthesis to continue to be primarily a computer process. But there is no way of telling how the music produced by computers will be controlled. Some synthesizers are controlled by computers themselves, which do at least some of the composing (some of this technology was developed for the musical scores for computer games, where the music being produced must be automatically adapted to what the game player is currently doing in the game). Music synthesizers can also be controlled by dancers' positions in space. And they can be controlled by visual recognition systems watching the player conduct the instrument by hand gestures—full circle to the control methods used by the theremin. Eventually, music synthesizers may even be controlled by the player's brain waves.

REFERENCES

Bacon, Tony, and Paul Day. *The Gibson Les Paul Book: A Complete History of Les Paul Guitars.* Milwaukee, WI: Hal Leonard Publishing, 1993.

Brosnac, Donald. *The Electric Guitar: Its History and Construction.* San Francisco: Panjandrum Press, 1975.

Chadabe, Joel. *Electric Sound: The Past and Promise of Electronic Music.* Englewood Cliffs, NJ: Prentice-Hall, 1996.

Douglas, Alan. *The Electronic Musical Instrument Manual.* 5th ed. London: Pitman & Sons, 1968.

Mathews, Max V. *The Technology of Computer Music.* Cambridge, MA: MIT Press, 1969.

Vail, Mark. *Vintage Synthesizers.* San Francisco: Miller Freeman, 1993.

Fasteners

Two twentieth-century inventions began in the domain of clothing but now have literally hundreds of other applications: the zipper and Velcro.

THE ZIPPER

Elias Howe, inventor of the sewing machine, patented an "automatic continuous clothing closure" in 1851 but never produced it. In 1893 Whitcomb Judson marketed a "clasp locker." Judson didn't use the term "zipper," but his device was a complicated hooking shoe fastener that connected two rows of hooks and eyes by means of drawing a catch-tab upward. Thus the basic logic of the zipper entered the realm of production. Judson founded the Universal Fastener Company to produce his clasp lockers.

Gideon Sundback was hired as Universal's head designer and given the task of improving the design of the clasp locker, now designated "the c-curity fastener." Sundback reduced the size of the locking elements and increased their number per inch, fashioning two facing rows of teeth pulled together by a slider. In 1917 he patented his "separable fastener" and designed a machine to produce it. The teeth are clamped onto strips of cloth tape, and the slider brings the teeth together into a tight interlocking contact when moved upward, while breaking that contact when moved downward.

When the B.F. Goodrich Company began to market galoshes with Sundback's fastener installed, the term "zipper" first came into use, to designate the sound of the mechanism when being successfully fastened or unfastened.

The zipper took several more decades to move up and out from the boot to the general wardrobe. One 1930s application was in the area of children's clothing, where garments with zipper fastenings were touted as developing the virtue of self-reliance in the youngsters who could (with zipper assistance) dress themselves.

In 1937, men's clothing designers began to experiment with zippers in trousers. The zipper fly was praised by *Esquire* magazine as helping prevent "the possibility of unintentional and embarrassing disarray."

In the 1940s the Singer home sewing machine acquired an optional zipper foot attachment that allowed easy installation into home-sewn garments; this

Zipper fastener in the locked position. (Courtesy of Scott Speakes/Corbis)

encouraged the zipper to be incorporated into dress patterns and other sewing projects.

Though plastics are sometimes used for zipper teeth, metals are more common owing to their strength. Zippers are found in many types of garments, but also in luggage and purses, briefcases, sports and camping equipment, and in many other applications requiring a strong and neat, but not airtight, connection between two surfaces.

VELCRO

The story of the invention of Velcro has an almost folkloric quality. In 1948, Swiss inventor and outdoorsman George de Mestral returned from walking his dog as usual, and was as usual frustrated by the task of removing cockleburs from his clothing and his dog's coat. Frustration turned to scientific curiosity, as de Mestral began to explore exactly how cockleburs did their work so efficiently. Examining a burr under his microscope, de Mestral saw that its tines were each tipped with tiny hooks, capable of grasping on to fabric or animal fur with enormous efficiency.

Thus did Mother Nature provide the model for the hook-and-loop fastening tape that de Mestral would proceed to design. He worked on his idea for eight years, patenting Velcro in 1955; the name comes from two French words, *velour* (velvet) and *crochet* (hook). The successful design consists of two strips of nylon, one having thousands of tiny loops and the other thousands of tiny cocklebur-like hooks.

This invention's name now has a generic application to many other types of hook-and-loop tape, even though the term "Velcro" still is proprietary to the company named after it; strictly speaking there is no such thing as velcro, only Velcro.

The product achieved enormous popularity and its characteristic ripping sound is heard around the world today, as shoes are unfastened, lunch bags and back-packs opened, even horse blankets and boots removed. A "Best Use of Velcro" contest was held by an upstate New York radio station in the late 1990s. The winners were a third-grade class who performed "Yankee Doodle Dandy" by opening and closing their shoes.

REFERENCES

www.velcro.com
inventors.about.com/cs/famousinventions

Food Containers

For most of human history, the securing, preparing, and eating of safe and nutritious food was essentially a race against time. From the moment a potential food item (animal or vegetable) was spotted to the moment after it had been consumed, mortal risk was always present. Would the food be secured without a battle? Would it be prepared in such a way as not to cause disease, poisoning, sickness, or even death? Would its consumption occur within the window of safety from spoilage?

Several inventions of the late nineteenth and early twentieth centuries allow this risky business of food handling to become much more relaxed and much safer: the refrigerator greatly increases the safekeeping time window for food items; the can allows for processing out of bacteria that cause spoilage; and plastics lend themselves to many different applications for the safe packaging and preserving of perishable food.

CANNED FOOD

The basic process of food canning was discovered in 1809 by a Frenchman named Nicholas Appert. Although the causes were not understood, it was found that heat processing of food items in glass jars greatly enhanced the shelf life of the food. The original metal food cans were quite thick and heavy, and required hammers and chisels for their opening. Canned food was essentially a luxury item, affordable only by the very wealthy and used only in unusual circumstances, for the first century and a half of its existence.

A metal-canning operation in Bermondsey, England, was the first commercial venture to apply the canning preservation technology to marketable foods; still heavy, bulky, and expensive, the canned foods were nevertheless of interest to the Royal Navy, which sought palatable nutrition alternatives for its men at sea.

Early food cans were made of iron dipped in molten tin; the tin produced a nonreactive and shiny, appealing surface. The iron was soon replaced by steel, which could be rolled out into a thinner (thus lighter) layer.

Joseph Campbell was a pioneer in the American food canning industry. He began canning beefsteak tomatoes commercially in 1869. Campbell moved into

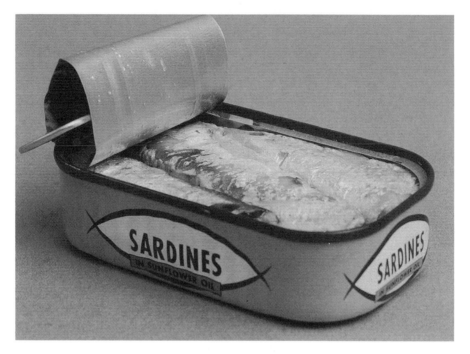

Some cans used key-openers to roll back lids. (Courtesy of Corbis)

soup canning, but business was slow until a young staff member named John Dorrance discovered a method of condensing the soup. By removing much of the water, the product could be marketed in a smaller, less costly can; it weighed less, was more easily transportable, took up less storage space, and could therefore be sold for a lower price. Despite all these advantages, condensed soups were regarded with some suspicion by consumers. Dorrance mounted a personal education campaign, driving a wagon through the countryside and giving taste sample and lecture tours designed to persuade Americans to eat more nonhomemade soup.

In 1898 a Campbell's company executive attended a Cornell-Penn football game and was smitten with Cornell's red-and-white uniforms. His recommendation that the soup product line be packaged in simple red-and-white cans was probably the most fortunate marketing decision the company could have made. Campbell's soup in the red-and-white cans came to enjoy product recognition at a very high level, even being immortalized in artistic form by pop artist Andy Warhol, himself a confirmed and loyal soup eater.

Can production itself went through some crucial changes during the first half of the twentieth century. In the 1930s, electroplating the tin coating replaced the older dip technique. This in turn reduced costs for the can itself, as the tin could be applied in a very thin, yet uniform layer. And most importantly, mass production of cans replaced the hand construction method, enabling can producers to go from 6 cans a day per worker to many thousands of cans per hour of operation of an entirely mechanized production line.

Today most American households maintain, and rely upon, a pantry stocked with cans as a significant foundation for meal planning.

CANNED BEVERAGES

The first beverage to be presented in canned form was beer. Bottles of beer were popular, but had their liabilities: they could break, they were heavy, and they were offered early in the twentieth century on a return-for-deposit system (testifying to the expense of glass packaging), which generated additional costs.

Beer bottlers began to explore cans in the late 1920s, but faced a technical challenge: beer is highly reactive with metal, quickly undergoing chemical changes upon contact with it and acquiring a foul taste and smell. A nonreactive barrier or can liner would be needed. In addition, beer is pasteurized at very high pressures of 80–90 pounds per square inch, as compared with 25–30 pounds per square inch for food processing. The can would have to be capable of withstanding such pressure.

The American Can Company introduced a flat-topped, punch-opening beer can in 1934, lined with a plastic film to prevent the bad reaction between metal and beverage. Beer producers were attracted to the idea that the entire outside surface of the can could be used to advertise the product—as opposed to the limited label surface on bottles. Consumers needed a lot of persuading, and the move to canned beer was gradual.

Incentives were strong, however; cans were lighter and more quickly chillable. Cases of cans could be stacked, and breakage was minimized. And the inconvenient return-for-deposit could be eliminated.

The slogan "No deposits! No returns!" was prominent in canned beer advertising by the Krueger Beer Company in the 1930s. Krueger had initially been very cautious about investing in can marketing, but its first year produced a sales increase of 550 percent. This quickly convinced other companies such as Pabst and Anheuser-Busch to follow Krueger's lead, and today canned beer dominates the world market.

Cans took even longer to pervade the burgeoning soda-pop industry. Soft drinks are more acidic than beer, and are produced at even higher pressure. Continental Can tested canned Pepsi-Cola in 1948. It required the postwar change of lifestyle, with increased emphasis on recreation and leisure, to create a demand for transportable and disposable soft drink packaging. Coca-Cola, already an industry giant in the 1950s, initially allowed canning of its product only for shipment to American GIs overseas, in Japan and the Pacific region.

As with beer, the convenience of shipping and marketing the canned soft drink finally won manufacturers' commitment and today commands consumer loyalty worldwide. The preferred beverage can metal is now aluminum, which is light, soft, relatively inexpensive, and recyclable.

REFRIGERATOR CONTAINERS

The advent of the home refrigerator changed the storage potential for perishable food items and virtually created the category of the "leftover," savable remnants of meals that are the mixed blessing of the contemporary home menu. But how could foods and leftovers best be stored, so as to avoid the dehydrating effects of refrigeration, keep their flavor and color, and yet not spread their flavors and odors to other stored food items?

The answer, strangely enough, lay in a sludgy, staining, black petroleum by-product with a strong odor and greasy texture: polyethylene slag. Methods of processing this messy substance into plastics of numerous kinds produced a revolution in American consumer products, which is still ongoing.

In the 1930s, for example, Earl Tupper invented a method of purifying the black slag into a plastic that is durable, flexible, odorless, nontoxic, and lightweight. He used it to make plastic gas-mask parts during World War II. In 1946 he applied the new substance in the design and manufacture of food containers that were virtually airtight, thanks to a seal mechanism that he modeled on that used for paint cans: a slot runs around the lower surface of the lid, into which the can top fits under pressure.

Tupper's food containers were a hard sell at first. The virtues of their material and unique lid mechanism required more explanation and demonstration than a mere product label could provide; shoppers found them more puzzling and strange than appealing. Several salespersons for the Stanley Home Products Company, which sold via demonstrations, took up Tupper's containers and enjoyed such sales success that Tupper himself hired them. One was Florida housewife Brownie Wise, who pioneered the social gathering that came to be known as the "Tupperware party," a combination of friendly gathering and concerted sales pitch, at which the containers could be shown and ordered. Wise soon became a Tupperware Company vice-president and was largely responsible for the success of the direct marketing demonstration-based method of sale, which would guarantee the product's success and eventually give it huge name recognition worldwide. Today, a Tupperware demonstration begins somewhere in the world every two seconds, and 118 million people attended such demonstrations in the year 2000.

Tight-sealing plastic containers proliferated and became an indispensable part of any well-furnished kitchen today.

FOOD WRAPS

Plastic food wraps also come from that same unpromising black petroleum sludge that yields pretty pastel refrigerator containers as described above. The plastic wrap that is now widely available on rolls (in kitchen drawers often specially designed to hold them) was an accidental discovery.

In 1933 a college student named Ralph Wiley worked part-time at Dow Chemical as a laboratory dishwasher. One glass beaker he came across contained a substance that refused to wash out. This uncleanable stuff Wiley named "eonite," after a fictional indestructible material mentioned in the "Little Orphan Annie" comic strip. Dow researchers went to work on Wiley's "eonite" and developed a greasy dark-green film that came to be called Saran. Saran was used as a corrosion-retardant on fighter planes during World War II.

In 1953 a cleaned-up, nongreasy, no longer green Saran was approved for use in contact with food surfaces and Saran Wrap film was born, the first cling wrap designed for household use.

Saran Wrap and its many close relatives are made of polyvinyliden chloride, or PVDC. PVDC is made by polymerizing vinyl chloride with monomers such as acrylic esters and unsaturated carboxyl groups. In this process, long chains of vinyl chloride molecules are produced. This makes for a film in which molecules are so tightly bound together that very little can penetrate past them. In other words, PVDC is a great barrier. It is resistant to oxygen, water, acids, bases, and solvents. With all this barrier power it is nevertheless light, transparent, flexible, and highly resistant to degeneration.

Layers of PVDC are found in a great deal of food packaging, and are used in the packaging of many nonfood products as well. Hundreds of varieties of plastic bags, including food, trash, and grocery bags, are descended from the same primordial petroleum sludge. Plastic films and packages are so successful that environmentalists regard them as a major concern; their strength is also a liability when we consider how long they will be blowing across beaches and settling in landfills all across our planet. Household plastics will certainly be among the twentieth century's most lasting legacies.

Frozen Foods

Frozen foods are of two types, those intended to be eaten cold, like ice cream bars, and those that are to be heated, like frozen peas or pizzas.

ICE CREAM AND FROZEN DESSERTS

While iced treats date back to the ancient Roman Empire (essentially flavored snow) and iced cream desserts were developed in the seventeenth century, these were rare and expensive. Homemade ice cream became possible in 1846 when Nancy Johnson of New Jersey invented a machine that can still be found in food specialty stores. Fresh cream, sugar, and flavoring are put into a metal can that has a hand crank that turns a paddle in the mixture. The can is placed in a larger wooden pail in which cracked ice surrounds the can. Salt is sprinkled on the ice, producing brine, which has a temperature lower than the freezing point of water. The brine is in contact with the entire surface of the metal can and so can chill the can more effectively than ice alone. Hand labor moves the liquid past the cold metal, and slowly it freezes in tiny crystals, making a creamy frozen concoction. Nostalgia for old ways keeps a market for these, although most use an electrically rotated paddle.

The first ice cream bar was invented in 1919 by candy maker Christian Nelson of Onawa, Iowa, who dipped the bar in chocolate, introducing it as the I-Scream-Bar. In 1921 Nelson joined another confectioner, Russell Stover, renaming his invention the Eskimo Pie. It was Harry Burt who first froze an ice cream bar on a stick, in 1920, selling it as the Good Humor Ice Cream Sucker. The "Good Humor Man" became familiar in many parts of America, pushing his refrigerated wagon through neighborhoods on hot summer days.

Popsicles were invented by accident. Frank Epperson left a glass of lemonade with a spoon in it on a windowsill through a cold night. He first called it an Epsicle (a play on *icicle* and his name) but patented his invention in 1924 to be marketed under its familiar name. These treats were instantly popular, and as dry ice became more readily available commercially after 1925, frozen storage at stands in amusement parks became possible. (Dry ice is solidified carbon dioxide with a temperature of $-109.3°$ F., $-78.5°$ C.) There have been many variations on these early inventions, but basically they are the same idea.

Unlike ice cream that was dispensed in scoops, these cones were filled directly from the mixer. (Courtesy of Corbis)

FROZEN FOODS

The story of other frozen foods is not so simple. Freezing meat for transoceanic shipping appeared in the nineteenth century, using the brine method. The disadvantage is that slow freezing—it could take days—forms large ice crystals that pierce the meat cells, and when thawed, the meat is mushy and often tasteless. The problem was solved in the early 1920s by Clarence Birdseye (1886–1956), who later said, "My contribution was to take Eskimo knowledge and the scientists' theories and adapt them to quantity production." Birdseye had direct experience with Eskimo food preservation, as he left Dartmouth College after two years to pursue adventure trapping and fishing in Labrador in 1912–1915. He noticed that when at temperatures as low as –50° F. Eskimos pulled their catch from the water, the fish would freeze immediately. More amazing, when thawed months later, they tasted fresh. Returning to Labrador in 1916, he experimented with preserving fresh vegetables by fast-freezing. The key, scientifically, was to pass below the freezing point of water (0° C., 32° F.) so fast that large ice crystals did not form and the food cells were undamaged.

Back in the United States Birdseye worked to find a manufacturing method that could freeze fish that quickly. By this time a number of mechanical refrigeration devices had been patented in Europe and America, but Birdseye used ice and salt to chill two metal plates between which the fish were placed, with fans to circulate dry, cold air. In 1923 he was ready to found Birdseye Foods Company to process frozen fish, and the following year with several investors, he established General Seafoods in Gloucester, Massachusetts. Among other improvements, Birdseye invented a belt to carry prepackaged foods through the freezing process. Expanding beyond fish to fruits and vegetables, in 1928 he marketed as much as a million pounds of frozen foods.

The success attracted the interest of the Postum Company (Postum, a non-caffeine coffee substitute of roasted grains, was the invention of Charles W. Post (1854–1914), who also invented Post-Toasties and Grape-Nuts cereals). The Postum Company was scouting around for expansion into other food products industries. Birdseye's company looked like a good growth area, and Postum bought Birdseye's 168 patents for $20 million, $2 million for other assets, and almost another million for the right to use Birdseye's name, which they divided into the two words "Birds" and "Eye" imprinted on the familiar emblem of a soaring one-eyed white dove. Postum's new food conglomerate was renamed General Foods Corporation. Unfortunately for them (if not Mr. Birdseye, who, incidentally, continued inventing throughout his life), the deal was made in 1929, just before the stock market crash that brought on the Great Depression. This caused a setback on expanding sales of frozen foods.

There were many other problems challenging the industry, some technical, others economic. Unlike canned goods, which can be transported, stored, and shelved at markets and at home without any special care, frozen foods must be kept at the very least below the freezing point of water until they are actually prepared for serving. Furthermore, unlike canned foods, whose heat processing kills bacteria, frozen bacteria turned out to be as well preserved as the food around them, and contamination and illness were and are very real concerns about thawed foods. The problems were compounded by the requirement that ideally, all links in the chain from production to consumer had to be refrigerated at once. Home refrigerators with small freezer compartments were available as early as 1919, e.g., General Motors' Frigidaire, and the number sold in the United States rose from 10,000 in 1920 to 800,000 in 1929. But few grocery stores had freezers; Birds Eye had only ten outlets in 1931; the rise to about 12,000 by 1940 may sound large, but this represented only 2 percent of retail food stores at that time—every neighborhood or village might have three or four "ma and pa" corner groceries. In the mid-1930s Birds Eye began to confront these challenges by furnishing freezers and packaging equipment to producers of canned foods and also by supervising production at key market areas throughout the nation. Next they contracted with the American Radiator Company to develop a frozen foods display case that retailers could rent at low cost. Transportation by rail of fresh meats had since the late 1800s been by rail cars with large ice compartments, or drums filled with ice and salt. Mechanical refrigeration came slowly in the twentieth century so until around 1940 the largest sales of frozen foods were to institutions such as hotels and restaurants close to the frozen food factory. The breakthrough was by Minneapolis engineer Frederick McKinley Jones (1892–1961), who, after several tries, patented in 1940 a tough, shockproof refrigeration unit for trucks. Other improvements were made to insulate railway cars and trucks so that perishable and frozen foods could be transported long distances without much change in temperature. In 1944 Birds Eye began to lease refrigerated railroad cars to ship frozen foods anywhere in the United States.

All these developments by 1940 had frozen foods poised for expansion, but World War II (1941–1945) interrupted growth as almost all production of vehicles and appliances was directed toward the military. Nevertheless, sales of frozen foods increased during the war. Partly this was due to food shortages on the home front: when canned or fresh foods were unavailable, people who hadn't considered the more expensive frozen foods had no choice. Also food purchases were rationed during the war (i.e., in addition to having the money to buy food, consumers had to have "token" coins that limited the number of cans of food or pounds of meat they could buy), but frozen foods were taken off the rationed list seven months before canned goods. With the end of the war, innovations in popular frozen foods began in earnest.

TV DINNERS AND FAST FOOD

Precooked frozen foods were available to restaurants in the 1930s (although they kept this secret from their customers). But in 1945 William L. Maxson invented a complete cooked dinner, frozen on a divided paper plate for Pan American Airlines. These were heated in an electric oven on the plane. Nine years later in 1954 this concept revolutionized American eating habits. The Swanson brothers, Clarke and Gilbert, of Omaha, Nebraska (who had brought out a frozen chicken pot pie about 1951) introduced the "TV Dinner." Although not the first "heat and eat" dinner, it capitalized on the new habit of watching the family's one television set while eating. The first dinner packages showed the platter enclosed in a TV screen. It sold for $1.09, but with many competitors entering the market prices soon dropped to three for a dollar. Choice was simple, such things as sliced turkey, mashed potatoes, and peas or sliced beef, mashed potatoes, and corn. Variety increased later with the introduction of ethnic menus, gourmet meals, low-calorie meals, and others. It is interesting to note that the same decade that saw these easy-preparation home meals also spawned the large fast-food franchise chains, such as Dunkin' Donuts (1950), Kentucky Fried Chicken (1952), Burger King (1954), McDonald's (1955), Pizza Hut (1958), and others. To a large extent, these were made possible by frozen foods as transporting uncooked ingredients from central factories guaranteed consistent quality and flavor. Together fast foods and frozen entrees changed Americans' eating habits from homemade meals to "convenience" foods.

There probably is no end to the possible variety of prepared frozen foods, from Japanese sushi to Ukrainian pierogies, but here are a few of the early landmarks:

Minute Maid frozen concentrated orange juice (1946), Sara Lee cheesecakes (1949), Mrs. Paul's fish sticks (1952), Eggos frozen waffles (1953), frozen pie crusts (1962), Cool Whip (1965), Jeno's Pizza (1966). With all the variety, however, Clarence Birdseye's inventions remain basic.

FREEZE-DRIED FOODS

A frozen food process that is less important to popular consumption is freeze-drying, in which the organic material (it was first used for preserving biological specimens in Sweden in the 1930s and for human blood in World War II) is quick-frozen in a vacuum, causing the water content to sublimate (convert to vapor directly), thereby eliminating any ice crystals. One of the experimenters with freeze-drying food was American inventor George Speri Sperti (1900–1991) of the St. Thomas Institute for Advanced Studies. The foods are not actually "frozen foods," being sold at normal temperatures. Reconstituting is a mere matter of soaking them in water if they are precooked or boiling them if not. Freeze-dried coffee is the most common product, but campers, mountain climbers, and astronauts are familiar with a wide variety of soups, stews, and other foods that are extremely lightweight until soaked in water of the appropriate temperature.

REFERENCES

"The American Century in Food." *Bon Appétit,* Millennium Special, September 1999.
Anderson, Oscar Edward. *Refrigeration in America: A History of a New Technology and Its Impact.* Princeton: Princeton University Press, 1953.
Danforth, Randi, Peter Feierabend, and Gary Chassman. *Culinaria. The United States: A Culinary Discovery.* Könemann: Köln, Germany, 1998.
Williams, E.W. *Frozen Foods: Biography of an Industry.* Boston: Cahners Publishing Company, 1963.

Glues and Adhesives

The problem of sticking things together is a very old one, and has been solved by similar technology for many centuries. Traditional glues are derived from rendered parts of animals or plants; collagen, the principal protein constituent of animal hides, lends itself to the making of hide glue, for example. Hide glue has great strength and water resistance, but it dissolves with alcohol, which makes it indispensable for such things as wooden stringed instruments, which must be taken apart for repair. Plant glues can be derived from mucilaginous layers on seed casings, or from boiled and macerated stem materials of certain flora. Such adhesives have been in use for at least 4,000 years.

PAPER, SAND, AND GLUE

Significant advances in glue production awaited twentieth-century developments in the understanding of adhesive chemistry. Stickiness is a property of certain kinds of molecules. The ability to isolate outstandingly stickable molecules and suspend their adhesion until a desired time (outside the tube or bottle, for example) enabled the production and mass marketing of a wide variety of glues for consumers.

Major adhesive researches in the early years of the twentieth century were driven by the desire to build a better grade of sandpaper. Attaching mineral grit to a paper surface strongly enough to withstand the rubbing and pressing of a sanding operation was a challenge addressed by the Minnesota Mining and Manufacturing Company (today's 3M Corporation). As with so many other everyday inventions, better consumer glues and other adhesive products were often the unanticipated side benefit of industrial research (see **Adhesive Tapes**). Some of the glue-based products to be discussed below were examples, including Super Glue and Post-it notes. However, the century began with much less sophisticated adhesives in the home.

MUCILAGE

The LePage's Company (originally named the Russian Cement Company) developed and marketed mucilage, a plant-derived, amber-colored, transparent adhesive in a small glass bottle with a rubber top stopper. A slit in the stopper could

Multi-purpose white glue is one of the most popular adhesives. (Courtesy of Scott Speakes/Corbis)

be pressed from opposite sides to create an opening from which glue would emerge when the bottle was tilted. Like many such glues, mucilage hardens when it loses water on contact with air; thus, clogging of rubber stoppers had to be prevented with careful cleaning after use.

ELMER'S GLUE-ALL

In 1947 the Borden Company began to market a synthetic PVA-based white glue for home, school, and general everyday use. First named Cascorex Glue, it was presented in a glass bottle with a wooden applicator paddle attached by a rubber band. The Borden Company was enjoying great popular success for its logo "Elsie the Cow" on quite another front; however, it was decided to find a comparable representative for the white glue product line. Thus was created Elmer the Bull, conceived as a sort of spouse for Elsie, and Cascorex became Elmer's Glue-All within a few short years. This product enjoyed huge popularity, not least because of its cleanup convenience; it washes off hands, desktops, and out of hair with soap and water. Today 47 million elementary school students use Elmer's Glue-All at least once a week.

Elmer's and other synthetic glues are made from polymers, large molecules that present themselves in strands. Some polymers are naturally sticky; others must have "tackifiers" added in order to initiate adherence.

SUPER AND CRAZY GLUES

The amazingly sticky substances marketed as SuperGlue and Crazy Glue consist of cyanoacrylate. It is actually a plastic that hardens upon contact with air. The original discoverers of cyanoacrylate were searching for a transparent plastic for use in gun sights during World War II; they quickly rejected it for this purpose, as it stuck irrevocably to everything and created a terrific mess.

In 1951 Eastman Kodak researchers Harry Coover and Fred Joyner rediscovered cyanoacrylate as it thoroughly ruined a costly refractometer in their lab. Naming it Eastman Kodak #910, they recommended that it be explored for its remarkable adhesive properties. The glue became famous via television in 1958, when Coover appeared on the show *What's My Line?* and lifted host Gary Moore completely off the stage floor with a single drop.

In recent years, formulas for the products SuperGlue and Crazy Glue have been developed that avoid their previous problem of adhering to human skin. Cyanoacrylate is a glue for permanent joining, and its strength has made it a favorite for hundreds of kinds of home repairs.

POST-ITS

Post-it notepaper is one of the most popular products of the Scotch line of 3M pressure-sensitive adhesive products. While most of these products have been invented in response to needs in other businesses, Post-it notes were not invented because of industrial needs. The problem was age-old and familiar to most of us. Chemical engineer Art Fry of 3M sang in a church choir, using scraps of paper as bookmarks in his hymnal. Loose bookmarks are prone to falling out or slipping down between pages where they can't be seen.

Fry remembered a demonstration a few years before by another 3M researcher, Spencer Silver, of a peculiar acrylate adhesive that would stick firmly but peel off with ease and without residue. The key to Dr. Silver's 1968 invention was that the adhesive gathered into tiny spheres, each the diameter of a paper fiber, that were not connected, and therefore the entire surface was not actually covered with the sticky medium. At the time, no one, including Silver, had any idea for using a glue that didn't hold.

However, Art Fry thought this adhesive might be used for a nonslip bookmark. He developed the idea of applying the adhesive to the edge only, so that the marker had a nonstick handle for picking it off.

Post-its were not an immediate success, and several 3M executives recommended their untimely demise before mass production. Fry and several friends mounted an aggressive market-testing campaign that involved taking Post-it prototypes out onto the streets and getting responses from passersby. Wherever free samples were distributed, people found as many uses for Post-its as they had found for masking tape and cellophane tape. These responses were favorable enough that initial production began.

Today the Post-it Note is a ubiquitous and indispensable component of office and school work worldwide. The notes attach smoothly and readily to many types of surface, though most reliably to paper; they remove without leaving a visible trace of adhesive, and can be reapplied to the same or different locations dozens of times. Generically referred to as the "sticky-note," they constitute one of the most rousing success stories of any twentieth century invention; in its product niche, the Post-it Note conquered the world. Post-it Notes are commonly used for reminders on bulletin boards, refrigerators, bathroom mirrors, car dashboards, shirt fronts, backs of hands; they are used by editors to mark copy, by students to highlight texts, by writers for inserted revisions, by scientists to mark specimens, by managers to arrange and rearrange schedules, and, of course, by choir members to mark hymns.

REFERENCES

Benedek, Istvan. *Development and Manufacture of Pressure-Sensitive Products.* New York: Marcel Dekker, Inc., 1998.

Huck, Virginia. *Brand of the Tartan: The 3M Story.* New York: Appleton-Century-Crofts, 1955.

Hair Care Products

Hair care inventions of the twentieth century have primarily been applications of electricity and developments of chemical substances. While basic hair care has to do with cleanliness and neatness, the influence of fashions on inventions is considerably greater. The influences are sometimes reciprocal, as when an invention makes a different style available, or as a new fad spurs inventions of products to serve the fad. The main concern has been scalp hair, but for males facial hair and for females body hair receive attention as well. Of course, the manipulation of hair for practical, ornamental, and ritual reasons is worldwide and reaches back to earliest human societies, but the pace of changing fashions accelerated during the twentieth century. In the Western world, the century began with fashionable male facial hair and female long hair, elaborately arranged in piled-up braids and buns, for ladies' hair was never seen full-length except in young girls or in the privacy of the bed chamber.

SHAVING PRODUCTS

The first revolutionary invention of the century was neither electrical nor chemical. This was the disposable safety razor blade, invented by King Camp Gillette (1855–1932) in 1901. The term "safety" was used in contrast to the kind of razor that had been in use since ancient times. These straight (or "cutthroat") razors were 4–8 inches long, honed (naturally) to razor sharpness, and extremely dangerous. To be effective, they were honed against a leather strop, often more than once during the shaving operation. Gillette, who worked for William Painter, the inventor of the crown bottle cap (still used for beer and some other beverages), was advised by his boss to invent something disposable, so that continuing sales were guaranteed. Safety razors had been invented before, but with fixed blades that could not have been as easy to hone as a straight razor. The 1902 Sears, Roebuck catalog offered "travel sets" with seven interchangeable wedge-shaped blades, one for each day of the week after which they could be rehoned for another week's shaving.

Gillette's invention was a double-edged steel blade so thin that it was flexible and could be clamped into a T-shaped razor that allowed only the edges of the

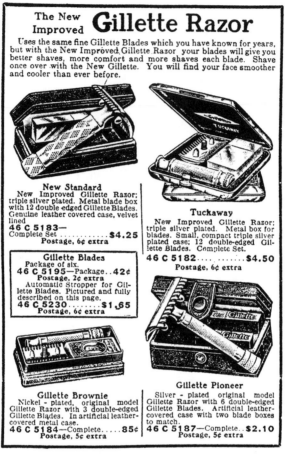

The New Improved **Gillette Razor**

Uses the same fine Gillette Blades which you have known for years, but with the New Improved Gillette Razor your blades will give you better shaves, more comfort and more shaves each blade. Shave once over with the New Gillette. You will find your face smoother and cooler than ever before.

New Standard
New Improved Gillette Razor; triple silver plated. Metal blade box with 12 double edged Gillette Blades. Genuine leather covered case, velvet lined
46 C 5183—
Complete Set **$4.25**
Postage, 6¢ extra

Gillette Blades
Package of six.
46 C 5195—Package..**42¢**
Postage, 2¢ extra
Automatic Stropper for Gillette Blades. Pictured and fully described on this page.
46 C 5230 ....**$1.65**
Postage, 6¢ extra

Tuckaway
New Improved Gillette Razor; triple silver plated. Metal box for blades. Small, compact triple silver plated case; 12 double-edged Gillette Blades. Complete Set.
46 C 5182............**$4.50**
Postage, 6¢ extra

Gillette Brownie
Nickel - plated, original model Gillette Razor with 3 double-edged Gillette Blades. In artificial leather-covered metal case.
46 C 5184—Complete.....**85¢**
Postage, 5¢ extra

Gillette Pioneer
Silver - plated original model Gillette Razor with 6 double-edged Gillette Blades. Artificial leather-covered case with two blade boxes to match.
46 C 5187—Complete..**$2.10**
Postage, 5¢ extra

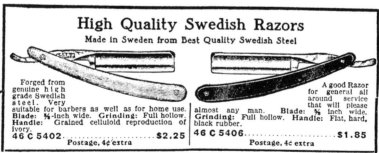

High Quality Swedish Razors
Made in Sweden from Best Quality Swedish Steel

Forged from genuine high grade Swedish steel. Very suitable for barbers as well as for home use. **Blade:** ⅝-inch wide. **Grinding:** Full hollow. **Handle:** Grained celluloid reproduction of ivory.
46 C 5402 .... **$2.25**
Postage, 4¢ extra

A good Razor for general all around service that will please almost any man. **Blade:** ⅝ inch wide. **Grinding:** Full hollow. **Handle:** Flat, hard, black rubber.
46 C 5406 .... **$1.85**
Postage, 4¢ extra

The transition from "cutthroat" straight razors to safety razors with disposable blades was slow. The Gillette had been on the market for over 20 years, yet a 1922 Montgomery Ward catalog offered 14 different straight razors.

blade to be exposed. The technology for production of these steel blades was developed by William Nickerson. Sales began in 1903 and America soon became familiar with King Gillette's signature and visage (he wore big muttonchop whiskers), which appeared on every package of disposable blades. A London office was opened in 1905 as well as a factory in Paris. In World War I the U.S. Armed Forces included safety razors in every doughboy's kit, representing sales in 1918 of 3 million razors and 36 million blades. They were still hazardous, as users had to unwrap each blade; it was 1946 before a dispenser was introduced to keep fingers away from the edges. Safety razor design continues to try to fulfill King Gillette's dream of unending sales: in 1971, for example, a twin-bladed model was introduced, promising at one stroke two slices off the whisker. The new design also required buying a new razor body. The ultimate in disposability came in 1975, when Baron Marcel Bich, who had brought out the cheap Bic ballpoint pen in 1945, introduced the Bic disposable razor. All blade razors require wet hair, and many products were invented to keep moistness while shaving and produce a lubricated surface for the razor blade to ride on. Burma-Shave cream was the most popular because of the imaginative advertising campaign that exploited automobile travel with series of small signs along highways that added up to a jingle (as "His Face was Smooth—And Cool as Ice—And Oh, Lucille—He Smells so Nice—Burma-Shave").

ELECTRIC RAZORS

An electric razor promised a dry shave. The story is that Colonel Jacob Schick got the idea of freeing the daily ritual from soap and water while in a cold climate (Alaska or British Columbia by different accounts). His invention was not the first electric shaving device, but his 1928 patent was the first successful model, brought on the market in 1931. Individual hair stubble was caught in tiny slots and a rapidly moving reciprocating cutter (later multiple cutters) sliced the hair. As with so many electric appliances, a lightweight but powerful motor was required. Schick's invention had perfected such a motor. Within a few years, some fifty competing models were introduced. The Remington company, which had been well-known for typewriters and firearms, was one of these, introducing in 1940 the somewhat daring "Lady Remington" for legs and armpits, as well as a shaver that could be plugged into an automobile cigarette lighter—a genuine boon for traveling sales personnel. Innovations continued, notably in 1960 Remington's Cordless "Lectronic," powered by a nickel-cadmium battery (see **Batteries**). Now men and women can shave electrically in the Gobi Desert or in their home showers. As with all earlier innovations, competing models followed quickly, but the technical design of most electric razors with a light, fast-reciprocating motor still derives basically from Schick's invention. However, the Philips corporation of Netherlands had developed a razor along somewhat different lines with a rotary-action, round-headed razor with six self-sharpening blades. This was introduced in the United States as the Norelco in 1948. The reciprocating blade is now called a "foil" to distinguish it from rotary designs. Other refinements have included trimmers for sideburns and for mustaches and beards.

HAIR STYLING PRODUCTS

There seems to be no end to the possibilities for arranging long hair. But insofar as twentieth-century inventions are concerned, the main problems have been that people with straight hair want it to be curly, and people with curly hair want to straighten it. Applying heat with pressure on the hair can change the natural form. The curling iron, a metal cylindrical clamp, was invented in 1866 by Hiram Maxim (1840–1916)—better known for his later invention of the machine gun. Shortly after, in France, Maurice Lentheric and Marcel Gateau used the hot curling tongs on damp hair with hot-air drying, and Gateau gave his name to the deep tight curls that resulted—marcelled curls. These were not "home perms." The problem with curling irons was heating them. Home users usually heated them just as they did their flatirons for pressing clothing, placing them on hot kitchen stoves. Electrically heated curling irons were exhibited at the 1893 Chicago World's Fair. *Scientific American* magazine reported that in 1887 special electric "stoves" were to be found backstage in Berlin theaters, where flames from gas or alcohol heaters were strictly forbidden. Fire hazard probably was the reason that fashionable American hotels provided electric heaters for guests' curling irons in 1904. Exactly when self-heating curling irons (with a cord attached) first appeared is unclear, but they were available from Montgomery Ward's catalog in 1922.

While the application of a hot shaping iron to damp hair was effective, it was temporary and required redoing. The quest for a "permanent wave" process was, paradoxically, first satisfied in a hair-straightening invention. Many black Americans desired to iron out the natural kinks in their hair and achieved this by the rather hazardous method of using a flatiron on an ironing board. Not only were burns possible, but hair loss was common. Sarah Breedlove Walker (1867–1919), a washerwoman at a St. Louis hotel, invented a process using a hot iron comb along with a softening emollient pomade. This was in 1905, by which time she had moved to Denver. In the next five years she had established a beauty school for training assistants in the Walker Method (she now was called Madame C.J. Walker), and in 1910 built a factory in Indianapolis. By 1917 she had over 3,000 workers in the nation's largest black-owned business and had become a millionaire. In her last years of life, Madame Walker devoted her time and money to numerous philanthropic projects from her home in the Harlem neighborhood of New York City.

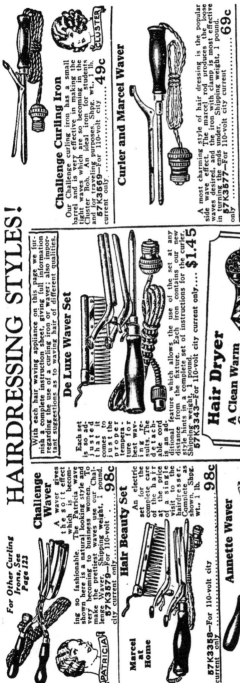

In the "Roaring Twenties" short "bobbed" hair was the latest style. This 1927 Sears, Roebuck catalog illustrated four popular styles along with electric curling irons and marcel wavers. Notice two technological details: these only work on "city current" (farms that were electrified had their own small power plants), and each curler is supplied with detachable plugs so houses without wall receptacles could screw them into a light socket. (Courtesy of Sears Roebuck and Co.)

Meanwhile, in London, England, a German hairdresser, Charles L. Nesser, invented in 1906 a 12-hour process of using borax paste and curling irons to produced a "permanent" wave. Various improvements were made to speed and improve "perming" so that multiple electric curlers could be attached to a head of hair, and drying was done under a helmet-like heater. Variants on these processes continue in commercial hairdressing salons.

Cold permanent waving was a development of the French cosmetic giant corporation L'Oreal. One of their chemists, Eugene Schueller, found a means of softening keratin, the protein in hair that makes individual hairs hard. Keratin has sulfur-containing amino acids that "cross-link" providing the structure of individual hairs (e.g., straight, wavy, etc.). Thyloglycolic acid breaks these cross-links, leaving the hair without "body." The hair is then wound around curlers or other shapers. Finally, the sulfur is encouraged to form new cross-links by the application of sodium hypobromite or other chemical that causes a rebonding of the disulfides, but in the shape imposed by the curlers. Schueller's 1945 invention is basic to modern professional hairdressing, but it quickly made possible home permanents, needing no heating or drying devices or professional assistance. The characteristic odor of the process comes from the thyloglycolic acid. The Toni brand of cold permanent waving was introduced in 1947, boosted by a very popular advertising campaign featuring women twins, one of whom had a salon perm, the other a home perm: "Which Twin has the Toni?"

HAIR DRYERS

Another essential invention in hair care is the hair dryer. Before its invention, women's very long hair had to be dried in the sunshine or beside the kitchen stove, a process that took hours and kept the lady from other activities. In 1906, one vacuum cleaner manufacturer showed the exhaust hose from a tank-type vacuum as a hair blower, which of course was not heated. As lightweight small motors became available in the 1920s and household current more readily available, handheld dryers were introduced, such as the "Cyclone" of the Hamilton Beach Company. For some years in mid-century, "bonnet" dryers were popular. The user put on a plastic bonnet with a hose connected to a heater-blower. However, the standard design became lightweight, handheld, pistol-grip devices that combined a heating element with a fan and various settings for different degrees of heat and fan speed.

In addition to these major inventions in twentieth century hair care, there have been many other devices that have responded to current fashions, such as prestyled synthetic hair wigs, plastic soft curlers, lacquer hair sprays, electric hair untanglers, mousses and gels, hair dyes, depilatories, and hair restorers. The influence of entertainment media has been profound, one of the most famous being the child actress Shirley Temple, whose curls in 1930s movies encouraged a generation of permanents for little girls. Because of such fads and novelties, the future in hair care is certain to be changeable. But the trend toward easy care styles and products that facilitate speed and convenience is likely to continue in this multibillion-dollar industry.

REFERENCES

Consumer Reports, October 1995.
Lifshey, Earl. *The Housewares Story.* Chicago: National Housewares Manufacturers Association, 1973.
McGrath, Kimberly A. *World of Invention.* 2nd ed. Detroit: Gale Research, 1999.

Home Video

Throughout the twentieth century, motion picture film remained the primary medium for recording theatrical productions (see **Motion Pictures**). Photographic film can provide the excellent resolution and contrast needed for high-impact display in theaters. Film was also the medium chosen by home movie makers for the first three-quarters of the twentieth century. However, film is expensive, bulky, and difficult to edit. Film cannot be erased and reused, and it requires expensive photo developing before it can be viewed. It is not surprising, then, that home movies were displaced by a new technology developed in the second half of the twentieth century.

The new technology was developed because another form of motion image had appeared: television. Television signals have a relatively low-resolution image, compared to film, so a recording medium did not require the special abilities of photographic film. Early television was live, or was expensively recorded on motion picture film using machines that synchronized the video image with the film frame rate.

In 1927, Scottish inventor John Logie Baird (1888–1946) was the first to record a video signal. This achievement may seem surprising, since this was before electronic television and tape recording. Baird's television system was mechanical, and used an image with just 30 lines. Baird was therefore able to record this low-frequency signal on a phonograph record—hence the name Phonovision for this system.

VIDEOTAPE RECORDING (VCRs)

Baird's mechanical television was replaced by electronic television in the 1930s. In the same period, **audio recording** was first used in radio broadcasting. After World War II, many people were interested in recording the television video signal. The main technical problem was the very large amount of information that is in a video signal, as compared to an audio signal—the video signal has very high "bandwidth." Recording this high-frequency signal requires that tape pass the record head of a tape recorder at a very high relative speed. In 1951, Crosby Enterprises (owned by crooner Bing Crosby [1903–1977]) demonstrated an experimental video tape recorder with 12 heads and a tape speed of 100 inches per second. In late 1953, RCA demonstrated a videotape recorder that used a tape speed of 360 inches per second. These tape speeds required very heavy-duty motors. Great care was needed to avoid damaging the thin, fragile tape, which was held on enormous reels to record even short segments of video.

A leading commercial tape recorder manufacturer was Ampex, in Redwood City, California. Ampex had introduced its first audio tape recorder in 1948. By 1951, after debate by the president and main technical officers, Ampex decided to do research on an innovative alternative tape recorder design in which wide recording tape would move slowly past a spinning head. The head-to-tape speed could remain very high, but the tape itself could move at a manageable 30 inches per second. Most importantly, a half-hour TV broadcast could fit on a single reel. The machine was developed over the next four years by a design team that was led by Charles Ginsburg (1921–1992) and included then-student Ray Dolby (whose name later became well known for his work on noise reduction systems for audio tape recording). The work was sporadic and surmounted many difficulties. Ampex finally demonstrated prototype machines using 2-inch (50-mm) wide tape at the television broadcasters' convention in April 1956. It was an immediate sensation, and orders poured in for the machines, which cost up to $75,000. The first broadcast of a videotaped program was the evening news on the CBS network, in October 1956. Soon RCA and Ampex pooled patents to make color video recording possible. Toshiba and Ampex both claim credit for developing, in the late 1950s, the now standard "helical scan" system, where each head on the spinning drum scans a full image in a pass. Thus the basic technology for video recording was developed by 1960.

These large and expensive video tape recorders (VTRs) did not appear in many homes, apart from Hugh Hefner's Playboy Mansion. The first VTRs were larger and wider than washing machines. Size reduction was rapid, however. Ampex introduced a portable recorder in 1959. Sony, a pioneer at using transistors to shrink the size of home electronics, introduced the first home VTR in 1963, an open-reel deck using half-inch-wide tape, priced at $995. In 1969, Sony introduced its first system with the tape in a cassette, the U-Matic videocassette recorder (VCR), which could record one hour of video on ¾-inch-wide tape. These still expensive systems were largely for commercial and educational users.

In 1975, Sony's Betamax consumer VCR was introduced. This $2,295 machine used cassettes with half-inch-wide tape that could hold an hour of video. Sony advertised that its machines would permit viewers to record programs off the air for later viewing, as many times as one wished. In 1976, Universal Studios and Disney sued Sony for abetting copyright infringement. This suit went to the U.S. Supreme Court, and, partly on the basis of testimony by PBS children's show host Fred Rogers, Sony eventually won the suit. From that time on, American consumers could legally make copies of broadcast programming for their personal use.

Movie studios initially panicked, but soon discovered a developing substantial market for prerecorded movies. At first these were largely supplied by video rental stores, which sprang up in neighborhoods. The first video rental store franchises were sold in 1978. The most successful of the rental chains, Blockbuster Video, began in 1985. By the end of 1987, Americans were spending more on video rentals than on going to the movies.

The growth of VCR sales featured a format war. By 1976, JVC introduced VHS, a rival format to Betamax, for under $1,000. Sony then licensed other manufacturers to produce Beta machines—the war was on. By 1977, RCA was touting VHS machines that could record four hours of video on a single cassette, double the previous two-hour time, by using a slower recording speed and taking advantage of new tape formulations. Sound on early VCRs was monophonic and low quality, since the tape moved at a slow speed past the nonspinning audio head and recorded a narrow audio track with low fidelity. Hi-fi stereo sound was added by Sony in 1983, and shortly thereafter VHS manufacturers introduced their own version of stereo Hi-fi. These systems recorded the audio using the rapidly moving video head drum.

Well into the 1980s, the two formats, Betamax and VHS, competed side by side, and stores and video rental outlets had to stock prerecorded movies in both formats. By the end of the 1980s, VHS emerged as victor of the format wars. It is believed that this was largely due to the longer, if lower-quality, recording time that VHS permitted—and, in particular, sufficient time to record a complete American football game.

VIDEO DISCS AND DVDs

In 1972, Philips, having earlier developed the audio **compact disc** along with Sony, introduced a video laserdisc system. Like an audio CD, these systems were playback only. Unlike CDs, video disc systems were analog. In 1978, Philips introduced the model 8000 LaserVision player under its Magnavox name in the United States. These large discs could hold a movie, though some movies required more than one disc. RCA had long been working on video discs, and in 1981 it finally introduced its CED 100 SelectaVision video disc player, with a price of $499.95. RCA's system did not use a laser; it used a diamond stylus in a groove. A pickup guided by the stylus could detect changes in capacitance in the groove of the spinning disc.

RCA was surprised by consumer enthusiasm for VCRs and for tape rental. After huge losses, RCA terminated its laser disc system in 1984. Japanese manufacturer Pioneer was undaunted, and in 1984 introduced the model CLD 900 combination video disc and CD player. Pioneer remained a major manufacturer of video disc systems. The most common form of video disc was 12 inches in diameter, with a fairly large center hole. These discs could hold up to an hour of material on each of two sides.

In the 1990s, higher-frequency solid-state lasers were developed. These could create a smaller spot of light than the lasers used for audio CDs, and so could

DECK EXPLODED VIEW

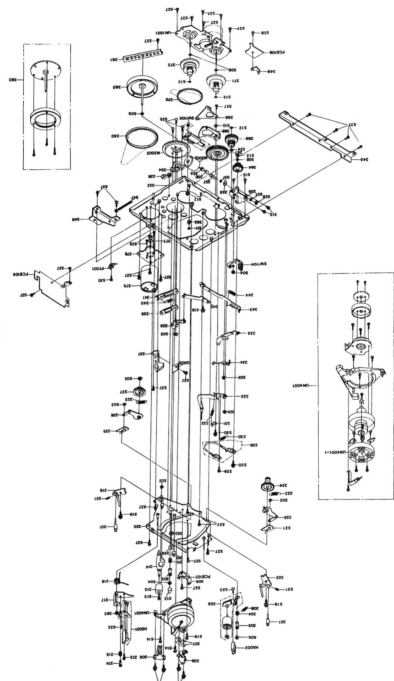

Exploded diagram of the tape transport and head assembly of an early 1980s Japanese VHS videocassette recorder. Note the spinning drum, titled at an angle, which holds the video heads. Tape loading is complicated: the machine opens the front of the cassette and metal fingers pull a loop of the tape out against the heads.

A videotape cassette in the VHS format introduced by JVC in 1976. This format emerged victorious over Sony's rival Beta format, largely because it could record a complete American football game. Inside the cassette are two small reels holding half-inch wide magnetic tape. The cassette is inserted into the cassette player/recorder (VCR). Once inside, the VCR opens the hinged door on the cassette (at top in the figure), and pulls the tape out and around the video and audio heads. (Courtesy of Corbis)

allow much more information to be recorded on the same conveniently sized disc. Rival formats for video compact discs were proposed, and it took several years for manufacturers to agree on a standard format known as digital versatile disc (DVD). The compromise format adopted allowed the digital signal to be stored on up to two layers on each of two sides of a disc. Production was delayed by work on an anticopying encryption system to allay the fears of the movie studies that movies on DVDs would be easily copied.

The first DVD player appeared in Japan at the end of 1996, and in the United States the following spring. By the end of 1997, DVD sales in the United States surpassed laser disc sales. By the end of the decade, DVDs, many priced under $20, were displacing prerecorded videotapes in stores. DIVX was an interesting but short-lived experiment, introduced in 1998 and gone within the next two years. DIVX discs (played in a DIVX player) were limited by the manufacturing process to a couple of viewings—in effect providing a pay-per-view video disc. Movie studios loved this idea, but consumers chose DVD.

CAMCORDERS

In 1980, Sony introduced the first consumer video camcorder. Integrated circuits, improved batteries and tapes, and shrinking of the mechanical components including the spinning drum allowed the portable combination camera and video-cassette recorder to rest on a shoulder. Machines of this size are still preferred by television news crews and other professionals.

Camcorders rapidly became more compact. In 1985 Sony introduced camcorders using tiny cassettes that had 8-mm-wide tape (the same width that had been common for the film used in home movie making). The VHS manufacturers responded with a small "VHS-C" tape format for camcorders. The VHS-C tape could only record 20 minutes of video, but unlike Sony's 8-mm tape, it could be played back in standard home VHS VCRs, using an adapter cassette. In 1989, Sony introduced a "Hi8" format with improved images. These two camcorder formats, VHS-C and 8-mm, continued to compete until the end of the twentieth century.

The end of the twentieth century saw the digital revolution throughout the electronics industry. The audio compact disc, introduced in the early 1980s, was digital. In 1987, digital audio tape (DAT) recorders were introduced. In the last decade of the twentieth century, digital video camcorders were introduced with substantially improved picture quality. At the outset of the twenty-first century, these existed alongside inexpensive camcorders and home VCRs that were analog, and DVD players that were digital.

It seems clear that the future of home video is digital and on disc. DVDs largely replaced prerecorded videocassettes at the end of the twentieth century. Home recording of CDs, both audio and data, was common. DVD recorders appeared at the very end of the century, and costs were expected to drop. It is reasonable to suppose that these will replace videocassette recorders, just as audio CDs had been displacing audiocassettes. Digital media is more compact, provides higher quality, can be edited on computers, and can be transmitted over the Internet. Digital broadcast television was introduced at the very end of the century.

It is also reasonable to expect that camcorders will eventually move from tape to disc, or include other forms of compact internal data storage, and will transfer their images by digital connection to home computers or digital video recorders. It is also likely that "on demand" video programming will be supplied in digital form over the Internet, bypassing both the disc and tape physical media that dominated the twentieth century.

REFERENCES

Graham, Margaret. *RCA and the Videodisc: The Business of Research.* Cambridge: Cambridge University Press, 1986.

Lardner, James. *Fast Forward: Hollywood, the Japanese, and the VCR Wars.* New York: W.W. Norton & Co., 1987.

Luther, Arch C. *Video Recording Technology.* London: Artech House, 1999.

Morita, Akio. *From a 500 Dollar Company to a Global Corporation: The Growth of Sony.* Pittsburgh: Carnegie-Mellon University Press, 1985.

Nmungwun, Aaron. *Video Recording Technology: Its Impact on Media and Home Entertainment.* Mahwah, NJ: Lawrence Erlbaum Associates, 1989.

Taylor, Barbara. *Charles Ginsburg: Video Wizard.* Vero Beach, FL: Rourke Enterprises, 1993.

Jukeboxes

Jukeboxes are coin-operated automatic players of recorded popular music. They are still common, but in their heyday (c. 1934–1970) there was hardly a diner, café, truck stop, soda fountain, bar, or tavern that did not have a jukebox blaring out popular tunes from selections that went from a dozen to 200 choices.

Although the name "jukebox" did not become current until the 1930s, the ancestry goes all the way back to 1889 at the Palais Royal Saloon in San Francisco. Louis Glass of the Pacific Phonograph Company set up an Edison cylinder **phonograph** with an electric motor powered by a storage **battery,** and connected four "listening tubes" to the reproducer (the term is a forerunner of "tone arm" or "pickup"). Each tube could be activated by inserting a nickel in a slot. There was only one selection on the phonograph, but as four listeners could invest their nickels, Glass could earn twenty cents for each play. Glass's device was so successful that he was able to set up a dozen more in other locations. A similar one was in the Edison exhibit at the 1893 Chicago World's Fair, but despite the attraction of its two songs, "Daisy, Daisy" and "After the Ball," it proved too delicate for the rough Fair crowds and so it and several other machines were installed in Chicago saloons. It is difficult today to picture the attraction of listening to songs, comic monologues, and virtuoso whistlers through a rubber tube held to the ear (though the same acoustic process has been used on thousands of jetliners), but in France "phonograph parlors" became popular, one Parisian parlor with 40 employees playing selections from a stock of 1,500 musical cylinders for customers upstairs. For a coin, each customer was given a desk, a chair and a speaking tube to convey requests below and thereupon to listen to the selection. In the United States, one of the early deluxe movie theaters, the Vitascope Hall in Buffalo, New York, installed 28 Edison machines in the theater lobby.

The main challenges facing inventors and marketers were to increase the number of choices, to provide convenient access to the machines for customers, to have efficient maintenance of heavily used phonographs, to have sufficient volume for noisy locations, and to face up to competing technologies. As to the last challenge, there was a period from about 1910 to 1925 when the competition from mechanical music machines actually killed off production of coin-operated phonographs.

MUSIC BOXES AND PLAYER PIANOS

Another type of disc player was derived from the technology of music boxes reaching back to the early nineteenth century in Germany. A large metal disc is punched with holes in such a way that the metal is not completely punched out, but a metal prong is left to protrude from one side of each hole. When the disc revolves, powered by a spring-wound motor, the prongs strike tuned metal strips. The Regina Music Box Company of Rahway, New Jersey, in 1908 introduced a large coin-operated music box, with dozens of 27-inch diameter metal discs and a piano sounding-board that produced rich, loud tones. In the same year Regina appears to have also made a coin-operated machine that had a carousel of six Edison cylinder recordings, played in a set sequence. In 1906, John Gabel of Chicago introduced the "Automatic Entertainer," a spring-wound machine that had 24 phonograph discs that for the first time allowed the customer to select the record to be heard—and although the customer had to wind up the spring motor, the handle also changed the record and the phonograph needle with one turn. This earliest of all "real" jukeboxes had a 40-inch horn, dispensing with the individualized ear tubes. Maintenance was a problem with all the early machines, as needles and records wore out rapidly. But Gabel, who now held many patents that would affect the future, stopped production of the Automatic Entertainer by 1910 or so, because of a rival coin machine, the Peerless Player Piano.

The technology of the player piano was not unlike that of a music box, with holes punched in a roll of paper and a vacuum pump that activated the keys of a real piano. Precursors had required that the human player pump the air with foot treadles, but the coin-operated machines had electric motors. The Peerless came out in 1908, and coin-operated phonographs were not to reappear until 1925. It is interesting that during this period, several of the most important manufacturers of jukeboxes of the future were producing coin-operated player pianos. Rudolph Wurlitzer, who came to America in 1856 from Germany, imported musical instruments from his family's business, and began to manufacture drums and bugles for the Union Army in the Civil War. In 1880, he added pianos to the production of his Cincinnati factory, and in 1896 produced the first coin-operated electric piano. AMI (Automatic Musical Instrument Company) was formed by combining two 1909 enterprises of the Rowe family of Grand Rapids, Michigan, one which manufactured player pianos, the other which leased and serviced these coin-operated instruments. Among their patents was one that made possible automatically selecting piano rolls from a magazine. By 1925, they had installed over 4,200 pianos nationwide.

A third big name in jukeboxes of the future was Seeburg. Justus P. Seeburg (1871–1958) emigrated from Sweden, learned the piano manufacturing trade, and in 1910 came out with the Seeburg Orchestrion, a player piano that was also equipped with violin, mandolin, flute, and various percussion instruments. Wurlitzer outdid this versatility with theater organs to accompany silent films; the "Mighty Wurlitzers" could produce sounds of church bells, tom-toms, and other dramatic effects along with all the stops of a great pipe organ. (This of course was not a coin-operated machine.)

COIN PHONOGRAPHS

The rebirth of coin phonographs occurred in 1925 when the advances in radios, especially the vacuum tube, finally gave sufficient sound amplification for a crowded room. This effectively ended the era of player pianos, though there were now over two million player pianos in American homes and gathering places. With amplified recording microphones and electrically driven dynamic loudspeakers, the records were clearer and capable of recording the full spectrum of orchestral and band sounds. Seeburg in 1927 introduced the first all-electric coin-operated phonograph. In 1928 the Seeburg Audiophone gave a choice of eight records. This was in the U.S. historical period known as Prohibition (1919–1933), when the sale of alcoholic beverages was illegal. However, there were an abundance of illegal drinking establishments known as "roadhouses" or "speakeasies" primarily in the north, and as "juke-joints" in the southeastern states. The word "juke" derives from the black Gullah dialect term "jook," which in turn derives from a West African word *dzugu*, denoting disorder. The association with both illegal booze and prostitution as well as slot-gambling machines made the new slot-fed phonographs morally suspect, but the name "jukebox" stuck, even after the 1933 repeal of the prohibition amendment made taverns, bars, night clubs, and cocktail lounges legal. With repeal came a vast new market for jukeboxes, and many manufacturers entered the business.

Among them was the Canadian-born David C. Rockola, who had already entered the vending machine business and had patented a weighing machine as a Rock-Ola Scale. Rock-Ola bought up John Gabel's patents and in 1934 introduced the Rock-Ola Multi-Selector, which gave 12 selections. Wurlitzer countered in the same year with the Simplex, playing 24 records. In the 1930s, Wurlitzer was producing 45,000 jukeboxes annually. Another pioneer in coin phonographs was Homer Capehart of Indiana, who produced a good machine in 1927, but as the "juke" association tarnished the image, Capehart perfected an automatic record changer for home use and turned to producing high-quality, high-priced radio phonographs. Others entered the field. Most failed, and Seeburg, AMI, Wurlitzer, and Rock-Ola dominated the business with a bewildering variety of innovations.

At first, the machines could play only one side of a record; then devices were invented to flip the record over, doubling the number of selections. In some machines, the selected record was brought out of a stack and lowered onto a turntable, in others the pickup arm was moved up and down to the record. Jukeboxes were made with glass fronts so customers could watch these clever operations. In 1939 Seeburg bypassed the lines of customers waiting at the machine with the "Playboy," the first remote-control selection box that could be installed

Remote control selection boxes such as this one could be located at counters and in booths in restaurants and bars. The actual jukebox containing the phonograph records was centrally located and could be accessed directly, but the convenience of the remote was that friends could discuss what selections they would like to hear, insert coins in the slot, and punch in the codes of each choice. Like most jukeboxes of the 1940s and 1950s, this has a streamlined art deco design. (Courtesy of Corbis)

at each dining booth or along the bar or counter. Wurlitzer made the jukebox an object of visual delight; in 1940 bubble tubes were introduced with colored lights; their most popular Model 1015 in 1946–1947 had eight bubble tubes. Every manufacturer vied to increase the number of selections. In 1941, Ed Andrews invented a method of playing records vertically (AMI had in 1927 introduced a machine invented by B.C. Kenyon that stacked the records vertically, but flipped them to a horizontal turntable.) Andrews' invention was purchased by Seeburg, but with the interruption of World War II, it was not available until 1948.

Seeburg first employed the Andrews device in a machine that could play 100 records, both sides, intermixing 10-inch and 12-inch discs. This was not a coin-operated machine, but a forerunner of background music for commercial establishments. By the end of the year, though, Seeburg's "Select-O-Matic" jukeboxes were offering 100 choices. Almost immediately, the industry was faced with another technical challenge: Columbia records introduced the 33⅓-rpm microgroove disc, and in 1949 RCA Victor countered with the 45-rpm microgroove. Manufacturers now had to contend with three record speeds, two kinds of pickups (for microgrooves and for "old" 78s), as well as the 45s' unusual 7-inch diameter and large spindle hole. Select-O-Matic was a natural for 45s, which took up so little space, and Seeburg recognized that the new lightweight pickups with diamond needles would tremendously extend record lifetimes and reduce maintenance expenses. The first all-45s came out in 1950 from Seeburg and Wurlitzer. In 1952–1953 the "Wurlimagic Brain" intermixed 78s and 45s. In 1958 all four major companies introduced 200-selection jukeboxes.

Hi-fi enthusiasm brought in multiple loudspeakers, and another challenge came with the advent of CDs in the early 1990s. But for many reasons, the era of jukeboxes had declined, though by no means ended. In 1974 Wurlitzer closed its U.S. factory, retaining operations in Germany. In 1977 the Antique Apparatus Company began to make "nostalgic jukebox" replicas, and most significantly, in 1992 combined with Rock-Ola. There is a major market for jukeboxes as antiques, and suitably converted, they remain popular in nostalgic fifties and sixties "theme" restaurants and bars. This backward look is probably the "future" for jukeboxes. The factors contributing to the decline are complex. Fast-food restaurant chains do not want to encourage customers to linger. Better restaurants prefer silence. Local taverns prefer to have a television set playing behind the bar. Upscale cocktail lounges and coffee houses draw customers with live performers. Travelers carry their own preferred music by way of miniature personal radios or compact discs or audio tape players in their cars, trucks, backpacks, and shirt pockets. But the technology of jukeboxes lives on: now there are many "jukebox" CD changers in the home, holding 100–200 CDs, while smaller 6–12 disc changers bring jukebox features to automobiles.

REFERENCE

Read, Oliver, and Walter L. Welch. *From Tin Foil to Stereo: Evolution of the Phonograph.* Indianapolis: Howard W. Sams & Co., 1959.

Kitchen Appliances: Heat Generating

Using electric current to generate heat for cooking was one of the earliest ideas after electricity became available to homeowners. The advantage of a flameless, smokeless, odorless heat source coincided with one of the culinary fads of the early twentieth century: chafing dish cooking, which was done at the dining room table or sideboard. Electric chafing dishes were available as early as 1901, and H.W. Hillman's 1905 "all-electric" house boasted an outlet for one. The physics is simple: electric current passing through a copper wire of a given gauge forced into wire of smaller gauge, or one made of a material with higher resistance than copper, produces heat. (**Microwave ovens** have a different physics and technology.) At the Columbian Exposition of 1892 in Chicago, electric saucepans, broilers, and boilers were exhibited, and by 1904 stoves, ovens, teakettles, griddles, cake irons (i.e., waffle irons), toasters, and coffee urns were all available.

There were problems: cost was one deterrent because using electricity for heat consumes a great deal of current, and the price per kilowatt was high. A second problem was that the wires in the heating elements burned out quickly. This was solved by the invention of nichrome, an alloy of nickel and chromium that was patented by engineer Albert Marsh in 1905. A third problem was that until electric appliance plugs developed in the mid-1920s, the heating devices had to be wired into the household current or screwed into an electric light socket. Another problem was achieving precise heat control, and this delayed the successful marketing of toasters and frying pans for decades.

TOASTERS

The earliest toasters had their heating elements exposed and required that the slice be turned manually to do both sides. Sometime in the early 1920s a four-slice toaster for restaurants was developed that allowed for flipping the slices over. In 1922, a toaster resembling today's was introduced by the Best Stove and Stamping Company of Detroit. This had the electric heating elements safely enclosed. Two slices of bread were placed in slots on a platform that could be lowered to expose the bread to heat on both sides. By smell and guesswork about doneness, the cook would raise the platform with the toasted bread.

The pop-up two-slice toaster design remained basically the same as it was in the 1930s. On this model, the "frozen" button reflects the introduction of convenience foods such as frozen waffles, tarts, and bagels in the 1950s. (Courtesy of Corbis)

An automatic toaster for restaurants was invented in 1919 by Charles Strite of Stillwater, Minnesota, incorporating a spring, a motor, and a switch. Each toaster was custom built, with production at a rate of one toaster per day. The company that manufactured these registered the name Toastmaster in 1925 and in the same year hired Murray Ireland, who designed a household model that came on the market in 1926. This model had a spring-powered clock mechanism that popped the toasted bread up after a measured period of time, but the manufacturer, Waters-Genter of Minneapolis, urged users to first run it empty to heat the coils before inserting a slice of bread. Incidentally, until 1930 all home bread was sliced by hand; the introduction of presliced Wonder Bread undoubtedly contributed to the reliability and popularity of electric toasters.

For the next quarter-century various manufacturers made refinements to allow the toaster to "read" such variables as hot and cold starts and the temperature of the bread, adjusting the toasting time appropriately. This was done by means of a bimetallic strip such as is used in thermostats (two strips of metal having different degrees of expansion when heated are bonded together, causing the bonded strip to bend to a point of touching an electric contact that switches off the current). The switch also releases the spring that was compressed when the bread was lowered into the toaster. As a result, the toast pops up when done. Other refinements have been made, some purely for fashion, others for increased versa-

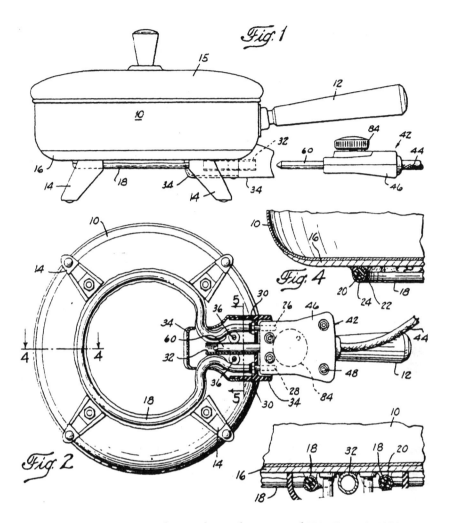

Electric frying pans were invented around 1900, but not until H.K. Foster's 1954 invention could they become popular because he solved the problems of washing up and maintaining variable degrees of heat.

tility in toasting buns and bagels, defrosting waffles, Pop-Tarts, etc., toasting more than two slices, and with push-button settings for different functions.

ELECTRIC FRYING PANS

The electric frying pan took much longer to develop positive heat control. Without some method of setting different levels of heat for different foods, and maintaining optimum heat, there was no advantage over stove-top cookware. Furthermore, frying pans are one of the most troublesome pieces of cookware to clean and often require soaking and scrubbing. Immersing any electrical device in water is not recommended. In 1953 Sunbeam introduced an automatic fry pan with a temperature dial and a printed "Fryguide" on the handle. By their second-year sales were approaching one million, but washing the pan was still a problem. This was solved in 1954 by engineer H.K. Foster of S.W. Farber, Inc., who developed a "probe" independent heating control that could be slipped out of its connecting sleeve in the frying pan, thus allowing the entire pan, with the actual heating elements molded into the bottom, to be dunked in the dishpan.

Many refinements in size, appearance, nonstick surfaces, and programmed settings made electric frying pans one of the most useful and versatile gifts for young people setting up household in small apartments and dormitory rooms. As with the rudimentary chafing dishes of a half-century earlier, these allowed for cooking and serving at the table. Curiously, at this same time, chafing dishes over alcohol lamps (Sterno) came back into fashion, and electric chafing dishes were "reinvented." Oriental cooking was also one of the fads introduced in the 1950s, so it didn't take long for electric woks to appear.

Other small appliances enabled people to get along without a kitchen range. Tabletop electric broilers were introduced as early as 1934; the Broil-King, introduced in 1937, had the basic elements of a rack to hold the food, a detachable heating coil beneath it, and beneath that, a drip pan. Several companies introduced various types of covers for smoke control and two heating elements so that both sides of meat could be seared simultaneously, and in 1946 Robert Kemelhor and Charles Green introduced the Rotissimat, a tabletop motorized spit. It didn't catch on as a home appliance, but it marks the beginning of the commercial chicken rotisseries that by the 1980s were a standby in delicatessens, supermarkets, and convenience stores.

Several hybrid appliances combining toaster and oven, broiler and oven, toaster and broiler, or ultimately "toaster-oven/broilers" were brought on the market in the 1950s and years following. The first appears to have been General Electric's Toast-R-Oven in 1956. Most of these toast the bread horizontally, as many as six pieces at a time.

ROASTER OVENS AND COOKING POTS

Electric roasters or roaster ovens were invented in 1924 by Ted Swartzbaugh of Toledo, Ohio. However, the concept goes back to ancient history. Many foods, especially dried beans and tough meats, benefit from slow cooking at even temperatures. Potages and stews combining these with other ingredients become most savory with similar treatment. Many cultures found that covered earthenware pots surrounded by hot ashes provided this sort of steady cooking, while others simply plastered whole fish or game with wet clay and buried them in coals. The clay baked evenly, and after the coals were raked away, the hard cover was broken off to expose tender meat steamed in its own juices. The ancient Romans used both methods, and their word for cooking pot (*olla*) survives in Spanish and New World cooking for both the pot and the potage. Germans developed an earthenware covered pot—the *Romertopf* (Roman pot)—unglazed so that it can be soaked in water before being filled with food and placed in an oven. Essentially, these, as well as heavy bean pots, are low-pressure cookers. Swartzbaugh's father had in 1884 started manufacturing heavyweight tin six-quart pots with copper bottoms that could slowly cook a one-dish meal on top of a coal- or wood-burning range. These "Peerless" cookers sold well, but Swartzbaugh carried the idea one step further with the "Fireless Cooker." Actually there was a fire, as the food was first heated in an aluminum pot, then removed from the heat and slipped into a tightly fitting, heavily insulated sleeve, where the cooking was completed from its own pressurized heat. In 1918 an electric hot plate was added to the bottom of the pot.

The younger Swarzbaugh's invention, the Everhot Electric Roaster, had a six-quart cooking pot, wrapped in asbestos insulation. This was wound with "over six hundred inches" of copper wire, which was sealed in a special cement, padded with another layer of insulation, and finally encased in a smooth enameled metal jacket. When plugged in, the Roaster could be set for either 350 or 100 watts; either way, the length of the heating wire prevented it from getting red hot. Imitators soon competed with different shapes (oval or rectangular prevailed), differing capacities, timing devices, variable heats, and accessories. Although quite large, they were so much more versatile than kitchen ranges of the 1930s and 1940s that the various roaster brands were found useful in many home kitchens. Large versions are commonly used by caterers (they are portable and can be plugged in at any social function); while many homemakers continue to use them for roasting turkeys and full hams that won't fit into a conventional oven. Smaller versions have been made possible by greatly improved insulating products, and a neat Crock-Pot became very popular in the 1970s. These slow cookers could be filled in the morning before work or school and eight or ten hours later would have a complete main dish ready for serving a small family or a single person.

COFFEEMAKERS

Until 1800 coffee was brewed in the manner that many campers still like. Ground coffee was placed in a pot with cold water and boiled until it smelled good. In 1800 the percolator was invented in France, taking the name of its inventor, M. Biggin. The biggin concept was to have the coffee in a separate compartment above the pot. Boiling forced the water up through a tube to be released above the coffee. It then slowly dripped through, extracting the essence and color without the grounds. Until 1908, percolators generally required twenty minutes before the heated water would pump. In that year the Landers, Frary & Clark Company brought out a "Universal" brand percolator with a "cold water pump." The pot had a small reservoir at the bottom where the electric heat was concentrated, producing the pumping action in two or three minutes. Variations on this concept continue in electric percolators.

Sometime around 1915 a "vacuum-drip" percolator made of the new Pyrex heat-resistant glass was introduced under the trade name Silex. Lifshey says the invention may have been English or German. The advantage of glass, other than allowing one to see the color of the brew, is that it is chemically neutral, imparting no flavor to the coffee. The water boils in the lower vessel as with other percolators, but as it empties, a vacuum is formed by the condensing steam and the water is sucked rather than dripped through the coffee grounds. These highly breakable coffeemakers were very popular for home use (especially in World War II when metal was in short supply), but the bulb-shaped, Silex-style pot remains a familiar sight in restaurants and jetliners worldwide.

In the early years of electric percolators, burnouts were common because of lack of a thermostat shutoff. From 1924, on various manufacturers developed different solutions, one of the more curious of which was by S.W. Farber's inventor F.J. Murphy, who in 1932 patented a carousel of eight fuses: when one fuse blew, you just turned the carousel to the next one. In 1937 Farberware introduced the "Coffee Robot," which not only shut off the current when the coffee was done, but set it to maintain an even warmth. The bottom of this vacuum-type machine was a chrome-plated urn with a spigot for serving. The next step seemed inevitable, but it was a good forty years before a clock/timer was incorporated so that morning coffee lovers could preset the coffeemaker to brew while they slept and set off an alarm when it was ready. Several manufacturers introduced these around 1980, but the most heavily advertised American brand was Mr. Coffee. Solid-state circuitry and quartz timers were the enabling technologies.

In the last decade of the century gourmet coffee making expanded from a rather narrow segment of the population to broad popularity for custom-ground blends and espressos. Hand-operated grinders had been available for a century and electric grinders in grocery stores were common by the 1930s. Preground vacuum-packed coffees dominated, though, and following World War II many Americans preferred the convenience of "instant coffee" powders. A home electric coffee bean grinder was introduced by KitchenAid in 1937 (although mixers and blenders had had coffee grinder attachments a quarter-century earlier). A problem was that special varieties of coffee beans were not generally available until the late 1970s.

Espresso coffeemakers are not a twentieth-century invention: rather elaborate machines of gleaming metal with gas heat were common in *caffe* bars throughout Italy. Enthusiasm for Italian cuisine in the 1980s spawned the production of many varieties of home espressos, European and American, stovetop and electric. The common principle is finely ground, tightly packed coffee through which steam is forced quickly (Italian: *espresso*), thereby extracting the coffee essence without the oils and chemicals that purportedly are products of slow percolation.

Two coffeemakers may not belong here, as the water is heated entirely outside on a range or hot plate. In 1908, Frau Melitta Bentz cobbled together a filter from a tin can, in which she had punched holes, and a piece of ink-blotting paper. With proper filter paper, this became the Melitta coffee maker. Another German, chemist Dr. Peter Schlumbohn, emigrated to America in 1939. In 1941 he invented the simplest coffeemaker of all based on the laboratory practice of filtering liquids through a circular filter paper fitted into a glass funnel. His Chemex coffee maker was made of Pyrex glass, so he had clearance to manufacture it despite wartime shortages. He also marketed Chemex devices himself.

DEEP FRYERS AND CORN POPPERS

There have been many specialized appliances that are more faddish than essential, hot dog cookers, rice cookers, and meat smokers among them. At least two specialized electric appliances have shown more lasting popularity: deep fryers and corn poppers. These, like so many others, date back to the early twentieth century, but as with frying pans, their success waited for positive heat control, and for deep fryers, detachable electric controls and nonstick surfaces.

Corn poppers present several design challenges. Popcorn requires high heat to pop, but it will scorch if left exposed to the heat after popping. Simple electric poppers use a wok principle: a small amount of oil is heated in a well at the bottom. As the kernels pop, they expand and are pushed above the heat source. A later design, largely a fad, was the hot-air popper. This used very hot air to pop the corn, which was blown out a chute into a bowl. The resulting popcorn was low calorie, but a bit like Styrofoam packing beads. A design popular at the end of the century returned to the use of oil, but had a large heated surface and a motorized paddle to stir the popcorn kernels.

Since the introduction of solid-state circuitry, high-impact plastic housings, and nonstick cooking surfaces, the designs of small kitchen appliances have changed little. How far these technologies might go is suggested by the introduction in 2000 of a "Fuzzy Logic" rice cooker, with "a host of programmed settings including sushi rice, brown rice, regular rice, soft grains, slow cooking (for stews and soups), steaming (for vegetables and fish)" as well as a programmable twenty-four-hour timer. Still, there is room for improvement in ease of cleanup, especially cooking spatters, and although generating heat from battery power is problematic, cordless appliances are indicated as a direction for development.

See separate articles on **Bread Machines** and **Microwave Ovens.**

REFERENCES

Beard, James, et al. *International Cooks' Catalogue.* New York: Random House, 1977.

Franklin, Linda Campbell. *300 Years of Kitchen Collectibles.* Iola, WI: Krause Publications, 2002.

Lifshey, Earl. *The Housewares Story: A History of the American Housewares Industry.* Chicago: National Housewares Manufacturers Association, 1973.

Schroeder, Fred E.H. "More Small Things Forgotten: Domestic Electrical Plugs and Receptacles, 1881–1931." In *Technology and Choice,* edited by Marcel C. LaFollette and Jeffrey K. Stine. Chicago: University of Chicago Press, 1991.

Kitchen Appliances: Motorized

Most applications of electric motors to kitchen chores were adaptations of manual processes that are common in less industrialized countries and are still preferred by some gourmet cooks. Mixing doughs and other food combinations with bare hands, beating eggs and cream with a fork, wire whisk, or hand rotary beater, chopping and dicing with a knife or cleaver, blending beverages in a shaker bottle or jar, and grating vegetables by hand are the manual antecedents to products such as the Sunbeam Mixmaster, Waring Blendor, or Cuisinart food processor. However, the technological breakthrough that made these appliances possible was not for kitchen operations, but for a massage vibrator of a kind that is still used in health spas and some homes. In the early years of the century vibrators were a fad, and the first demonstration "all-electric house" in Schenectady, New York, in 1905 included one.

The enabling invention was a lightweight motor that ran at high speed and could operate either on direct current such as Edison's power companies provided or on the alternating current supplied by Westinghouse dynamos. In 1904 two entrepreneurs in Racine, Wisconsin, Fred Osius and George Schmidt, formed a company to manufacture vibrators. Shortly after, they hired a farm boy, Chester A. Beach, as a mechanic, and as advertising manager, a steamboat cashier, L.H. Hamilton. Together, Hamilton and Beach invented a successful "universal" (AC/DC) motor for vibrators. By 1910, the company reorganized as Hamilton-Beach. Perceiving a new fad for "milk shakes" and "malteds" (Racine was the American home of Horlick's malted milk powders, which had been introduced as a health food in the late 1880s by William Horlick), the inventors developed a high-speed mixer for restaurants and soda fountains. These had a vertical spindle driven by the high-speed (7200 rpm) motor. At the end of the spindle was the mixer, resembling a miniature boat propeller. For most of the century, the Hamilton-Beach mixers were the standard device at soda fountains.

Other uses for the lightweight universal motors were on the inventors' minds. In 1912 they sold little motors (about the size of a fist) sitting on four steady legs as the HOME motor. The spindle came equipped with a rubber tire that could be placed against the hand wheel of a foot-operated (treadle) sewing machine, and the old machine was instantly converted to electricity. Other attachments were made available so that the HOME motor could sharpen knives, buff silver, and mix cake batter, too.

"....And I thought I knew all about it"

More than a "Mixer"...
a Complete Food Preparer

Beats—Eggs (1 or 10), icings, batters for cakes, waffles, etc.

Whips—cream (little or much).

Mixes—dough for bread, rolls, biscuits, pies and pastries.

Extracts—juice from oranges, lemons, grapefruit.

Grinds—coffee and cereals.

Strains—fruits for butters, jellies, sauces.

Sieves—vegetables for soups and purees; pumpkin, etc.

Slices—potatoes (thick or thin), vegetables, firm fruits.

Chops—meats (cooked or raw), nuts, raisins, figs.

Freezes—ice cream, sherbets and other frozen dainties.

Makes—mayonnaise, candies, fruit whips, applesauce (without paring or coring).

Shreds and Grates—vegetables, cheese, cocoanut, chocolate, etc.

Chips ice — Shreds cabbage — Mashes potatoes — Creams butter.

All these things—and many more

"I'd heard of KitchenAid for years. I have friends who use and praise it—but I imagined their enthusiasm was based somewhat on the human tendency to defend their purchase.

"I'd seen KitchenAid displayed, but had never actually used it myself. Somehow it seemed to me it might be complicated—it seemed there might be too many things to wash, and so on. But now I find it's *the simplest thing in the world.* And just imagine, I thought I knew all about it.

"The revelation came when I permitted a KitchenAid representative to show it to me *in my own kitchen.* I saw it take flour and shortening ... whole vegetables ... cream and butter ... eggs, milk and flavorings and transform them into finished creations so quickly and simply that I realized *I had really known nothing about it before.*

"*Now* I wonder why I denied myself the pleasure and satisfaction of KitchenAid all this time. From snowy-white mashed potatoes to wondrous angel-food cake and tempting desserts, it covers the whole range of food preparation. *I have only to put in the materials and snap the switch.*"

This reaction to the use of KitchenAid on the part of one owner is typical of expressions from thousands now enthusiastically using it, who hesitated to have it explained to them in their own kitchens because they, too, had felt, from superficial impressions, "they knew all about it."

You will find much of interest in our descriptive matter, sent without obligation, of course. Just sign and mail the coupon.

The KitchenAid Manufacturing Co.
223 Olive Street   Troy, Ohio

KitchenAid
REG. US. PAT. OFF.
Electrical Food Preparer for the Home

Sales Representation in Principal Cities
Distributing Agencies:
173 King Street East, Toronto, Canada; 38 Charterhouse Street, London, E. C. 1, England.

The KitchenAid Manufacturing Co.,
223 Olive Street, Troy, Ohio.

Please send, *without obligation,* your free descriptive matter on KitchenAid.

Name....................................

Street..................................

City.................. State..............

March 1931 Good Housekeeping

The KitchenAid mixer was introduced in 1920, but many housewives thought that all it could do was mix doughs and cake batters. This 1931 advertisement touts its versatility and offers home demonstrations for skeptical women. Extra attachments were needed for many of the processes. (Courtesy of Whirlpool)

MIXERS

With this last function we have the earliest form of a home mixer, but it must have been very awkward to use. In 1920 Hobart Manufacturing Company of Troy, Ohio, introduced the self-contained KitchenAid mixer mounted on its own stand. The next step in convenience and versatility was to make the motor and mixing blades assembly detachable so that the cook could move a handheld mixer to another bowl. Several manufacturers brought these out in the 1920s and the single beater (usually a modified wire whisk) was replaced with dual beaters that were more effective at folding in the batters. In 1931, the Chicago Flexible Shaft Company introduced the "Mixmaster," which incorporated all the improvements above and had a sturdy and steady cast metal base, and under the Sunbeam label, would advertise that it could mix, mash, whip, beat, cream, stir, and blend, and with attachments, could extract and filter fruit juices, chop food, grind meat, peel potatoes, open cans, mix drinks, and grind coffee. The Sunbeam Mixmaster became the mixer of choice for the next three decades. Improvements in the several brands of kitchen mixers have primarily been the conversion to solid-state circuitry allowing for push-button speed controls and lighter weight. Design changes have been made with the use of color plastics and streamlining. However, with fewer homemakers making cakes and whipped toppings from scratch, mixers declined in popularity, as several of their functions were taken over by blenders and food processors.

BLENDERS

The food blender also came out of Racine, Wisconsin, and also was planned for the commercial market for milk shakes. The inventor was Stephen J. Poplawski. In 1922 he was issued a patent for an appliance that had the essential characteristics of the modern blender. Instead of a motor at the top, as in a mixer or milk shake maker, it had the motor in a base. Instead of inserting the mixing blade into a container of ingredients, it had the mixing blades as part of the container. Poplawski brought his patents to the Greene Manufacturing Company in Racine in 1932, and it was in that year that it was first used to chop and liquefy fruits and vegetables as well as to mix shakes and malts. The food blender was born, soon to be known as the "Osterizer" as the Greene Company's mixer production was taken over by John Oster Manufacturing Company.

How the blender became popular in home kitchens takes the story back to Fred Osius, the entrepreneur who started Hamilton-Beach. Osius had an idea for his own blender design. He also had an associate who was related to the publicity agent for Fred Waring, whose "Pennsylvanians" band and choir were to be popular radio stars well into the 1940s. Osius demonstrated his model in 1936 to Waring, and Waring had invested $25,000 in Osius' invention before he realized that Osius was incapable of bringing out a production model. Fred Waring turned the problem over to Ed Lee, who identified several engineering and manufacturing shortcomings that had to be addressed: the shape of the container, leakproofing, and coupling the mixing blades and the driver. In 1937 the Waring "Miracle Mixer" was introduced at a restaurant trade show as a machine for making frozen daiquiris. The Ron Rico rum company promoted the Waring Blendor to bars and restaurants. A California health food advocate, Martin Pretorius, also promoted the Blendor for liquefying foods. This was all before World War II; when production resumed after the war, blender sales were modest because the public regarded them as a bar fixture. To counteract this prejudice Oster and Waring issued recipe books and demonstrated food preparation in department stores. Improvements in design and color helped to make blenders a rage for "in" consumers. Push buttons for different speeds were made possible by solid-state circuitry in 1965, after which some sixty-seven manufacturers engaged in a "battle of the buttons" reaching well over a dozen speeds by the time that sales peaked in the early 1970s. Blenders continue to be popular for mixing drinks, whether alcoholic or for health diets.

FOOD PROCESSORS

Although the food processor derives from a French chopping-mixing machine used by restaurants, the home appliance is quite American. Carl Sontheimer (1915–1983) had retired from a career as a physicist to continue an avocation as a gourmet cook. On a trip to France in 1971 Sontheimer and his wife saw a demonstration of a food preparation machine. On returning home, he decided to start a company that would import high-quality European cookware. He named the company Cuisinart. The following year Sontheimer worked on improvements to the food preparation machine to make it more suitable for the American home market, adding safety features as well as improving the cutting blades. In 1973 Cuisinart unveiled the machine at a National Housewares Exposition, introducing the term "food processor," which would cover the wide array of functions that it could perform in the kitchen. Sales were slow, until Sontheimer gained support from some of the leading American cooking stars such as Julia Child, James Beard, and Craig Claiborne. Television demonstrations, recipe books, and later videotapes attracted consumers to this new appliance.

By 1977, not only did Cuisinart's business boom, but more than a dozen other manufacturers brought out competing models of food processors. The industry continues to refine and diversify the machines, especially in offering different sizes, but essentially they are chopping machines with a motor base similar to that on a blender, a horizontal chopping blade that fits within a food bowl, and an opening through which raw materials can be introduced. The variations include different speeds and blades for chopping and grinding hard materials such as ice and coffee, blending mixtures, grinding soft materials such as meat, and pureeing and liquefying fruits and vegetables. Some machines also have grating and slicing discs that are elevated above the food bowl.

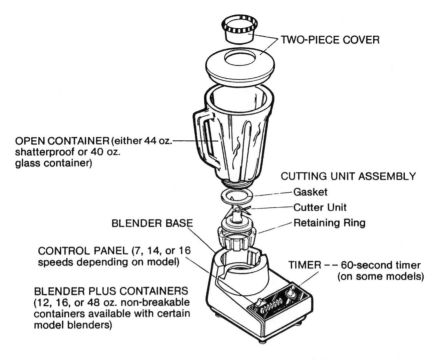

Typical blender components. The base contains the motor and electronic speed controls. All other parts can be easily separated for washing. (Illustration courtesy of Hamilton Beach/Proctor-Silex, Inc.)

GARBAGE DISPOSERS

One motorized appliance that is not an adaptation of a manual task is the garbage disposer. Large garbage grinders had been developed in the 1920s for municipalities to reduce garbage to a mash that could be processed with sewage. The impetus for a home version came from right at the top at the General Electric Corporation, with President Gerard Swope challenging his engineers to compete with one another for a design. The Chicago laboratory won, crediting one of its engineers, J.H. Powers, for important contributions. Production and sales began in 1935 with the introduction of the General Electric "Disposall" (the registered trademark became the popular generic term, as with Kleenex, Frigidaire, Band-Aid, Scotch Tape, etc.). This was of course, the middle of the Great Depression, and both the machine and installation were expensive. Furthermore, there was considerable controversy among sanitation engineers and public works officials about whether mixing garbage and sewage was a good idea. Would the accepted way of treating human wastes work on garbage? Would the influx of ground garbage from thousands of homes overburden treatment plants? World War II stopped all production of home units, but GE engineers continued to refine Disposalls, partly because the navy had requested a larger Disposall. By the end of the war, Disposall engineers had reduced the size and complexity of the machine, had found ways of reducing the noise level, and had worked a method of chilling fats with cold water so that they wouldn't clog systems.

The real test came in 1950, when the town of Jasper, Indiana, voted to require the installation of garbage disposers in all homes. They were motivated by health issues, as there had been an outbreak of cholera from garbage-fed hogs, and a polio epidemic was thought to have been fostered by the municipal garbage dump. Other cities followed, although as recently as 1967 *Consumer Reports* cautioned prospective buyers that some communities prohibited disposers. There are many health and convenience advantages to having a disposer in the kitchen, yet problems with retrofitting and installation in rural home septic systems (the majority of which were not perfectly effective for human wastes even at the end of the century) indicate that eliminating the garbage can take time.

The motorized mixer, blender, food processor, and disposer have proved to be the most popular appliances, but there are many other single-use appliances, some of which, like ice crushers, can openers, knife sharpeners, orange juicers, and coffee grinders, were anticipated as attachments to Mixmasters and other machines, but a few others, such as the electric knife, trash compactor, and cookie dough shooter, were unique. All are inherently useful, and for persons with physical disabilities such as arthritic hands, they may be essential, but to many consumers they may be regarded as fad items that add to kitchen clutter.

The future will doubtless see more cordless appliances, more easily cleaned components and with changing tastes, different colors and designs. The miniaturization of many products is limited in food preparation appliances. Unless people are miniaturized also, the size of these machines is limited by food serving sizes.

For partially motorized kitchen appliances, see articles on **Dishwashers, Bread machines,** and **Microwave Ovens.**

REFERENCES

Hoy, Suellen. "The Garbage Disposer, the Public Health, and the Good Life." In *Technology and Choice,* edited by Marcel C. LaFollette and Jeffrey K. Stine. Chicago: University of Chicago Press, 1991.

Lifshey, Earl. *The Housewares Story: A History of the American Housewares Industry.* Chicago: National Housewares Manufacturers Association, 1973.

Microwave Ovens

"Now you're cooking with gas!" At the beginning of the twentieth century, gas cooking was an enormous convenience compared to coal and wood-fired stoves. Slowly, the electric oven became an alternative. Electric ovens are very simple: a squarish sheet metal chamber with a door, and a simple electric heating element at the bottom and top. The heating elements are just a loop of resisting wire—electric currents always produce heat when they flow through a resistance, as in the equally simple incandescent light bulb.

As a supplement to large electric ovens (and an alternative where space is very restricted), small countertop toaster ovens were produced (see **Kitchen Appliances: Heat Generating**). These are typically small uninsulated metal boxes, have a heating coil underneath a grid, and double as a toaster or, using a small tray over the grid, as an oven.

But in the middle of the twentieth century, an interesting alternative to gas and electric coil heating suddenly emerged. In the last two decades of the century it had an enormous surge of popularity, and became near-universal in kitchens across America: the microwave oven.

In 1939 Sir John Randall and Dr. H.A. Boot at Birmingham University in England invented a device called a magnetron to produce high-energy microwaves. Microwaves are short-wavelength radio waves, overlapping the television band at the low-frequency end, and extending up toward infrared light. Microwaves range in length from about 0.1 to 30 centimeters (about 0.04 to 12 inches). The immediate application for the magnetron was to improve radar (radio detection and ranging). Radar was developed by the British and Americans for use in World War II (in particular, to detect invading German aircraft and rockets). After the war, microwaves, relayed from station to station using dish antennas, were widely used for long-distance telecommunications.

An American company, Raytheon in Massachusetts, was the first to mass-produce magnetrons, and during World War II Raytheon became the leading producer of magnetrons and radar systems. Raytheon sales went from $3 million in 1940 to $168 million in 1945, and the firm remained a major defense contractor thereafter. Raytheon had been founded in 1922 and their first product was the tube used to allow radios to run off house current rather than batteries (see **Radios**). In addition, Raytheon made the first mass-produced transistor, the CK722. (More recently, they produced the Patriot missiles used in the Gulf War in 1991.)

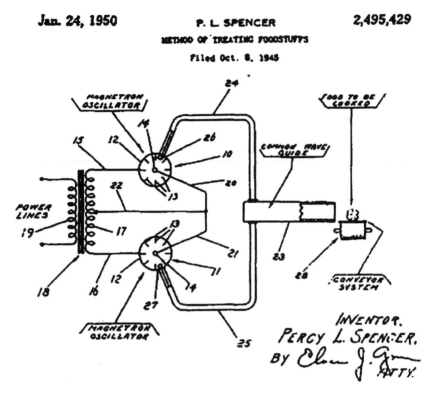

Percy Spencer's 1945 patent drawing for a "method of treating foodstuffs"—the Raytheon Radarange. The first microwave oven used two very expensive water-cooled magnetrons to generate the microwaves, and it cost many thousands of 1954 dollars. Its use was largely confined to luxury restaurants and ocean liners.

Percy L. Spencer (1894–1970) was an employee at Raytheon working around magnetrons just after the end of the war. One day he noticed that a candy bar in his pocket melted when he walked near one of the magnetrons. Spencer asked for a bag of popcorn—and he quickly discovered that the microwaves from the magnetron could pop the corn! Spencer immediately saw the possibilities for cooking, and the patent for microwave cooking was applied for in 1946. Spencer and his team developed the first microwave oven, the RadaRange, in 1947. Its name was determined in an employee contest. The RadaRange stood five and half feet tall and weighed in at 750 pounds. Its twin magnetrons required a water supply for cooling. This large, expensive device was not a great commercial success; its use was confined to a few restaurants and especially unusual food preparation sites such as railroad dining cars and ocean liners.

In 1955, Tappan, an Ohio stove manufacturer, introduced the first home microwave oven. It was 24 inches wide, operated on 220 volts, and was priced at around $1,200. This was far too expensive to lead to wide use in home kitchens. The microwave evangelists at Raytheon did not abandon their hopes; they looked for a strategic opportunity to enter the home market. They found it in a Midwest refrigerator manufacturer.

Amana was founded in 1934 by George Foerstner (1908–2000), a young entrepreneur in Amana, Iowa. The Amana Colonies were a religious community settled in 1855 by a group of German immigrants belonging to the Community of True Inspiration. They originally practiced a communal lifestyle, with most assets owned collectively by the community. They voted to abandon this arrangement in 1932, and became a joint stock company. Foerstner then founded the Electrical Equipment Company and drew upon the talented local cabinetmakers to build a commercial beverage cooler. In 1936, the operation was renamed Amana Refrigeration as Foerstner sold the company to the Amana Society, remaining as head until he retired in 1982. In 1954 the company added air conditioners to its product line of refrigeration appliances.

Raytheon saw Amana as the source of the appliance manufacturing capability it needed, and acquired Amana in 1965. In 1967, Amana introduced the first home countertop microwave oven, the Amana RadarRange. This new home Radarange, which retailed for $495, weighed 91 pounds and was about 15 inches tall. It was powered by a 115-volt current, had 650 watts of cooking power, and featured two control knobs, one for cooking food in 5 minutes or less and the other for longer times. Amana went to elaborate measures to introduce the product, including presentations by home economists around the country.

The first American competitor, Litton, another military contractor and corporate conglomerate, introduced a model in 1969. The Japanese company Matsushita had marketed a microwave oven in 1963, and soon it too was producing countertop models (sold in the United States under the Panasonic brand name). By the end of the 1970s, these manufacturers were joined by American firms General Electric, Magic Chef, Tappan, and Westinghouse, and Japanese manufacturers Sharp and Sanyo. A decade later, Korean companies Samsung and Goldstar had significant market presence. Over the years, magnetrons in home microwaves had increased in power from about 650 watts to 1,100 watts.

In 1975 Amana introduced the first touch controls on microwaves. Digital touch pads became the most common type of control panel, with an LED display showing time and other information. Since the microwave oven doesn't brown food well, microwaves have been combined with other methods of heat generation to produce hybrid ovens. Some of these used browning coils in the roof of the oven; more common at the end of the twentieth century was microwave plus convection cooking—the latter blows heated air around the food, browning the surface and assisting with the cooking. The countertop microwave oven was the most common form, but microwave ovens were also available designed to be mounted over a conventional cooking range. In this form a wide cooking cavity is combined with a light and exhaust fan to form a range hood—at a cost of at least twice that of countertop models.

A microwave oven has a cooking chamber that is between 0.5 and 2 cubic feet, much smaller than conventional cooking ovens. Typically no racks are provided. Electronic components are typically to the right of the oven cavity. The main components are a control panel and timer, the magnetron, high-voltage power supply for the magnetron, a fan, and safety fuses and switches. The safety fuses typically are thermal, and one may be mounted on the wall of the cooking cavity, another on the magnetron itself. A safety switch is provided at the door so that the microwave will not operate if the door is opened. The door is transparent, but the view is through a metal grid that reflects microwaves back into the cavity.

When high voltage (around 3,000 volts) is applied to the magnetron, it produces a beam of microwaves. These travel down a metal horn, the waveguide, into the cooking chamber. In the chamber, the microwaves reflect off the walls and door, bouncing around until they hit something that absorbs them. Food, especially water, is good at absorbing microwave energy. The water in the food rapidly heats up, and heat is transferred by conduction to other parts of the food. When popcorn pops, the moisture in the popcorn kernel is converted to steam, is held by the outer hull as the steam pressure builds, and the kernel eventually explodes into a puffy edible. Soon "microwave popcorn" was introduced, pre-buttered and packaged in a special paper bag that has a layer of microwave-absorbing material on one side.

A fan blows air across the magnetron and into the cooking cavity. The cavity has an exhaust vent, usually near the back. The airflow cools the magnetron, keeps steam away from the electronics, and exhausts steam from the cooking cavity. Microwaves tend to be directional and uneven; in cooking this is not desirable, so some means of diffusing the microwave energy is required for cooking to be even. Two methods are used—a rotating paddle wheel in the top of the case (which may be turned by the air from the fan blowing across the blades), or a large turntable mounted in the floor of the cooking chamber, powered by a separate motor. Separate spring-wound turntables were also produced in the 1980s, for ovens lacking a built-in turntable.

To produce different cooking "levels," the timer simply cycles the magnetron on and off—several seconds on, a variable time off. High power would be continuous on, while for defrosting, the magnetron might receive power only 10–20 percent of the time. While this is the near-universal method of controlling cooking, in the late 1990s Panasonic produced ovens with "inverter technology" that varied the power output of the magnetron itself. Simple microwave ovens have a timer that shuts them off after a specified number of minutes. Additional controls have been tried, including temperature probes that were stuck into the food and turned off the oven when a preset food temperature was reached. At the end of the 1990s a preferred method of automatic control used in some of the more expensive ovens were humidity sensors detecting steaming from the food.

With the cost of computer technology continuously dropping, the expectation is that appliances will get "smarter." A prime candidate is the microwave oven. In 1993 Amana produced a microwave that read bar-coded cooking instructions directly from product packages (see **Barcodes and Magnetic Stripes**). General Electric introduced an Advantium oven that can recognize and respond to voice commands. Another GE microwave can scan UPC labels on food items to get cooking and nutritional information; microwave ovens appear to be a natural appliance to use the Internet to get information (see **Digital Telecommunications**), recipes, and cooking instructions. These brave new appliances may be one of the first to use network technology to enhance people's lives.

REFERENCES

Barham, Peter. *The Science of Cooking.* New York: Springer-Verlag, 2001.

Cowan, Ruth. *More Work for Mother: The Ironies of Household Technology from the Open Hearth to the Microwave.* New York: Basic Books, 1983.

Gallawa, J.C. *The History of the Microwave Oven.* 1996, 2000. http://www.gallawa.com/microtech/history.html

Hardyment, Christina. *From Mangle to Microwave: The Mechanization of Household Work.* New York and Oxford: Blackwell Publishers, 1988.

Webb, Pauline, and Mark Suggit. *Gadgets and Necessities: An Encyclopeida of Household Innovations.* Santa Barbara, CA: ABC-Clio.

Motion Pictures

Although motion picture photography was invented at the end of the nineteenth century, it was transformed from a novelty to a major form of entertainment and information in the twentieth century. Four significant innovations were: multi-reel feature films, synchronized sound, color photography, and wide screen. Lesser innovations included drive-in theaters, 3D, and, of course, improvements in all areas from safety film to computer animation and Dolby surround sound. As a result of these technological breakthroughs, a performance that might have been viewed by an audience of at most a few thousand people could be viewed by a billion or more people once recorded on film. The effect on the content of entertainment was enormous, as mass audiences justified production of expensive spectacles. The sociological and cultural effects of motion pictures were also great, as masses of people shared theatrical experiences once confined to small numbers.

Zoetropes were a mid-nineteenth century novelty in which apparent motion was produced by a short series of drawings viewed through slits in a rotating cylinder. Eadweard Muybridge (1830–1904) then used photography to capture motion. Muybridge, funded by California railroad magnate Leland Stanford, in 1877 set up a series of cameras triggered in succession to photograph a running horse (originally to answer the question of whether the horse ever has all four hooves off the ground while running). Then in France in 1882, Etienne Marey (1830–1904) invented a "photographic gun," a single camera that could capture a series of photos on a disk of photographic paper. This was developed over the following six years into a camera that used a strip of photographic paper.

Many others worked on the move to transparent celluloid film. Thomas Edison (1847–1931) was the first to achieve commercial success after much work in the early 1890s. A key was to exploit the nitrocellulose film introduced in 1889 by George Eastman (1854–1932) for his Kodak cameras. Edison introduced the Kinetoscope in 1894, a coin-operated peepshow in a wooden cabinet that allowed about 15 seconds of viewing of motion captured as a series of photographs on a maximum of 50-foot-long loop of film. These early motion pictures were very short, and were exhibited in arcades.

The development of electric lamps encouraged many to work on motion picture projectors. Thomas Armat (1867?–1948) made many projector improvements, including introducing a loop of film above and below the projection opening and then having the film pause briefly in the projection aperture, allowing a brighter

An early projector for silent motion pictures. (Courtesy of www.comstock.com)

image on the screen. Edison built on Armat's patents, settled on 35-millimeter wide film, which became standard, and in 1896 the resulting Vitascope projector made possible theatrical presentation of short films in vaudeville houses. Motion pictures, "movies," had finally arrived as a short theatrical novelty.

FEATURE FILMS

The first film copyrighted in the United States was the 1894 Edison *Kinescopic Record of a Sneeze*. It was a far cry from a sneeze to the full eight minutes of director Edwin S. Porter's *The Great Train Robbery* in 1903. This landmark movie was one of the first films shot in segments and then edited to tell a story. By 1912 the first feature-length film shown in the United States was *Queen Elizabeth*, featuring Sarah Bernhardt. The 1912 Italian film *Quo Vadis?*, at almost two hours, was the longest early film. These were soon followed by D.W. Griffith's spectacles *Birth of a Nation* (1915) and *Intolerance* (1916). To present these multireel films without interruption, theaters needed two projectors; as one projected a reel of the film, the other could be loaded with the next reel. But the expense was justified; the movies had become a popular storyteller, taking a place alongside stage plays and novels. In this second decade of the century several genres besides spectacles had appeared, including Westerns, horror (beginning with the 1919 German film *The Cabinet of Dr. Caligari*), and romance (including *The Sheik* with Rudolph Valentino and films starring the vamp, Theda Bara). Some of the most popular movies of the period were the comedies, typically two-reelers, including films by Charlie Chaplin, Mack Sennett's Keystone Cops, Buster Keaton, Harold Lloyd, and a host of films turned out by the Hal Roach studios, including many with Stan Laurel and Oliver Hardy.

TALKING MOTION PICTURES

For the first three decades of the twentieth century, almost all films were silent. Music was provided in the theater by an organist, often at the mighty Wurlitzer. Sound was attempted, using the technology of the phonograph, but synchronization was difficult. Records were shorter than reels of film, and the unamplified phonographs available before 1910 were ill-suited for theaters. Lee De Forest (1873–1961) invented the Audion amplifier tube, and after World War I De Forest turned his attention to motion picture sound, recording sound directly on the motion picture film. By 1923 he was exhibiting "Phonofilms." The sound is recorded in a narrow band to one side of the picture. In the projector, the film passes between a small separate lamp and a photocell, and the varying light intensity is converted into an electrical signal, amplified, and turned back into sound by speakers. The film must move at a smooth fixed rate between photocell and lamp. Thus the sound accompanying an image is located on the film a short distance from the part of the film where the image is being projected. As the film passes in front of the image projection lamp, the motion of the film is jerky, since each frame must be held stationary for a fraction of a second as light passes through it and the image is projected onto the screen. Therefore, the sound recording is offset from the images—and if the film loop in the projector is not the correct size for the offset, the sound will be out of sync with the images.

Meanwhile Bell Telephone laboratories had persisted in the phonograph approach to sound movies well into the 1920s, using 13–17-inch-diameter phonographs. Warner Brothers used this system in its 1927 film *The Jazz Singer*, featuring the popular vaudeville star Al Jolson. This was the first feature-length film with segments with synchronized sound, and its popularity both saved Warner Brothers from bankruptcy and encouraged a shift of all major studio motion picture production to sound by 1930. Walt Disney produced the first sound cartoon, *Steamboat Willie*, in 1928. By 1930 Warner Brothers converted to the De Forest system of sound-on-film, which became the standard thereafter.

The sound is recorded in a narrow stripe between the left sprocket holes and the images. The sound stripe is either variable in width, looking under a magnifying glass somewhat like a filled-in oscilloscope image of the waveform, or has a fixed width with varying density from black to transparent. In either case, when a light shines through the sound stripe on the moving film, the light passing through is caused to vary in intensity at exactly the frequency and varying amplitude of the original sound signal. The reproduction circuitry is fairly simple, made possible by the development of the selenium photocell. Recording the image was more complicated. Incandescent lamps do not change brightness rapidly enough to allow them to be used directly to record the sound signals' rapid variations.

Later sound developments included stereophonic sound pioneered in the 1930s, and developed by Disney for the 1940 animated musical film *Fantasia*. There followed multitrack sound in the 1950s, magnetic sound stripes (used in Cinemascope in 1953), various forms of noise reduction, including work by Ray Dolby (see **Audio Recording**), and digital sound (see **Compact Discs**).

TECHNICOLOR

Color can greatly enhance the experience of watching a motion picture. Color motion pictures, using film with emulsions sensitive to different colors, was described in the 1860s by Louis du Hauron, long before there were black-and-white movies! In the early twentieth century, some films were colored by hand, frame by frame. Pathé introduced a system using stencils in 1905. In 1906 the Englishmen Charles Urban and G. Albert Smith patented a two-color "Kinemacolor" process that used regular black-and-white film running at double speed (32 fps). Alternate frames were shot (and later projected) through red and green filters.

Herbert T. Kalmus (1881–1963) and associates from MIT founded Technicolor in 1915. They too initially used a two-color process. The incoming image was passed through a prism that separated it into two images, one emphasizing light toward the red end of the spectrum, the other emphasizing light toward the blue end. The two images were filmed separately. During processing, the two films were dyed, then laminated to produce a two-layer multicolor film. The first commercial film to use the process was produced in 1922. This early color was an expensive novelty that faded quickly; feature films continued to be produced in black and white. In 1932 Walt Disney was the first to use a new three-color Technicolor process. Only with the success of *The Wizard of Oz* and *Gone with the Wind* (1939) did the expensive color process become popular. Technicolor dominated color film in the United States until the 1950s when Eastman Kodak and Ansco produced single "monopack" films with emulsions sensitive to all three colors (Kodak had developed Kodachrome film in 1935 for still photography). A development that promoted the use of these new tricolor emulsions on a single strip of film, rather than the multiple film strips of Technicolor, was wide screen movies shot on wider film.

WIDE SCREEN

Fred Waller (1886–1954) was an engineer at Paramount (he also patented the first water skis). He experimented with wide-screen production in the 1930s, initially using an array of eleven 16-millimeter cameras. This work culminated in a successful wide-screen gunnery training film used by the U.S. military in a simulator during World War II. Convinced that the tremendous visual impact made by wide-screen would have commercial appeal, Waller redid the system to use three 35-millimeter cameras and projectors, each displaying a 50 percent taller-than-normal image. The projectors were in sync and displayed their images side by side on a huge curving screen encompassing 146 degrees of arc. A fourth 35-millimeter projector carried only the sound information, in a system developed by Hazard Reeves with an amazing 7 channels—5 played back through speakers behind the screen and 2 on the side walls of the theater. The result was Cinerama, aptly premiering with *This Is Cinerama* in New York City in fall 1952.

The immersive impact of the wide-screen presentation, and the multichannel sound system (along, perhaps, with the competition of television for viewers' eyes), spurred the other studios to come out with their own systems. Fox, with Bausch and Lomb, rapidly developed a single-film system, using anamorphic distorting lenses that had been invented in the late 1920s by French Professor Henri Chrétien. During filming, an anamorphic lens in front of the normal camera lens compresses a double-wide image onto normal 35-millimeter film, and during projection a corresponding lens expands the image back to its original proportions. Fox also developed a 4-channel sound system, carried by 4 magnetic stripes along both edges of the film (the sprocket holes were reduced in size). This CinemaScope system premiered with *The Robe* in 1953. Most of the Hollywood studios decided to use this wide-screen format, which was substantially less expensive than Cinerama.

Waller's idea of multiple cameras continued to be used in various small productions, including a 360-degree surround tour of America featured for many years at the AT&T display in Tomorrowland at Disneyland. Most of the filming was done with the camera array atop a moving car. The success of another multicamera presentation, at Expo '67 in Montreal, inspired its Canadian developers to create a new single-camera format, Imax. This system used 70-millimeter film, but ran the film sideways, with the result that each image had about 10 times the area (and image detail) of 35-millimeter film. In addition, a new film advance system was used that permitted each frame to be projected for a longer time, transmitting more light. Imax premiered at Expo '70 in Osaka, Japan, and then was adapted to dome-shaped "Omnimax" theaters with the 1973 opening of the Reuben H. Fleet Space Theater in San Diego, California. In the dome theaters, the projection room is below steeply sloped seats, and at show time the projector is raised to a small cubicle set in the center of the seating. By 2000, there were over 200 permanent Imax theaters and a catalog of about 150 films in the format.

FLICKERING FORMATS

The really big screens were found in drive-in movie theaters. This peculiarly American innovation consisted of a huge outdoor screen in a flat fenced lot. Patrons drove their cars in through a box office gate and parked in rows on slightly inclined parking spaces. A speaker was taken from a stand and hung on the partially lowered side window of the car. Patrons could watch a large-screen movie from the (relative) privacy of their own cars—an arrangement popular with teenagers. Over 4,000 drive-in movie theaters had been built in the United States by the 1960s. These helped slow the loss of movie revenue to television. But by the end of the century, the rise of home theater and multiple televisions had driven drive-ins nearly to extinction. Not even 3D had saved them from decline.

3D motion pictures were demonstrated at the 1939 World's Fair. In 1952 3D was revived in the low-budget film *Bwana Devil*. The film was shot with separate red and blue images; viewers wore glasses with a red cellophane filter over one eye and blue over the other, separating the images. A short-lived 3D fad ensued. "Smell-o-Vision" was even shorter-lived.

Even if movie content was sometimes lacking at mid-century, the film itself was improved. In the first half of the century films were shot on nitrocellulose film. This film is highly flammable. If the film breaks in the projector, the intense light of the projection lamp will often ignite the film. A fire in a crowded theater is very dangerous. In 1908 acetate safety film was introduced and became widely used by amateur moviemakers, but it was not until over forty years later that it displaced nitrocellulose film in commercial motion pictures.

By the end of the twentieth century, computer animation played an important role in motion picture production (notably in Disney's *Toy Story*). The future likely holds increasing use of computer technology to create images of ever-more-lifelike characters and ever-more-spectacular special effects. Home theater is expected to continue to compete with presentations in theaters. Studios have come to rely on the secondary market of direct purchase by consumers of videotape and DVD copies of movies (delayed until after theatrical release). High-speed data links may permit direct download of movies ("view on demand"), bypassing the need for renting or purchasing physical copies of films. Optical film may be finally replaced by digital media, if the resolution can be great enough for projection. Virtual reality is a natural extension of wide-screen presentation, with viewers either wearing special goggles or sitting in a display booth. In this way, 3D may yet return to play a role in future film production.

REFERENCES

Basten, Fred. *Glorious Technicolor: The Movies' Magic Rainbow.* New York: Barnes & Company, 1995.

Belton, John. *Widescreen Cinema*. Harvard Film Studies. Cambridge: Harvard University Press, 1992.

Crafton, Donald. *Talkies: American Cinema's Transition to Sound, 1926–1931*. History of the American Cinema, 4. Berkeley: University of California Press, 1999.

Friedman, Jeffrey, ed. *Milestones in Motion Picture and Television Technology*. Scarsdale, NY: Society of Motion Picture and Television Engineers, 1991.

Kalmus, Herbert, and Eleanor Kalmus. *Mr. Technicolor*. Absecon, NJ: Magic Image Filmbooks, 1993.

Ryan, Roderick. *A History of Motion Picture Color Technology*. London: Focal Press, 1977.

Sanders, Don, and Susan Sanders. *The American Drive-in Movie Theater*. Osceola, WI: MotorBooks International, 1997.

Personal Hygiene Products

Tampons, sanitary napkins, disposable diapers, and condoms are all products that have a relatively low-tech predecessor going back into the very distant past. However, each of these personal hygiene products also transformed itself in the twentieth century, using newly available materials, advertising, and mass marketing to achieve universal and global presence in contemporary life.

CONDOMS

Ancient Egyptians are pictured wearing brightly colored penis sheaths, possibly as a form of personal adornment. Ancient Greeks and Romans made condom-like objects out of dried animal intestines and fish bladders, and these were used for their two modern purposes: prevention of pregnancy, and reduction of disease risk from sexual intercourse. In the nineteenth century condoms were made of treated linen or other fabrics. A latex rubber condom or "rubber" was marketed in the 1930s, and designs gradually became thinner, more pliable, and more comfortable as the decades passed.

Initial opposition to widespread use of condoms came from conservative organizations such as the American Social Hygiene Association, whose members argued that the consequences of "illegitimate" sexual activity should be visited upon the participants. Such thinking held sway during World War I, when American troops abroad were the only military force not supplied with condoms. By the time of World War II, however, military thinking had changed, and condoms were lavishly distributed; educational films shown in military training promoted their use and extolled their merits.

Condom manufacturers fell upon hard times during the 1960s, as widespread use of birth control pills rendered them less necessary for pregnancy prevention. But the advent of the AIDS epidemic brought condoms back vigorously, as in 1986 the U.S. surgeon general endorsed their use as "the only currently available effective barrier against AIDS." Safer-sex educational campaigns, such as those advocated by Planned Parenthood, now feature condom use as a crucial component.

In condom manufacture, glass molds shaped like expanded condoms are repeatedly dipped into vats of liquid latex, removed, dried, and vulcanized. The con-

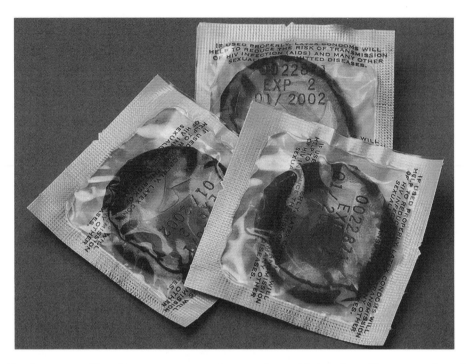

Condoms were illegal in some states and were often sold elsewhere "for prevention of disease only." (Courtesy of Corbis)

doms are then removed by air pressure, dried, and powdered before being packaged in hygienic aluminum wraps. Currently, the indispensable condom is available in a variety of colors, textures, and even flavors; a glow-in-the-dark condom was introduced in 1990 by the Global Protection Corporation. The product name is "Knight Light."

SANITARY NAPKINS

The history of how women through the ages have managed menstruation and its hygiene is a fascinating study. The isolation of menstruating women as "unclean," practiced in many cultures both in the past and still today, is predicated on menstruation being socially detectable. Twentieth-century developments in menstrual hygiene have been designed to make the process invisible and to reduce its inconvenience. Prior to the development of the sanitary napkin and the tampon, menstrual blood was collected in household rags attached by various means to a woman's underclothing. These rags were then laundered and reused.

During World War I, bandage cotton became a scarce commodity and cellulose wadding was introduced as a substitute. This bandage material was made available in hospitals and first-aid stations by the Kimberley-Clark Company. Enterprising nurses began to use the bandage material in place of cloths for menstrual purposes as well. In 1920, the Kotex disposable sanitary napkin was marketed. An elastic belt was designed with center buckles for attaching the napkin's thin gauze-like ends.

Advertisers faced the challenge of educating the consumer about this product without mentioning the still-largely taboo subject of menstruation explicitly. Many creative euphemisms were used: menstrual periods were referred to as "those critical times," in napkin ads both in the United States and abroad. Fully clothed women were pictured at graceful ease (comfortable) or disporting themselves athletically, above the product's name and manufacturer. The actual appearance of the product remained a mystery to the purchaser until she bought it and opened the box. A certain reticence in packaging of "feminine hygiene" products persists today.

Today's sanitary napkin tends to be flatter and smaller than the originals, and incorporates a barrier layer of polypropylene or polyethylene for the side away from the wearer. Although belt-attaching napkins are still available, they have been largely superseded by self-adhesive ones that require nothing other than an underwear surface to which to attach.

TAMPONS

The tampon, an entirely internal menstrual hygiene device, also has ancient predecessors. Tampon-like objects had medicinal uses in ancient cultures, soaked with various herbal treatments for a range of disorders (some physical, some mental). The first modern tampon was the Fax, marketed in the 1920s as an "internal sanitary napkin" and "modern woman's best friend." The Fax had no applicator and also lacked the attaching string that makes for convenient removal in most modern tampons. It was packaged so discreetly that it lacked the manufacturing company's name; consequently, it is now a matter of some mystery who actually made the Fax.

On September 12, 1933, Dr. Earle Haas (1888–1981) secured a patent for a tampon within a cardboard applicator tube; the tube had two sections, one slightly smaller in diameter than the other. When pressure is applied on the smaller tube, it slides within the larger tube and presses the tampon out. In addition, Haas designed a machine for compressing the tampon material to become highly absorbent owing to its density. Haas's tampon was not a commercial success until the rights were purchased from him and the product was aggressively advertised and marketed as Tampax. Tampax became an extremely popular product, spawning many imitators with various shapes and types of applicators.

DISPOSABLE DIAPERS

The use of some kind of absorbent material to catch and absorb babies' natural products is probably as old as communal living. Records exist of ancient cultures using soft mosses and milkweeds for such purposes. Cloths specially cut and designed for babies' bottoms appeared in households during the nineteenth century, and diapers of 100 percent cotton were manufactured in the United States in the 1920s. They were simple soft cloth rectangles, 20 by 40 inches, and required folding and pinning.

Disposable diapers began to appear near the end of the nineteenth century. They were expensive and impractical for any but the shortest lengths of wearing time, owing to their design: they used 15–20 layers of tissue paper with a heavier outer layer. Their shape was rectangular and they required pinning or taping. These first disposables were used for trips to the doctor and the like, and were a luxury item.

In 1950 a New York woman named Marion Donovan made a prototype disposable diaper by cutting up a shower curtain and stuffing it with absorbent material. She also attached snaps to the plastic outer layer. Manufacturers remained uninterested in the product, so she started her own business and marketed the product herself to New York department stores.

At around the same time, Procter & Gamble asked one of its engineers to recommend a use for a paper pulp mill it had recently purchased. The engineer, a grandfather named Victor Mills, decided that clean absorbent paper would make a nice disposable diaper; the resultant product was named Pampers. Pampers still was rectangular in shape and required pinning or taping, but its increased absorbency made it popular during the 1960s.

Competition between Procter & Gamble and Kimberley-Clark, the two giants of the disposable-diaper trade, produced rapid innovation and improvement: resealable fastening tapes elastic at the legs to reduce leaks; lighterweight, superabsorbent gel materials inside; spunbound topsheets for a cloth-like feeling; girl and boy specialized designs; a larger number of sizes including a toddler/training version; disposable diapers designed for the beach; fragrances; all these and more modifications helped make the disposable diaper achieve 93 percent market penetration in the United States by 1998.

Environmental concerns about disposable diapers, which have become a huge-volume item in landfills, have prompted the industry to explore biodegradable materials. As yet no completely biodegradable composition has been discovered, and cloth diapers remain the choice of preference for the environmentally conscientious consumer.

REFERENCES

www.gpoabs.com.mx/cricher/history.html
www.kotex.com
www.mum.org
www.pg.com

Phonographs and High Fidelity

Phonographs are devices for recording and playing back sounds by converting sound wave vibrations to and from variable grooves in a disc. Essentially this is a mechanical process, differing from magnetic (**audio recording**), light wave (**motion pictures**), and digital (**compact disc**) recording systems. While the phonograph is a nineteenth-century invention, the improvements and changes that made it an important part of everyday life were twentieth-century developments. Thomas Edison (1847–1931) invented the phonograph in 1877, and, although he used tinfoil wrapped around a metal cylinder on which sound vibrations were indented at varying depths by a stylus, Edison's patents included the possibility of recording on discs, belts, or strips fashioned from a wide variety of materials.

Like the telegraph and telephone before, the phonograph was conceived as an instrument for business rather than entertainment. Recorders for dictating letters continued to be office fixtures until the 1970s, when they were replaced by cassette tapes. The requirements for these "Dictaphones" are limited: they don't need amplified sound as they are listened to by one stenographer, they don't need to record or reproduce sounds with a range beyond a single speaking voice, they don't need to be duplicated for marketing, and they don't have to be designed as living room furniture. All these things had to be addressed before phonographs could become popular as anything beyond a novelty. All the early cylinder phonographs could be used both to record and to play back, so a hobbyist could record friends' amateur performances. There were more serious amateurs, among them the Italian Lieutenant Gianni Bettini (1860–?), who procured an Edison phonograph—probably illegally, as nineteenth-century phonographs were leased, rather than sold—and set forth to record major vocalists, especially opera stars. The sound quality was so poor that Bettini invented a better "reproducer" in 1889. The reproducer receives the sound waves and converts them to a vibrating diaphragm that in turn wobbles a stylus to make an impression on the record surface. Bettini's invention was not generally accepted but it is one example of the many patented inventions that proliferated, finally leading to an absolute standstill in the recording industry in 1901, when there were so many lawsuits and countersuits about who had the right to use inventions that a court injunction was issued forbidding any manufacture of phonographs and records until the rights were sorted out.

DISCS

The problems were these: Thomas Edison had the basic patents, but his method of embossing the sound waves on tinfoil produced a very soft record surface. Furthermore, there was no way to duplicate, much less mass-produce, cylinder recordings. But in 1886, Chichester Bell (brother of Alexander Graham Bell, the telephone inventor) and Dr. Charles Sumner Tainter patented a much superior method of recording on cylinders. The Bell-Tainter method was to use a wax surface, and instead of embossing the surface, they used a needle to cut a groove in the hard wax. In both the Edison and Bell-Tainter (which became the Graphophone Company) methods, the grooves were of an even width, and the vibrations were vertical, shallower, or deeper in what came to be called "hill-and-dale" recording.

In 1887 Emile Berliner (1851–1929), who had migrated from Germany to the United States as a young man, patented what he called a Gramophone. Although his first model used a cylinder, he quickly changed to a flat circular disc. In recording, the disc was covered with a thin layer of wax as with Bell-Tainter's graphophone, but the grooves were all of an even depth, the vibrations wobbling laterally. On the cylinder, the grooves described a corkscrew pattern, while on the disc, the grooves were a long spiral, usually going from the outside perimeter to the inside. (The French Pathe-Freres firm chose to go inside out when they added discs to their products.)

The clear advantage of Berliner's flat record is that it had the potential to be duplicated simply by pressing a soft material onto a master disc. The problem was that Bell and Tainter had the rights to the method of incising onto hard wax. To get around this, Berliner neither embossed nor incised but etched the grooves into a zinc disc. Etching was a sixteenth-century method of making possible multiple copies of drawings. A metal plate is coated with a gummy acid-proof "ground." The artist uses a sharp stylus to draw onto the plate. Then the plate is placed in an acid bath, which "bites" into the exposed metal. The plate is then washed clear of the ground, etched lines are exposed, ink is rubbed into the grooves, and the plate is pressed against paper. The etched phonograph recording was not perfect, as the acid could bite under the ground, producing sound not so clear as incised hard wax.

Making a copy of the original recording, however, required that first a negative mold be made, something like a waffle iron. This was done by electroplating the etched zinc original with another metal, peeling it off, stiffening the electroplate negative, and then pressing a soft substance onto the negative, thereby producing a positive copy. Electroplating is a method of applying a thin—sometimes only a molecule in thickness—cover of a valuable metal onto a baser metal, as in silver-plating iron spoons. The base serves as a cathode in a solution of a metal salt such as silver nitrate. The anode is a bar of pure silver. An electric current is passed through the anode, ionizing the solution and depositing atoms of silver onto the base.

It was discovered that one could electroplate a wax original (which by itself couldn't conduct an electric current) by coating it with powdered graphite, which is a conductor of electricity. Thomas Lambert of Chicago patented such a means of copper-plating wax in 1899. Edison claimed to have invented it some time earlier, and Eldridge R. Johnson (1867–1945), a New Jersey mechanic, devised a method of gold plating on graphited wax for Emile Berliner. Johnson came into the picture a short time earlier by solving Berliner's problem of finding a spring-powered motor that would keep the recording disc spinning at a constant speed even as the spring unwound (Berliner's first Gramophones were turned by hand).

In short, by 1901, almost all the requirements for improved recording and mass production were poised, but the manufacturers' hands were tied because of conflicting claims to prior inventions. And nobody was selling any of their products because of the court injunction. The answer was to pool all patents and withdraw from litigation. This the "Big Three" did in 1902, these being Edison's National Phonograph Company, the Columbia Phonograph Company, which had merged with Bell-Tainter's Graphophone, and the Victor Talking Machine Company, which combined the patents of Berliner's Gramophone company with those of Eldridge Johnson. It should be noted that all three companies had English and/or European branches, so the Western world was ready for the "first golden age" of recording.

ACOUSTIC RECORDING

A problem with all recording until 1925 was that it depended upon acoustic power. Acoustic, from the Greek for "hearing," meant that there was no way to amplify sound except by means of megaphone-like conical horns. The recording artist (usually a vocalist) stood in front of the wide end of the horn and bellowed into it, the sound vibrations being carried down to the reproducer, which in turn vibrated the embossing or incising stylus. With cylinders, to manufacture a dozen copies, the artist would have to sing twelve times, in other words, each wax record was an original! The Edison Company developed a "pantograph" method of making four copies at once (the pantograph, one version of which had been invented by Thomas Jefferson for making a copy of his correspondence while he was writing, was used in architects' studios to copy drawings). As the original was drawn or traced, a lattice-like linkage to a pencil duplicated it on another sheet. By a similar device, styluses were connected in tandem to four phonographs. Another method of duplication was transcription—playing the recording into another horn—but as the recording was not amplified to anywhere near the original loudness, transcriptions were much weaker than the original.

Attempts at molding copies of a cylinder were frustrating. Making a mold in two or more sections that could be opened to release the copy left mold marks such as can be seen on bottles; the mold marks, of course, made pops or skips when played. Many experiments searched for a material that could be pressed into a cylindrical sleeve, but would shrink when cooled. The cooled copy could then be slipped out of the sleeve. The disadvantage was that the copy was smaller, and required a different size and speed for the playback phonograph. Berliner's

Very early horn-type electric loud speaker. (Courtesy of Corbis)

discs had none of these problems, although there were many failures with such materials as hard rubber. Finally, a new material that was invented for the Durinoid Button Company of Newark, New Jersey, was tried. This was a mixture of shellac, lampblack (fine carbon), and cotton fibers; it was so successful that with variations, it became the standard for decades with black "shellac" records.

Acoustic playback was another problem. Phonographs were sold without a horn (one could listen by means of a flexible ear tube); many designs and materials for horns were available to attach the reproducer. The "morning-glory" horn, immortalized in the Victor Talking Machine's famous trademark of the terrier "Nipper" listening to "His Master's Voice," was the most common. However, the Victor Company abandoned these big intrusive horns in 1906, for Eldridge Johnson saw a German-made phonograph that had a horn built into a cabinet that could be set on a table. Doors opened for listening and closed to hide the internalized horn. Johnson's adaptation gave a new word to the home entertainment vocabulary, the Victrola, which was produced in many sizes and styles, and was a welcome addition to living-room decor.

The acoustic period was marked by many competing products and methods. Cylinders continued to be produced all the way to 1929, though their popular-

The 45 rpm phonograph shared some characteristics with LPs, such as microgroove unbreakable vinyl discs and slower speeds than the old 78 rpm shellac discs, but their small size and large spindle hole were unique. This suitcase model suggests its attraction for young people to carry their phonographs and pop music to dorm rooms and parties. (Courtesy of Corbis)

ity decreased rapidly in the United States, while continuing to be a choice in England. But both cylinders and discs were made in different sizes, speeds of rotation, and kind of groove. There were usually good technical reasons for each variant, but eventually the confusion of choices led manufacturers and consumers to settle on standards of black shellac two-sided discs with laterally cut grooves, spinning at 78 revolutions per minute (rpm), with 10-inch discs for popular songs, dance music, ethnic music, and novelty humor, while operatic and other "classical" music was recorded on 12-inch discs.

ELECTRICAL RECORDING

As broadcast radio developed rapidly in the 1920s (see **Radios**), the record companies were at first antagonistic, not allowing their recording artists to perform on radio. Opera stars in particular were jealously kept to their contracts. The most famous of these had been the Italian tenor Enrico Caruso (1873–1921). Berliner-Victor recorded ten songs on wax in Europe as soon as the patent pool was arranged, and the discs pressed from these originals were immensely popular, leading both Caruso and Victor on to millions of sales and riches. Victor and Columbia created their influential "Red Seal" and "Masterworks" lines, signing exclusive contracts with stars. The initial objection to radio was that it would cut into record sales, but the reality was that hearing a song on radio led to increased sales.

More important technologically was Lee De Forest's invention of the vacuum tube. This brought an end to the acoustic age, for it made possible amplification at each stage of production: the original sound was converted into electrical current by the microphone, amplified electronically, and sent to the reproducer (now more properly called the cutting head). Then when the record was played, the pickup on the tone arm transduced the vibrations from the laterally cut groove back to electric pulses; these were again amplified, and sent to a loudspeaker. By this time, many homes were provided with electric current, so the windup Victrola was relegated to the attic or junkpile. In 1927, the Radio Corporation of America acquired the Victor Talking Machine Company, and RCA Victor became one of the first giants of the music entertainment industry.

Sound quality and volume were vastly improved, and at last full orchestral sounds could be recorded. In acoustic days, the orchestra or band accompanying a soloist had been crowded together in a "vee" behind the singer producing a thin distant sound. With microphones placed around the recording studio, balanced sound and the true quality of each instrument could be heard. Phonographs were in a new golden age.

HI-FI AND LP RECORDS

With standardization and electric recording and playback, music lovers and the industry became more demanding about the fidelity (faithfulness) of recorded sound. European companies had so improved the quality of acoustic recording that even into the 1940s, some English music critics preferred them to electrical recordings. One problem of distorted sound was created by the move from cylinders to discs. When a disc is played, the speed (angular velocity) of the turntable is constant, but the speed at which the spiral groove passes under the stylus (linear velocity) is not. In fact, the groove speed on a 10-inch disc diminishes 50 percent from the outermost groove to the innermost (whereas on a cylinder the groove speed is constant with the revolutions per minute). Since sound is transmitted by waves and the greater the frequency of the waves, the higher the tones, and vice versa, distortion is certain. Ironically this problem had been anticipated by Bell and Tainter in their nineteenth-century patents, but it seems not to have been implemented until the 1940s. This solution was a variable-speed recording turntable that changed the speed in coordination with the ever-tightening spiral groove. This did not require a variable-speed player, as the playback turntable plays what it "hears" on the record, not how it was recorded. The reason that this became important in the 1940s is because of the LP (long play) microgroove record. The spiral groove on a 12-inch LP disc was much longer than on a 78-rpm record because the grooves were thinner and closer together. The first LPs had 250 grooves per inch compared to the 78's 80 grooves per inch.

Credit for inventing the microgroove LP goes to Peter Goldmark (1906–1977), a Hungarian-born engineer (and musician) at Columbia records. The LP was introduced in the spring of 1948 along with a low-priced turntable. The first LPs were mostly classical, of course, since symphonic movements were usually much longer than the four to five minute per side on 78s. The first Columbia LPs were a Mendelssohn violin concerto, a Tchaikovsky symphony, and the Broadway musical *South Pacific*. The speed Goldmark chose was 33⅓-rpm, but it was the microgroove that was revolutionary, as there had been longer-playing records among the competing cylinders and discs of the early years. A 33⅓-rpm disc had been introduced by RCA Victor in 1931 (soon abandoned), and radio programs (transcriptions) were on 16-inch discs that revolved as slowly as 16 rpm. The third aspect of the LP revolution was that instead of being pressed out of a shellac compound, they were in a plastic compound called vinylite. This, again, had been anticipated. Edison used celluloid (an early plastic) for cylinders, and plastic was used for Dictaphone belts. RCA Victor had also introduced transparent red vinyl Red Seal records in the late 1930s, boasting of their smooth, scratchless sound.

RCA Victor was caught by surprise with Columbia's LPs, especially because they had since 1939 been developing their own microgroove vinyl records—these in 7-inch discs, with a speed of 45 rpm, and a big spindle on the turntable for ease of stacking on an automatic record changer. The band of recorded grooves was quite narrow, RCA arguing that in both speed and grooves, they had the optimum fidelity without distortion. RCA's introduction of the 45s did nothing to alleviate the problem of interrupting classical music every few minutes to drop a record. It turned into a "battle of the speeds," with a rather bewildered public confused about having to buy two different new machines—and what to do with all their 78s! The answer was three-speed changers, with a flip-over cartridge at the end of the tone arm, one side with a needle for 78s, the other for microgrooves. The dust settled, and 45s became the record of choice for popular "singles," while LPs were the choice for symphonies, operas, musicals, jazz—and eventually, pop "albums," possibly the most influential of which was the Beatles' *Sergeant Pepper's Lonely Hearts Club Band* in 1967.

A nagging question about high-fidelity sound was "fidelity to what?" The easy answer was to reproduce the sound experience of a concert hall. But the acoustics of concert halls differ greatly. The sound also depends heavily on where the listener is seated. And one didn't really want fidelity to the actual concert experience, with people coughing, ballet dancers' feet hitting the floor, accidental "bubbles" from French horns, and so on. For popular vocalists, who all used amplified microphones in performance by the 1930s, there wasn't even a "natural" sound. Furthermore, people argued, the real audio experience comes from both ears. This led to the next major innovation, stereophonic sound, in which two mi-

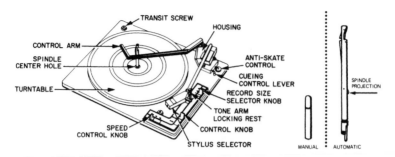

The ultimate answer to the "battle of speeds" was a phonograph record changer such as this model from the 1960s. It had settings for 16, 33⅓, 45, and 78 rpm, a knob to set the tone arm down for records of different diameters, a small spindle for playing single records (so the user could set the tone arm down on a selected groove), a long spindle to automatically drop a record from a stack, and an adapter (not shown) that could be slipped over the long spindle to play a stack of 45s, which had large spindle holes. (Courtesy of Emerson Electric).

crophones are placed at a distance apart (never as little as the one block between the ears). Some of the first stereos actually had a double tone arm to play two sets of grooves, but by the late 1950s the recording of left and right channels in a single groove (with all the extra components such as special amplifiers and dual loudspeakers) became the rule, and "monaural" records were obsolescent. Stereo recording was a British invention, primarily by EMI's engineer Alan Dower Blumlein.

However, by this time, any real "fidelity" was not a goal except for recorded "live" performances. The reason was that no one actually recorded directly on a master disc after 1950 (the first LPs in 1948–1949 were recorded first on a 16-inch disc and then transcribed to microgroove). Radio producers were first to use magnetic **audio tapes** for recording programs after World War II, and the advantages of being able to edit recordings were soon recognized. Thus, a symphony might have a recording made from only the best "takes" of each section. A soloist could be added after the band had recorded. Finally, in popular music, multitrack tapes and a sound mixer would create a recording where the performers might never have been in the same room. With various ways of "enhancing" sound, "hi-fi" became meaningless in its original meaning. And with digital **compact discs,** by the last decade of the twentieth century the age of phonographs came to an end.

As radio had advanced phonograph recording, so records did much to save **radio** after **television** had wiped out national network radio broadcasting by the early 1950s. Playing records was as old as radio broadcasting, but as television took over family home entertainment, the "spinning of platters" by "disc jockeys" (or deejays) on local stations became the dominant radio fare. And as the era of big "swing" dance bands declined, playing records at *discothèques* (a French play on the word for libraries—*bibliothèques*) swept Europe, and then, abbreviated to "discos," America as well. Another important technical and cultural aspect of phonographs is coin-operated phonographs (see **Jukeboxes**).

The twentieth century began with just one acoustically limited form of sound recording, its production halted by patent disputes. The century ended with music lovers enjoying a wide range of compact and high-fidelity media, including optical discs, digital memory chips (MP3 players), magnetic minidiscs, and audio cassette tapes.

See also **Electronic Musical Instruments.**

REFERENCES

Canby, Edward Tatnall, C.G. Burke, and Irving Kolodin. *The Saturday Review Home Book of Recorded Music and Sound Reproduction.* Englewood Cliffs, NJ: Prentice-Hall, 1952.
Read, Oliver, and Walter L. Welch. *From Tin Foil to Stereo: Evolution of the Phonograph.* Indianapolis: Howard W. Sams & Co., 1959.

Radios

Radios are everywhere. From high-fidelity living-room sets to tiny shirt pocket receivers for joggers, from push-button car radios to CBs in trucks, from walkie-talkies to battery-powered portables in the remotest corners of the earth, radios tune in on words and music from around the world. Scientists send radio messages to satellites throughout the solar system and receive radio messages from the stars.

ELECTROMAGNETIC RADIATION

To understand the inventions that made possible these indispensable instruments of communication and entertainment, we might start with the stars. In nature the stars, most particularly our star, the sun, are the main source of electromagnetic radiation, of which radio signals are a part. However, humans are equipped to tune in on only two parts of the electromagnetic spectrum. Our eyes are tuned to light and fine-tuned to color. Eyes do not perceive the entire range of light, for we cannot see infra- (meaning *below*) red, but we can still detect this form of radiation. Our skin is tuned to perceive infrared as radiant heat. For electromagnetic radiation other than light and heat rays, humans must use devices to convert the signals into forms that our senses can tune in on. For radio, this means conversion to sound waves. The story of the basic inventions is one of genius, inspiration, controversy, and tragedy.

The essential devices were invented early in the twentieth century. These were the wireless telegraph and the radio tube. Before these inventions could be made, people had to learn that there was such a thing as what we now call radio waves and how they relate to the electromagnetic spectrum. First, all electromagnetic radiations share the same velocity, traveling at the speed of light. Second, unlike sound, they travel by transverse waves; that is, the wave motion is perpendicular to the direction of the wave. (This can be demonstrated by fastening a fairly thick rope to a post or a hook and moving the other end up and down. The rope does not move forward, but the wave travels from one end to the other in an up-and-down motion.) A third characteristic common to electromagnetic radiation is that it is "wireless," needing no medium, whereas sound waves need molecules of air, water, or metal to travel from a source to our ears. Unlike sound, light and radio waves can travel in a vacuum.

Electromagnetic waves vary in two main parameters: wavelength and amplitude (the rope demonstration can illustrate these by varying the frequency and height [amplitude] of up-and-down arm motion). Wavelengths (the distance from crest to crest) vary tremendously. For example, visible light has tiny wavelengths ranging from 0.00004 to 0.00008 centimeters, while radio waves range from 0.01 centimeters to 18 kilometers. Ordinary radio broadcasting waves vary from 200 to 600 meters (waves equal in length to about two to six football fields). The frequency of a wave is the number of cycles occurring per second. The frequency is the velocity at which the wave travels, divided by the wavelength. Since all electromagnetic waves have a fixed velocity in empty space, the frequency has a precise fixed relationship to the wavelength: the velocity of light divided by the wavelength. Thus, as frequency increases, wavelength diminishes, and vice versa. Visible light waves oscillate in frequencies from as many as 750 million million cycles per second. Broadcast frequencies are much less, as can be seen on an AM radio dial where stations broadcast on set frequencies from about 540,000 to 1,600,000 cycles per second (usually abbreviated on the dial as 54–160, which is itself an abbreviation of 54–160 × 10 kHz). The k stands for kilo (1,000) and Hz stands for one cycle per second. It is pronounced Hertz, named after Heinrich Hertz (1857–1894), a German scientist who first sent a wireless electric impulse (a spark) across his laboratory in 1887, and subsequently measured the speed of this "Hertzian wave" as the same as the speed of light. A third variable in waves is amplitude, the height of the wave as measured from a line of no current flow. (Once again the rope can illustrate this. If it is pulled tight, obviously there is no wave, but when the rope is put into oscillations by means of arm power, the waves will have a "height" above and below the straightened rope—these are the positive and negative amplitude of the wave.)

WIRELESS TELEGRAPHY

Hertz's experiments inspired a young Italian, Guglielmo Marconi (1874–1937), to turn to practical applications. Marconi envisioned sending the dots and dashes of the Morse code of telegraph by Hertzian waves, thereby making possible communication where stringing wires or laying cables was impractical, especially for ships at sea. He drew heavily on others' discoveries and inventions. He adapted a powerful spark transmitter designed by his physics professor at the University of Bologna. As a receiver, he adapted a "coherer" that had been invented in 1892 by French scientist Edouard Branly and improved by Englishman Oliver Lodge. This was a thin glass tube with wires attached to each end and a gap between them. In the tube were metal filings that would stick together (cohere) when an impulse from a radio wave was introduced, thus completing the circuit. The system of "decohering" the filings by tapping the tube was a Russian invention. A regular Morse telegraph key closed and opened the transmitter impulses.

Marconi had the vision of wireless telegraphy; he improved the devices he had borrowed, and by accident he found a way to greatly improve the strength of signals. Hertz's antenna was elevated; Marconi noticed that when one end of the antenna touched the ground both transmission and reception were improved. It also was found that grounding made it possible to reduce the length of antennas to one-fourth of a wavelength. And as "ground" didn't have to be the earth itself, but any massive conductor of electricity, antennas on ships could be grounded to the hull (and when car radios were introduced in 1929, to the automobile frame).

By 1895, Marconi was able to send messages over a mile away, and he offered his invention to the Italian government. They were not interested. Marconi's mother packed up her son and his inventions and took him to her native England where family connections, influence, and money (the John Jameson Irish whisky distillers) quickly expedited a British patent in 1896 and the financial backing to form the Marconi Wireless Telegraph Company. Marconi was only twenty-three years old. By the end of the century Marconi equipment was on many ships, and in 1899 he was invited to America to report instantly the results of a yacht race from shipboard to a New York newspaper. He also formed an American Marconi Wireless Telegraph Company. On December 15, 1901 Marconi was in Newfoundland to attempt to receive a transatlantic signal. He did: it was *dot, dot, dot,* the Morse code for the letter "S." He continued to invent improvements on radiotelegraphy, and was careful to patent everything, thereby making rival inventors and companies liable to paying royalties or to lawsuits for infringement. Marconi shared the Nobel Prize in physics in 1909. When he died, all the world's radio stations paid a tribute of two minutes of silence. Ironically, Marconi had little interest in broadcasting or even voice communication.

VOICE TRANSMISSION

For voice transmission, the microphone and earphones were no problem, simply being adaptations of telephone technology that had been around for a quarter-century. The problems were mainly those of generating a continuous wave of radio frequency, and modulating that wave with an audio frequency signal. While radiotelegraphy worked by sending intermittent bursts of radio signals, voice and music require a continuous radio wave (called a carrier wave) to carry the complex lower-frequency audio signal waves. The combined signal and carrier are a modulated wave. The carrier is varied in amplitude in proportion to the amplitude of the audio signal (this is true for amplitude-modulated, "AM," radio; "FM" is explained below). Thus, if a carrier of 1 MHz is amplitude-modulated by an audio signal of 10 kHz, the carrier will have a constant frequency of 1 MHz, but will vary in strength or amplitude 10,000 times per second. The frequency of the carrier is fixed for AM, and in each country broadcast frequencies are assigned by a government

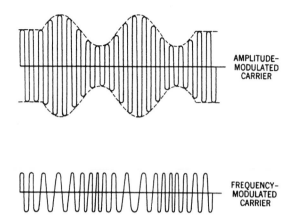

Amplitude-modulated (AM) and frequency-modulated (FM) radio waves compared. An unmodulated "carrier wave" would show equal wave height and equal intervals between waves. Diagrams such as these should not to be taken literally: ordinary broadcast wavelengths are as long as several football fields and wave frequencies oscillate thousands of times per second. Also radio waves are invisible.

authority (in the United States, the Federal Communications Commission, or FCC). In the receiver, the tuner is adjusted to respond to the carrier frequency, and then the imposed modulated audio signal is separated out by the "detector."

About 1902, two different methods of generating radio-frequency carrier waves were designed. Valdemar Poulson (1869–1942), a Dane who had already demonstrated magnetic wire recording, noticed that the flame from the two rods in a carbon-arc lamp emitted a continuous radio wave. His transmitters were widely used for several years, but Canadian-born Reginald Aubrey Fessenden's (1866–1932) design for a high-frequency alternator prevailed—at least for a while. Alternators (i.e, AC generators) for North American household current produced 60 cycles per second, but a carrier wave for voice required 100,000 cycles per second. Fessenden asked the great German-American engineer Charles Steinmetz of General Electric to build such an alternator.

Early attempts to achieve those speeds failed, but in 1904 General Electric's Ernst Alexanderson, a Swedish immigrant, started constructing one in which the magnetized armature was stationary around a whirling disc. At 100 kHz, this could carry the modulated voice waves. It was delivered to Fessenden two years later, and on Christmas Eve of 1906, the first real radio broadcast was made, with Fessenden playing some phonograph records and performing "O Holy Night" live on his violin.

THE VACUUM TUBE

In the meantime, the most important advance in radio was in the works. Back in 1883, while Thomas Edison was working on light bulbs, he noticed that a glowing carbon filament in an airless bulb caused a black deposit on the glass. To block this, he put a metal plate in the bulb. Curiosity apparently prompted him to attach a voltage meter to the plate. There was a small current. Edison patented this, although he had no use for it, and at this time could not know that what was happening was that electrons were "boiling off" the electrode, and as the plate had a slight positive charge, the electrons flowed toward it. This was called the "Edison effect."

John Ambrose Fleming, one of Edison's employees in England, did some experimenting with the Edison effect in the 1890s. In the new century, Fleming became a scientific adviser to Marconi and was handed the task of finding a better "detector" (receiver) for radio waves. Fleming thought that the Edison tube might be a key. What he discovered in 1904 was that although he fed AC into the filament, what came off the metal plate was DC. He patented this as an "oscillation valve." He also connected the plate to the positive pole of a battery. This markedly increased the flow of electrons; when he connected the plate to a negative pole, there was no flow (in electricity and magnetism, like charges repel, unlike charges attract). If we return to the rope demonstration, recall that the waves above and below the imaginary straight line are alternatively positive and negative. The cycles of AC through a wire likewise are alternatively positive and negative. When the plate in the Fleming valve is positively charged, the resulting current flow from filament to plate is DC.

In the United States, Lee De Forest (1873–1961), who had earned a doctorate in electrical engineering from Yale, was duplicating some of Fleming's work. But the revolutionary invention came in 1907 when De Forest added a third wire in the tube, close to the hot filament. This, when given a positive charge, actually accelerated the flow of electrons onto the plate. Because the wire was bent in a zigzag, De Forest called it a grid, and, indeed, as the vacuum tube developed, many of the grids actually were metal mesh. The two-element Fleming valve (a diode) had acted as a wave detector and a rectifier, converting the AC to DC. De Forest's three-element audion (triode) detected, rectified, and amplified the signal that was applied to the grid. No longer was the earphone sound limited by the weak current from the antenna. Amplification was further increased when it was discovered that "cascades" of triodes could produce multiple stages of amplification. The signal output from one triode circuit could be fed as input into another for further amplification. Then, in 1913, another important American, Edwin Howard Armstrong (1890–1954), invented the "regeneration" or feedback circuit. He added a wire coil in a "wing" of the path of current from the plate to the earphones. This generated a magnetic field in the coil producing AC that was in step with the DC to the earphones, thus greatly reinforcing the signal.

An unfortunate side note is that although Armstrong, still a student at Columbia University, filed a patent for the regeneration circuit in 1913, De Forest claimed that he had observed this in 1912. The lawsuit that ensued went through many courts and was not resolved until more than twenty years later in 1934 when the U.S. Supreme Court decided in favor of De Forest's claim. De Forest's audion had been his legitimate invention, but the science community and historians believe that the Supreme Court was wrong about regeneration. Armstrong also failed to include in his patent application another thing that he discovered in his experiments: when too much current was introduced, the audion tube emitted radio frequency oscillations. In short, the audion could operate as a detector, a rectifier, an amplifier—and as a radio transmitter!

These revolutionary inventions were still a long way from producing our familiar broadcast radio. All this circuitry was **battery** operated, requiring three expensive batteries, "A" for powering the glowing filament, "B" for the positive plate, and "C" for the De Forest grid. Receiving antennas were large frames wrapped with coils of wire. Listening to broadcasts was a one-person project, although some radio fans would place their earphones in a cut-glass punch bowl so the family could hear. Tuning was very complicated, requiring three or more dials because each amplification circuit in the set had to be tuned separately to the station's frequency. In 1919, this barrier to easy listening was eliminated. Armstrong, serving with the U.S. Army Signal Corps in France, perfected the "superheterodyne" circuit. The incoming modulated radio signal is mixed with a fixed frequency that is generated from the oscillations of a vacuum tube in the receiver. Other tubes amplify this "intermediate" frequency several thousand-fold, and finally the intermediate frequency (which still contains the audio information from the original broadcast signal) is rectified. This results in a pulsating DC signal that varies in amplitude at the frequency of the original audio signal; in short, the original audio has been recovered from the modulated carrier. When this signal is applied to the headphones, the original audio is heard.

BROADCASTING

Even after transistors were developed in the late 1940s, radio tubes were continuously improved and varied to perform tasks in radio, **television,** radar, and computers. More complete vacuums were developed, various gases were used in place of vacuum, and more elements than the triodes were introduced. In 1925 Raytheon's founders, Vannevar Bush (1890–1974, Dean of Engineering at Massachusetts Institute of Technology and later a pioneer in computers), Laurence Marshall, and Charles G. Smith invented a gaseous rectifier tube that allowed radios to operate on household current rather than on expensive batteries. In less than two years Raytheon had more than one million dollars in sales. Metal-enclosed tubes, pentodes, and space- and cost-saving dual tubes (two sets of filament/grid[s]/plates in a single enclosure) were developed for some uses and manufacturers strove to make smaller tubes for compact table radios and portables, and for the complex circuits of television.

The first portable radio was made by Edwin Armstrong for his new bride in 1923. It was the size of a large suitcase, could be closed up and carried by a handle, but it had a large loudspeaker horn almost two feet high. Except for specialty applications, including some guitar amplifiers, tubes are now obsolete in the

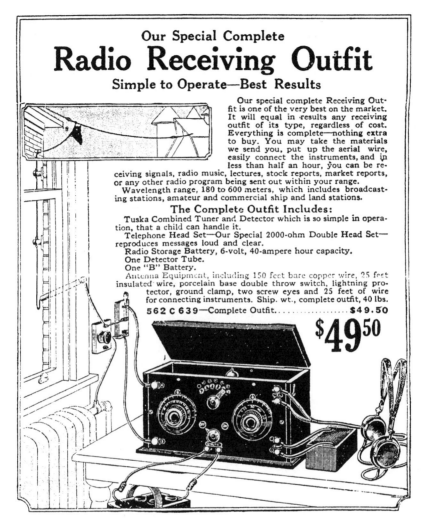

Early radios were not simple. This 1922 model didn't have a loudspeaker, its main power battery is on the floor, it required a second expensive battery on the table, it is grounded to the room-heating radiator, and its receiving antenna stretches all the way to the barn.

home, but the basic principles and functions of diodes, triodes and superheterodynes remain valid for the solid-state circuits used in radios and televisions.

The lone inventor, such as Marconi, De Forest, and Armstrong, fast disappeared as large corporations such as Marconi's company, American Telephone and Telegraph, General Electric, Radio Corporation of America, Westinghouse, and others set up laboratories for teams of engineers and scientists. These giants were able to buy up patents (De Forest was forced by the need to finance his many litigations—he had been sued by both Marconi and Fessenden—to sell the audion to

AT&T for much less than it was worth), and the giants could enter into prolonged court battles with independent inventors over infringements, or pick up ideas for commercial exploitation. In a sense, that is how modern broadcasting began.

In 1919 a Westinghouse engineer who was also a radio amateur, Dr. Frank Conrad, began to broadcast music (mainly **phonograph** records) regularly from his garage in Pittsburgh. Newspapers printed the times of his programs. A local department store advertised cheap crystal sets—they were World War I army surplus—to hear these concerts. Crystal sets were the simplest and most popular radios. It had been found that certain minerals can serve as rectifiers; connected to a wire antenna, such crystals as galena, germanium, quartz, etc. would detect a radio wave and convert it to DC that could power earphones. Westinghouse, which had paid Armstrong over one-third million dollars for rights to both his regeneration and superheterodyne inventions, decided that Frank Conrad's broadcasts might be a good way to create demand for Westinghouse radios. A radio station, KDKA, was set up on the roof of their factory, and on November 4, 1920, KDKA broadcast the results of the presidential election. Regular broadcasts started at 8:30 P.M. for an hour's time. Soon hours were expanded and such programs as church services were added. Westinghouse added more stations atop other factories and began to manufacture crystal sets.

By 1923 there were over 500 stations nationwide and it was estimated that 400,000 households had a radio. In 1927 RCA introduced a "light-socket" radio with tubes replacing the need for any batteries. By 1929 America manufactured 4.5 million radios—all with loudspeakers rather than earphones, the first blockbuster national radio show was well established (the serial comedy "Amos 'n' Andy"), NBC's monopoly on network radio was challenged by CBS, and commercial advertising had become the norm for financing radio programming. The first commercial was broadcast on New York City station WEAF on August 28, 1922. It advertised suburban real estate.

STATIC AND FM RADIO

In these pretransistor years, one more problem had to be addressed, radio interference (static). Especially in the summer season, with thunderstorms abounding, radio broadcasts often could not be heard because of the noise of crackling static. Most rural and small-town Americans listened to network programs from distant powerful stations, so if there was a storm anywhere between New Orleans and Panama City, or between Chicago and Green Bay, for instance, the interference for listeners in Panama City and Green Bay would affect them regardless of how clear the local skies were. Ironically, the regeneration circuit amplified the static as well as the broadcast. The problem of static interference is simple; the radiation by lightning varies in amplitude, just as nearly all pre–World War II radio was AM. The answer was also simple. It had been proposed by a few engineers, but was championed by only one, Major Edwin Howard Armstrong: use frequency modulation for radio.

Recall that the carrier wave was of regular frequency and amplitude; it had no modulation. The information signal that was superimposed on the carrier wave modulated its amplitude. The idea of FM was to maintain a fixed carrier amplitude, but vary the wave frequency. A diagram of an FM wave shows even height but waves variously compressed and expanded (bear in mind that a diagram cannot show thousands of cycles per second). Armstrong worked on the problems of designing transmitters and receivers for twenty years. He and his staff at Columbia University were almost alone in this research, because in 1922 a distinguished mathematician, John R. Carson at AT&T's Bell Laboratories, had "proved" mathematically that FM could not resolve the problem of static noise.

Everyone except Armstrong abandoned that direction of research. Finally, in 1934 Armstrong was ready to demonstrate the superiority of FM broadcasting. He sent identical audio material via AM and FM, while running a static generator. AM was noisy, FM was clear. Furthermore, FM was more faithful to the original sound. In fact, this was the birth of high-fidelity ("hi-fi") broadcasting, as the FM waves could transmit sounds of the entire range of human hearing. There were other advantages. One unforeseen one was that FM stations operating at the same frequency did not interfere (AM listeners were accustomed to hearing another program suddenly interrupting the one they wanted to hear). What happened with FM was the "capture effect"; the receiver would simply pick up the stronger signal. This made it possible to develop a network of relay stations of the same frequency, connected only by radio signals (the AM networks were relayed by phone lines).

Despite all this, opposition to FM came from many directions. Many people still were convinced by John R. Carson's mathematical theories, but most objections were more practical. It was the Great Depression and people were not likely to have money for replacing their radios. Likewise, FM required entirely new and different transmitting equipment. FM has a substantially shorter range than AM. Stations with good advertising revenue were skeptical about losing income. AT&T didn't like the wireless relays because their company made huge profits leasing long-distance phone lines to the AM networks. As for high fidelity, the general attitude was "who needs it?"

But the greatest opposition came from RCA, which not only manufactured AM radios and radio parts and equipment, but also owned two national networks (the Red and Blue, later named NBC and ABC) as well as RCA Victor records. According to Tom Lewis's *Empire of the Air*, the real source of opposition was David Sarnoff, the head of RCA, who had put his money into television research and development. Despite his having pioneered in radio networking and having been a longtime friend of Armstrong, Sarnoff believed that radio was doomed as television advanced. Nevertheless, in 1940 Sarnoff offered Armstrong one million dollars for his 1933 patents. Armstrong refused, preferring to receive royalties on sales of FM sets and equipment. However, General Electric believed in the future of FM, having brought out "Golden Tone" FM radios in 1939 with royalty payments to the inventor. Despite some opposition from army brass, Armstrong also had convinced the Signal Corps to use FM for communication

Until about 1940, radio cases were made of wood, and the vacuum tubes were large. Plastic housing and miniaturized tubes made this 1949 Philco "Transitone" table model a possibility, and just about as small as was possible until transistors were introduced some half-dozen years later. Notice that it only receives AM signals, but that its two simple controls, an on-off volume button and a large tuning knob are a major contrast with the 1922 home radio in the last figure. (Courtesy of Corbis)

between tanks. Other military uses soon followed. When war broke out in December 1941, Armstrong patriotically gave license to the government to use all his patents. RCA, on the other hand, made millions on government orders, and in 1944 announced that their researchers had invented a new FM system that didn't infringe on Armstrong's patents. Incidentally RCA's televisions all used FM for the audio.

In 1948, Armstrong brought suit against RCA and NBC for infringement of five basic inventions. RCA's lawyers used a strategy of trivial delays, because most of Armstrong's patents would expire in 1950, at which time they would become public property. Even so, the case was still in the courts in 1954, when Armstrong, almost bankrupt from legal fees and lost revenue in the war, discouraged and estranged from his wife, gave up all and committed suicide by leaping from a building. The end of this tale is that Mrs. Armstrong continued the fight, with all the radio manufacturers, won all settlements, and in 1967, thirteen years after the inventor's death, prevailed over the last holdout, Motorola.

Back in 1930, Motorola had come out with the first practical and affordable car radio, developed by the brothers Paul (1895–1959) and Joseph (1899–1944) Galvin. With the car battery supply of DC and the chassis for grounding, the invention was a natural. Still, automobile manufacturers didn't want to install radios, so the

Galvins sold them to car dealers for installation. In 1937, Motorola introduced a car radio with push-button tuning plus fine tuning and tone control.

From this point on the story of radio inventions is one of transistors, integrated circuits, miniaturization, and digital tuners. The vacuum tube is obsolete, but the functions of the tubes for detecting radio waves, rectifying, amplifying, and transmitting are as valid as the waves themselves.

REFERENCES

Carr, Joseph J. *Old Time Radios! Restoration and Repair.* Blue Summit, PA: Tab Books, 1991.

Herrick, Clyde N. *Radio: Theory and Servicing.* Reston, VA: Reston Publishing Company, Inc., 1975.

Johnson, David. *Antique Radio Restoration Guide.* 2nd ed. Iola, WI: Krause Publications, 1992.

Lewis, Tom. *Empire of the Air: The Men Who Made Radio.* New York: Edward Burlingame Books, 1991.

Refrigerators

Chilling food retards spoilage. In the nineteenth century, foods were often preserved by canning and by dehydration (salt and sugar curing). Some foods could be preserved in cold cellars, taking advantage of the modestly cool temperatures underground. These were very limited forms of food preservation. The impact of mechanical refrigeration on the range of foods in typical twentieth-century diets has been profound.

ICEBOXES

The immediate ancestor of today's refrigerator was the "icebox," a wooden cabinet lined with zinc or tin and insulated with sawdust or moss. Inside the icebox a small amount of perishable food such as milk or cream, meat, and butter could be stored along with a large block of ice. The ice was delivered by the iceman in a horse-drawn wagon, and it melted slowly into the drip pan kept below the icebox. The drip pan required daily emptying.

MECHANICAL REFRIGERATION

In 1805 Oliver Evans drew up a design for a refrigeration machine, which would work by compression of a liquid to gas, or in other words, by evaporation of the liquid. The gas would expand through tubes, drawing kinetic energy (heat) from the body of the machine and cooling the interior. Evans never manufactured his refrigeration machine.

In 1844 a Florida inventor named John Gorrie built a machine using Evans' design. But a marketable refrigerator was not produced until 1911, when the General Electric Company began manufacture in Fort Wayne, Indiana. This was the time when electric motors began to be introduced into appliances (see, for example, **Kitchen Appliances: Motorized, Washing Machines and Dryers, Calculators and Cash Registers**).

HOME REFRIGERATORS

In 1915 the Guardian refrigerator appeared. The earliest home refrigerators had belt-driven compressors that were typically attached to motors located in another room of the house than the refrigerator itself. This dangerous and breakage-prone system was not superseded until 1923 when Frigidaire produced the first entirely self-contained refrigerator. GE's most famous early refrigerator was the Monitor. This had the compressor and condenser mounted on top of the food case—a design that made physics sense because these generated heat, and heat rises. Aesthetics have resulted in a less efficient layout for home refrigeration, though commercial refrigerators often continue to use the compressor-on-top design.

These appliances resembled their icebox predecessors visually, having wood outer cases. Metal casings appeared in the 1920s and gradually eclipsed the wood exteriors. Coolants used in early models were ammonia and sulfur dioxide. These were replaced in the 1930s by the much safer Freon 12. The negative environmental impact of Freon 12 on the ozone layer in the upper atmosphere was not appreciated until much later.

Refrigerators have four main components: a box for holding food, a compressor, an evaporator, and a condenser. The latter two are essentially long lengths of metal tubing folded to occupy less space. The evaporator is inside the chilled food box; the condenser is outside, in contact with room air. The motor-driven compressor compresses a gas, the refrigerant, forcing it under pressure into the condenser. The compressed gas in the condenser is hot—as it passes through the condenser, it gives up its heat to the surrounding room air and condenses into a liquid. Some condensers are mounted on the back of refrigerators, some are mounted in the case with a small fan to blow cooling room air through the condenser coils.

The now-cooled pressurized liquid refrigerant is pushed through a tiny expansion orifice that separates the high-pressure tubing of the condenser from the much lower-pressure tubing of the evaporator inside the food box. At this low pressure in the evaporator, the refrigerant "boils"; that is, it changes from the liquid to the gas state, even though the temperature is below 0° F. Refrigerants are selected for their low boiling points. Whenever a liquid changes to gas, it absorbs heat—that is, it causes whatever is in contact with it to become cold. Thus the boiling refrigerant in the evaporator chills the inside of the refrigerator. The gaseous refrigerant is sucked from the evaporator into the inlet side of the compressor to begin the whole cycle again. Compressor, condenser, expansion orifice, and evaporator are connected to form a continuous loop. The refrigerant passes around this loop, at different pressure and temperature states in different parts of the loop. The refrigerator is thus a motor-operated heat pump, pumping heat out of the food compartment into the surrounding room air.

"FROST-FREE" REFRIGERATORS

A freezer compartment with removable ice trays became standard equipment in the 1950s. In most of these, the evaporator was formed as passages inside the double walled freezer compartment. This created the irksome job of "defrosting the refrigerator," or removing the accumulated ice and frost layer inside the freezer compartment. In early models defrosting meant turning off the refrigerator entirely, and risking spoilage of all stored food. Impatient defrosters hacked at their ice deposits with ice picks and in many cases damaged the freezer units in the process.

"Frost-free" and self-defrosting models eventually came to dominate the market. In frost-free models, the evaporator is usually concealed behind the back wall

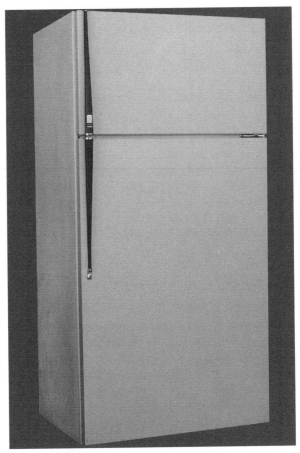

Refrigerator/freezer in the popular "up-and-down" configuration. (Courtesy of Corbis)

of the food compartment, and a small fan circulates air through it and around the food. A timer runs the defrost cycle: the compressor and all fans are turned off, and a heater mounted on the evaporator melts the frost that has formed. The resulting water drips into a plastic tray beneath the refrigerator. That water will evaporate, assisted by airflow from the condenser fan. After twenty-four hours, the defrost cycle will run again.

In the 1960s, luxury features such as icemakers and cooled-water dispensers began to appear. Refrigerators made for the American consumer are the largest in the world, with average capacity twice that of the British and French models, for example. The energy required to run today's refrigerator, with its extras and its large interior, is a considerable percentage of every household's electricity budget.

The refrigerator is the single most used appliance in the United States today, being found in 99.5 percent of American homes. With its large holding capacity, the American refrigerator changed the way we shop for groceries, cook, and eat. Quick daily trips to the grocery being no longer necessary, small neighborhood groceries have given way to huge supermarkets, where products are purchased in quantity and in sizes previously unheard of for household use. Milk, sold in pints in the days of the icebox, comes in gallons now. Refrigerators have even influenced the way food is grown: farmers breed fruits and vegetables for good storage quality. And the large freezer capacities have increased the consumption of ice cream, fruit juices from concentrates, and vegetables (see **Frozen Foods**). If we are what we eat, we are quite different people at the end of the twentieth century as a result of the invention of the refrigerator.

Remote Controls

The simplest and often the most natural place for a machine control is on the device being controlled. The user of a machine is usually holding or closely supervising the machine, and direct control is both convenient and safe. Sometimes, however, it is more convenient, and possibly safer, when a device is controlled remotely. In such cases, some form of remote control is needed.

Early remote controls were mechanical. A good example is the remote caliper brake control on a bicycle. A brake mechanism is located at the rim of both the front and rear wheel. It is most convenient and safest for the brake control to be on the handlebars. The solution is a cable linking a lever control mounted on the handlebars to the brake mounted on the frame forks holding the wheel. The lever and cable form a remote brake control. A complex machine such as an automobile will have many remote controls, including cable-operated mechanical remotes similar to those on bicycles (such as the remote hood release) and hydraulic remote controls (brakes).

Even computers have had mechanical remote controls! The original 1981 IBM PC placed the power supply at the right rear of the case, where the cooling fan could exhaust air to the rear of the case. The power switch for the computer was then inconveniently placed at the right rear of the computer. Several later personal computers used a metal rod as a remote control to connect a front-mounted button to the switch in the power supply at the rear of the case.

REMOTE CONTROLS OF HOME ELECTRICAL DEVICES

In the home, most controlled devices are operated directly. For example, home plumbing valves are still almost universally operated directly by a lever or handle mounted on the valve. Many electrical devices, such as table lamps, are also operated by local switches, often integral with the lamp socket that is controlled. But increasingly, it has been found desirable to operate devices and appliances in the home remotely.

One of the first examples was the electric light. Early ceiling-mounted lights were often remotely operated mechanically, by a string attached to the switch that was part of the lamp socket. Remote wall switches were soon added for increased convenience (they could be operated near the doorway where a room was entered) and safety (a good tug on the lamp cord might pull the lamp from the ceiling!).

Central heating also created a need for remote control—the furnace was typically in the basement, away from the rooms to be heated and their occupants. The solution is the remote thermostat, which can turn the furnace on and off. Both wall switches for lamps and thermostats require special wiring. Such wiring is expensive, and must either be planned for before the house is built so it can be placed inside walls, or added later as less-attractive visible wiring mounted on the surface of walls. Furnace control thermostats usually operate at a safe low voltage (24 volts AQ, and light-gauge wire can be used).

One of the first home appliances to have a remote control was the electric sewing machine. In this case, it is desirable when operating the machine that both hands be free to manipulate the machine and the workpiece, yet precise control of the motor speed is also needed. The solution is a foot-operated control, connected by wires to the motor. This control was just a variable resistor in series with the motor.

Remote control of lighting has also included expensive relay systems. These wired systems use low-voltage wiring between the remote switch and a relay that is near the device being controlled, such as overhead lights. In 1978, after digital integrated circuits became available, X-10 developed a system of home remote control (or "home automation") using digital signals carried over the power lines of the house. These Power Line Carrier signals were a development of earlier analog "wireless" intercoms, which send the audio signal over the existing house power lines. The X-10 system uses a small remote-control panel that can be plugged in anywhere in the building. It sends low-frequency digital radio signals over the house wiring to a receiver plugged in to a remote outlet. The receiver contains either a relay, for controlling motorized appliances, or a solid-state dimmer, for controlling incandescent lights. The receiver modules can also be permanently installed, replacing existing light switches or electric outlets.

Other schemes for turning appliances on and off remotely involved sound. These included The Clapper, a switch marketed in the 1990s that was turned on and off by a clap of the hands, and the WhistleSwitch, an earlier switch that was actuated by a small, light, handheld, squeezable plastic whistle.

TELEVISION REMOTE CONTROLS

Television is optimally viewed from a distance, and can be watched from the comfort of bed. For many people, the greatest desire for remote control in the home was for television sets. Televisions were watched for long periods of time, and the volume needed to be turned down when the phone was answered, and channels needed to be changed in the course of watching. Wired remotes were possible, especially for power. Most of the earlier remote controls in the home had been simply remote switches that control whether electrical current gets to the controlled device. In addition to "on" and "off," televisions invite remote control of volume and tuning. But control of these is much more complicated than control of power, and ultimately the near-universal presence of remote control in televisions required core design changes in the television itself. Even volume control is challenging: a wired remote potentiometer will pick up hum and noise. With the advent of voltage-controlled amplifiers (see **Electronic Musical Instruments**), a remote volume control need only control a voltage applied to the audio amplifier in the television set; the audio signal itself need not be taken out of the shielded circuits inside the television.

Tuning presented an even greater challenge. By far the most common tuner type from 1950 to 1980 in the United States was the turret tuner. Rather than have the continuously variable tuner common on radio receivers, the turret tuner was tuned by a large rotary switch that turned a 2–4-inch-diameter drum on which were mounted 12 coils and other components. As the switch was turned, 12 different sets of these components were in turn switched into the oscillator circuit in the tuner, permitting television stations on the assigned channels 2–13 to be accurately tuned very quickly. To provide remote control of a turret tuner, a solenoid must be added to move this turret approximately 30 degrees each time the user hits the channel change button on the remote. In addition, to save money, the turret could only be turned in one direction. Turning the turret made no provision for remote tuning of the UHF channels that began to appear in large urban viewing areas.

In 1950, Zenith introduced the "Lazy Bones" wired remote control—a push button connected to the TV by a wire could advance the tuner to the next TV channel. By 1955, Zenith introduced a wireless remote—the Flash-Matic. The remote was essentially a flashlight—the viewer could point the control to direct a beam of light at any of four photocells located at the corners of the television picture tube. This system could adjust the volume as well as change the channel, but it was susceptible to inadvertent operation by sunlight and other light. Eugene McDonald Sr., the founder of Zenith Electronics Corporation, asked his engineers to come up with an improved remote. A radio signal would work—but it might also change the channel on the neighbor's television.

Dr. Robert Adler, at Zenith, came up with the idea of an ultrasonic wireless remote control, which appeared on the market in 1956 as the Zenith Space Command 400. The small two-button version of this handheld remote (channel change and volume) included two tuned aluminum bars. This handheld remote was completely mechanical, needing no batteries. Pressing a button on the remote caused the bar to be tapped. Like a tuning fork, the struck bar generated sound—at a precise ultrasonic frequency. A microphone in the television set detected the sound. An advantage of such a remote is that it was omnidirectional (it did not need to be directly pointed at the television). Disadvantages were unreliability, false triggering, and cost: it added $100 to the price of a television set.

This handheld remote controls both a television and cable television box. The remote
control contains an integrated circuit chip and a light emitting diode (LED). When a
button is pressed, the IC causes the diode to emit a series of pulses of infrared light. The
pulses form a unique digital code controlling a specific function on a unique remote device.
Different manufacturers use different digital codes. (Courtesy of Corbis)

Remote controls for television could come into their own only after a breakthrough redesign of tuners in the 1970s: tuners had to become all electronic, and
solid-state infrared-light-emitting diodes had to be invented. Only after 1985 did
more than half of television sets have remote controls, almost thirty years after
they were first introduced. Solid-state tuners made possible direct-access remotes
(the user could punch in the number of the desired channel on a numeric keypad).
Initially, these tuners were solid-state versions of the turret tuner; electronic
switches replaced the mechanical switch of the tuner. But soon, completely digitally
controlled tuners appeared. The remotes themselves relied upon integrated circuits
and infrared-light-emitting diodes (LEDs) (see the discussion of digital displays in
Calculators and **Cash Registers**). LEDs had many advantages: they turned on and
off almost instantly, consumed little power, were low cost, and did not have a filament to burn out. A single LED could control multiple functions by having it send
out series of short pulses of light as a digital "code" for each function. These digi-

tal codes also prevent false triggering—it is very unlikely that stray infrared light will fall into the digital pattern of any of the control codes. However, strong light can mask the signal from the remote, and such remotes are not omnidirectional; they must be pointed at the photodiode receiver on the device being controlled.

As read-only-memory (ROM) integrated circuits came down in cost, it become possible to have remotes that stored the codes of many brands of device—"universal remotes." Some even more capable remote controls ("learning remotes") have a built-in receiver and can detect the codes sent by another remote and store them, and later mimic the "teaching" remote.

Radio signals are also a natural medium for remote control—with the complication that range is difficult to control. Lower radio frequencies are onmidirectional. The most common home application for radio remote control is the electric garage door opener. Earlier openers had been controlled by photocells. A light shone from a short post mounted on one side of the driveway and a photocell mounted on a similar post on the other side of the driveway detected the light beam. As the car entered the driveway, it broke the beam and actuated the garage door opener. Of course, a burglar strolling up the driveway could have a similar effect.

Radio controls became fully practical only after tubes gave way to solid-state circuits. By the 1960s these radio remote controls provided some security, but since only a few frequencies were used, a user of a radio remote control had a good chance of operating another's garage door. In one case, it was reported that a communications satellite inadvertently opened many garage doors on the earth below. The solution did not come until digital integrated circuits allowed digital security codes to be transmitted. Each transmitter and receiver has a set of switches (or jumpers) to set a matching code, hopefully unique to that pair, in the neighborhood in which they are used.

The older nonencoded radio remote is still common in toys: for example, radio controlled (RC) cars. More sophisticated hobbyist toys, including remote-controlled airplanes, use digitally encoded signals for security (to allow many planes to fly at a given location), and to allow more precise proportional control than the simple on/off signals used in mass-market toy radio controlled cars and boats. In the 1990s, digital radio remote controls became common in automobiles, to arm and disarm alarm systems, and to lock and unlock the car.

Summary of remote control types:

Mechanical (e.g., bike brake and gear shifter, and automobile parking brake)

Wired (sewing machine speed, some early TVs, dictating machines, tape recorders)

Acoustic (Clapper, WhistleSwitch, voice-actuated tape recorders)

AC wire carrier (X-10 home lighting control)

Ultrasonic (Zenith Space Commander; early X-10 wireless)

Infrared (by 1990 near universal for TV and VCR)

Radio (garage door opener, RC toys, automobile door locks, some home theater)

The most common form of "remote control" still consists of one person asking another to do something. But currently direct remote control of machines typically requires a special device, the handheld remote. These remotes are easily lost, and inconvenient to use. The future is likely to involve both wearable remotes and machines that incorporate voice recognition. Such machines will be controlled by verbal commands. A more remote future of remote control may hold machines that are controlled directly by thought.

REFERENCES

Bellamy, Robert V., Jr., and James Walker. *Television and the Remote Control.* New York: Guilford Press, 1996.

History and Operation of X-10. *http://www.x10.com/backgrounder.htm*

Horn, Delton. *Home Remote-Control and Automation Projects.* Blue Ridge Summit, PA: Tab Books, 1991.

People Weekly, "Button Man: Robert Adler Invented TVs Remote Control." Vol. 45, no. 10, p. 84.

Wohleber, Curt. "The Remote Control." *American Heritage of Invention and Technology,* vol. 16, no. 3, pp. 6–7.

Telephone Answering Machines

"We're sorry we missed your call; please leave a message after the tone."

This pervasive feature of modern telephone experience, the prerecorded answering machine message that invites the caller to record something in turn, may seem like a recent development. And it is true that answering machines proliferated and became standard for almost all businesses and private homes in the United States during the 1980s.

But the idea is much older. The basic function of a recording telephone was already envisioned by the inventor of the phonograph, Thomas Alva Edison, in 1878. Edison foresaw that a phonograph-like device could be used in "connection with the telephone, so as to make that instrument an auxiliary in the transmission of permanent and invaluable records, instead of being the recipient of momentary and fleeing communication." Thus Edison imagined, correctly, that telephones could become powerful conveyors of information not only limited to the live speaking voice, but also using various recording media to store and reissue indefinitely large amounts of data. It is this bold thought that underlies today's most striking application of telephony: the Internet (see **Digital Telecommunications**).

BUSINESS TELEPHONE MACHINES

A very early recording telephone used a steel tape or wire to record sound; this machine, invented by Valemar Poulsen and displayed at the Paris Exposition in 1900, was named the Telegraphone. Poulsen went on to develop machines that could answer the telephone and also record incoming messages. (See also **Audio Recording.**)

Later machines employed wax cylinders on which conversations were recorded. This technology was similar to that used in cylinder phonographs. It was cumbersome, though not intrinsically expensive. Wax-cylinder machines included Thomas Edison's own Telescribe (1914) and Dictaphone's Telecord (1926). In an interesting and not atypical move, the American Telephone and Telegraph Company (AT&T) initially denied consumers the right to attach the

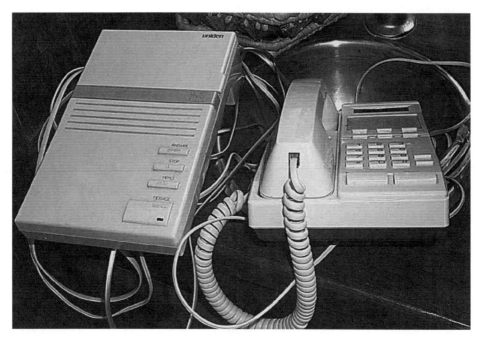

Answering machines like this one from Uniden quickly became so popular that you could find one in just about every home in America. (Courtesy of FreeFoto)

Telecord to the phone network, at that time, with government enforcement, entirely dominated by AT&T. In 1930, AT&T allowed Telecord use, with the stipulation that a PBX (or switchboard) also be used. This effectively prohibited home use.

Disc-recording and steel-tape recording technologies were also used in subsequent models of answering machines. Inventors continued to struggle with problems of size, as both disc and tape models required quite a bit of space and bulk, and tended also to be heavy. Thus, early answering machines were "installed" rather than merely being "plugged in," and once installed, they stayed put. The Swiss Ipsophon, invented in 1936 and marketed in the United States from 1946, is approximately the size of a small refrigerator.

Answering-machine research and development was stimulated during the years of World War II, when inventors raced to create machines that could record and replay tactical information. Bell Labs worked directly with government and military experts producing a profusion of prototypes from 1944 to 1948.

A suitcase-sized machine charmingly named the "Electronic Secretary" appeared in 1949. The Secretary used both wire and disc, with an outgoing mesage conveyed via a 45 rpm record and incoming ones recorded on wire. This machine was available to rent from Bell System and GTE during the 1960s.

HOME TELEPHONE ANSWERING MACHINES

A somewhat smaller answering machine designed explicitly for the private consumer and home use was the Peatrophone, which became available in 1951. Again AT&T presided over its presentation to customers, though the Peatrophone itself was made by the Gray Manufacturing Company. Peatrophones used discs exclusively, for both incoming and outgoing messages, and allowed their owners to accumulate discs with stored messages.

Throughout the 1950s and 1960s, it remained a costly proposition to indulge in an answering machine. Machine rental was about $12.50 per month, then a considerable sum, and installation about $15. AT&T also required customers to rent a "coupling device" from them, and to pay an additional installation fee for this. The device was later determined to be completely unnecessary.

The International Telephone and Telegraph Company (ITT) meanwhile developed the Code-a-Phone business answering machine. From 1958 to 1961, ITT worked on getting costs down for the Code-a-Phone so that individuals and small businesses could afford one. This machine was about the size of a cereal box and had the telephone set built in.

Also during the 1960s, magnetic tape became the preferred recording medium for most answering machines. The Ansaphone was developed by Dictaphone Corporation, the Robosonic Secretary by Robosonics, and Model 500 by Code-a-Phone, all using the relatively compact, lightweight, and lower-cost medium of tape recording. AT&T introduced a microcassette model in 1984. But back in 1975, the average cost of an answering machine hovered around $250. This makes the cost prohibitive for most households.

The telephone titan AT&T, a government-recognized monopoly since soon after its inception, was finally brought to the antitrust bar in the 1980s by MCI, a company that wanted the right to compete in the long-distance telephone market. After a lengthy trial, the courts finally forced AT&T to "divest," or sell off some of its powers and spheres of control to local companies. The so-called "modified final judgment" from the Department of Justice, issued in 1982, transformed the American telecommunications scene completely. The result is a proliferation of telephone models, forms of telephone service, and also, of course, types of answering machine. Intense competition both created a plethora of new models and drove costs down, bringing the answering machine finally into almost every telephone-owning home.

This transformation into everyday technology was materially assisted by the development of the integrated circuit, which controlled the operations of the tape transport. Machines with integrated circuits could have both outgoing message and incoming messages on a single microcassette tape. The complicated controller circuit on a chip could play the outgoing message that had been recorded on the beginning of the tape, then rapidly advance the tape past the end of the previously recorded incoming messages, produce a tone ("please leave your message after the tone"), shift to record mode, record the incoming message until it ended

Telephone answering machine utilizing computer-activated tape recording technology. (Courtesy of Corbis)

(detecting silence or dial tone), then shift from record to rewind mode and rewind the tape to the beginning to await the next incoming phone call. In 1996 sales of answering machines reached the billion-dollar mark.

DIGITAL ANSWERING MACHINES

While many home and business answering machines still use tape recording, digital solid-state technology is rapidly superseding the analog tapes and will (it is predicted) shortly make them obsolete. Integrated circuits can store very large amounts of digital information in a tiny space (as small as 1.5 square centimeters). First developed in the 1980s, digital signal processor (DSP) chips are specialized semiconductor chips that can digitize and compress speech, transmit data through modems, and perform many other telecommunication functions. DSPs are the brains behind today's digital cordless phones, digital answering machines, and Internet appliances.

ATT began marketing a half-digital answering machine in 1988 in it, the outgoing message cassette was replaced by a microchip. In 1990, PhoneMate (a Casio subsidiary) introduced ADAM, its All-Digital Answering Machine. ADAM eliminated moving parts within the recording/transmission operation. The caller's voice was converted into a series of digital signals, which were compressed and stored in the memory of electronic chips. ADAM was explicitly designed for the private consumer and was priced accordingly.

A DSP chip developed by Lucent Technologies (a Bell Labs offshoot of AT&T via divestiture) can simultaneously drive a caller ID display, a speakerphone, and a digital answering machine. This chip, called the DSP1609, operates at 100 million instructions per second (MIPS), has 2 kilowords of random-access memory (RAM), and 24 kilowords of read-only memory (ROM). Thus, a mere 20 years or so after business owners were scrambling to change tape reels after their twenty-first message had come in on the massive office answering machine, there were inexpensive, small, lightweight machines with the capability of recording or transmitting thousands of messages.

While some people still find the recorded message of an answering machine annoying, and some people certainly do create annoying messages (such as lengthy recitations of poems by young children, or political speeches), it cannot be denied that the answering machine has changed the way we communicate by telephone. Businesses can operate, to some extent, after staff hours; soccer coaches can contact their teams without speaking to a single human being; unwanted telephoners can be avoided; solicitations can be deflected.

Voice-mail, which is a computer-based sophistication of the answering machine, enables the sending of batch-messages, the sorting and storage of messages, and the forwarding of messages within proprietary voice-mail systems (see also **Digital Telecommunications**). This is accompanied by the familiar twin phenomena of convenience and alienation, so often encountered during times of rapid technological progress. Much business can take place, and much communication be made, without any direct human contact. Alexander Graham Bell (1847–1922), inventor of the telephone, made his first telephone call to his co-worker Thomas Watson: "Mr. Watson! Come here! I want you!" Paradoxically, he had just invented the very machine that would make it unnecessary for Watson to join him.

REFERENCE

Coe, Lewis. *The Telephone and Its Several Inventors: A History*. McFarland & Co., 1995.

Telephones

A large oak box bolted to the living room wall, with the only control being a big crank handle sticking out of the side, became a tiny plastic lump in the palm of the hand, with a complex keypad and a graphic display screen—the telephone changed literally beyond recognition in the twentieth century. And as it was transformed, this communication device changed lives, and built the largest and richest corporation of the world.

The technology of the telephone originated in the last quarter of the nineteenth century. Elisha Gray (1835–1901) and Alexander Graham Bell (1847–1922) can both lay claim to invention of the telephone, but the patent went to Bell. (Gray went on to cofound Western Electric, which ironically became the Bell Companies' manufacturing arm.) Bell's 1876 patent for "Improvements in Telegraphy" was arguably the most valuable patent ever granted, and there were many legal battles over the patent rights in the early years of the telephone.

The nineteenth-century telephone was an electromechanical device, a variation on the telegraph (indeed, Bell started his work on a quest for a "harmonic telegraph" that used tones instead of clicks). A telegraph sends pulses of a fixed voltage down a long wire to a remote receiver. A telephone sends a varying voltage—an audio signal. The crucial inventions were two transducers (a transducer converts energy in one form into another form): the microphone, which converts sound into varying electric current flow, and the earphone, which converts the varying electric current back into sound. Bell's first telephones used a single electromagnetic transducer: one spoke into it, then put one's ear to it to hear the reply. The later design with separate microphone, based on work by Gray, Thomas Edison, and others, worked much better.

Throughout much of the twentieth century, the telephone circuit was reasonably simple: a central telephone office provided bursts of pulsating DC voltage to an electromagnet that was located in the phone being called. This pulsating magnetic field caused an iron bar with an attached clapper to move, ringing the bell. If the called party answered, the central office connected the two wires going to the caller's phone to the two wires going to the phone being called. This completed a simple circuit, with all devices wired in series: caller's carbon microphone, caller's earphone, central office switchboard completing the connection, central office battery providing the current, called party's earphone, called party's microphone.

A wall-mounted telephone in a wooden case, common in the first third of the 20th century. To place a call, the crank on the right was used to turn a generator that rang the bells on the line (typically a multi-party rural line). Then the earpiece (left) was lifted from the "hook," a switch that connected the earpiece and microphone to the line. The carbon-granule microphone was permanently attached to the center of the case, forcing the user to stand in front of the telephone throughout the call. (Courtesy of Corbis)

The microphone consisted of loosely packed carbon grains behind a thin, flexible diaphragm. Speaking into the microphone vibrated the diaphragm, alternately compressing and decompressing the carbon grains. This motion varied the resistance of the microphone at the same frequency as the sound striking it. The earphone had an electromagnet beneath a metal disc. As the current in the electromagnet varied, the metal disc vibrated, recreating the original sound of the caller's voice. The central office provided the voltage; the two phones could each vary the current flow in the circuit. As a result, both caller and called heard his or her own voice in the headphone, as well as the voice of the other party.

The telephone set was permanently wired to a junction box on the wall. The early sets were often wooden boxes, and were attached to a wall or placed on a desktop. The microphone was affixed to the front of the box on a metal support that could be adjusted up and down. The earpiece hung from a hook on the side of the box—the hook moved up and down slightly, operating the main on-off switch inside the box. Thus picking up the earphone put the phone "off the hook" and connected the microphone and earpiece to the central telephone office. On some telephones, a hand crank, also on the side of the box, directly turned a generator inside the telephone. The voltage generated by turning the crank could ring the bell on any phone connected to the line. At the beginning, and much later in rural areas, phone lines were shared by several residences—a "party line." Distinctive rings were used for different intended-call recipients, but anyone on the line could pick up the phone and listen in on the conversation.

A more compact urban phone design without a generator was a desktop "candlestick" set. This much smaller set also had the microphone mounted on the telephone, at the top of a column, and it had a hook on the side for the earphone. To get the attention of the operator at the central office, one momentarily depressed the hook, causing a light to flash at the central office.

A human operator sat in front of a large "switchboard" at the central office with a large microphone on a rope around his neck. (Operators were originally all young men; they were almost all replaced by women operators before the twentieth century.) Using quarter-inch-diameter "phone plugs" (still used on electric guitars [see **Electronic Musical Instruments**] and many audio headphones), the operator connected to the caller's circuit: "Number please?" The caller would give a number such as "Madison 0349," a mix of an exchange name and a 3–4-digit number. The operator then completed the call using the switchboard. By this means, people were able to communicate as they never had before. Businesses were more efficient, and residential phone users were less isolated.

Americans embraced the telephone with much more enthusiasm than any other country—at the dawn of the 20th century, there were almost as many telephones in New York state alone as in all of Europe. In the United States, there was about one telephone for every 60 persons, whereas in many European countries there was only one phone, or less, for each 1,000 persons. The telephone changed the ways Americans lived, and more rapidly than it affected other nations.

DIAL PHONES

One of the first important telephone improvements was the dial phone. This was not a Bell company invention—it was the work of Almon B. Strowger, in Kansas City. Strowger was an undertaker, and so perhaps often mindful that life is short. Waiting for an operator to answer took time. However, another legend is that Strowger thought telephone operators were steering business to his competitors by giving false busy signals to potential Strowger customers. Strowger's solution, patented in 1891, was to eliminate the need for the telephone exchange operator by using a stepping relay: each pulse of current to an electromagnet ratcheted a rotating contact arm to the next contact in a bank of 10 circuits. The first automatic switching phones did not have dials—they had two buttons. They could call 2-digit phone numbers: depressing one button 7 times and the second

A dial telephone in a fancy case. The one-piece handset, combining earphone and microphone, came late to American homes. To place a call, the user placed their index finger in one of the 10 holes in the dial and rotated it to clockwise until their finger hit the stop, and then removed the finger. A spring and speed governor rotated the dial back to its original position. Gears on the rotating dial turn a cam that operates switch contacts, generating a series of electrical pulses on the line. The pulses operate switching relays back at the telephone exchange. (Courtesy of Corbis)

6 times connected the phone to line number 76. The buttons were soon replaced by a 10-digit alphanumeric dial. The dial was rotated with the index finger, and a spring returned the dial to its original position. The rate of return was controlled by a small centrifugal governor. The pulsing was done by a cam-operated switch during the dial return, providing evenly spaced pulses of equal length.

Although the Strowger automatic switch was a late-nineteenth-century invention, it was not widely deployed until well into the twentieth century. Smaller companies were the first to install dial phones. The Bell system continued to use operators, and only they had dials (callers spoke to the operator, who dialed the call). However, the conversion of the entire telephone system to direct dialing was inevitable. During the 1930s Great Depression, the total number of telephones in the United States declined. People could not afford this luxury. Western Electric's workforce would have been seriously reduced had it not been for the conversion of offices and telephones to dial phones, which, of course, resulted in a reduced need for operators, and hence permitted layoffs elsewhere in the system. The conversion to dial continued into the 1960s.

LONG-DISTANCE TELEPHONY

A telephone system must connect phones, but humans are not distributed uniformly across the globe. In urban centers, large networks of wires can connect phones with exchanges, and thus each other. Longer distances present a new set of problems, both technical and financial. Bell himself was interested in long distance from the start, and used borrowed telegraph lines for initial experiments and demonstrations. American Telephone and Telegraph, AT&T, which eventually became the largest corporation in the world, began as a subsidiary of the Bell companies to handle long distance. The man who, more than any other, built the Bell System, Theodore Vail (1845–1920), knew that dominating long distance would also give the Bell companies advantages against local competitors. The Bell system bought Lee De Forest's patents and perfected his triode tube for use in amplifying long-distance telephone signals. By 1915, the first transcontinental telephone line was in place, using 2,500 tons of copper wire.

Moving to long distance also got Bell System involved with the technology of **radio**. On January 7, 1927, the company used radio to establish the first commercial long-distance service between New York and London. Service to Tokyo in the Far East was added in 1934. Long cables were very expensive, and required periodic amplifiers ("repeaters") to take the signals over the long wires. This made the submarine telephone cable and expensive challenge. It was not until 1956 that the first transatlantic telephone cable was laid. At almost the same time, first the USSR, and then the United States, launched manmade satellites. In 1960 NASA and AT&T labs launched "Echo I," a giant reflective balloon that could bounce signals back to a distant earth surface receiver. In 1962, NASA finally agreed to launch the first active telecommunications satellite, AT&T's "Telstar." Within two weeks, Telstar was used not only for the long-distance telephone, but also to relay a television broadcast to Europe. Hundreds of communications satellites have followed, drastically bringing down the cost of long-distance communication.

Direct dialing of long distance began between some communities in the 1930s. But it was not available nationwide until a standard phone numbering scheme was in place, with prefixes assigned to areas ("area codes"). The first direct distance dialing service was available in Englewood, New Jersey, in 1951, and by 1965 90 percent of U.S. phones had access to direct dialing of long-distance calls.

TOUCHTONE PHONES

The telephone grew during the electronics revolution. Early telephones were not electronic; they were composed of magnets and coils of wire. The first applications of electronic amplifiers were in long-distance phones. However, by 1941, AT&T installed a switching system in Baltimore, Maryland, that used electronically generated audible tones, instead of pulses. As with early dials, only operators used the TouchTone pads to control the switching network.

Vacuum tube amplifiers, and the oscillators for making tones, are large and use a lot of electricity. Bell Labs was the site of the invention of the transistor, in 1947. One result of the transistor was that the cost of tone-based switching sys-

TouchTone telephones began to replace dial phones in the 1960s. These phones contained simple tone generator electronic circuits; combinations of a few tones operated switching equipment back at the telephone exchange. TouchTone "dialing" was faster than the older electro-mechanical dials, and added two additional buttons for special functions. Button pads can be made smaller than rotary dials, permitting small portable cell phones. (Courtesy of Corbis)

tems could be reduced. The first TouchTone phones for consumers were displayed at the Seattle World's Fair in 1962. (At the next World's Fair, in New York in 1964, IBM displayed Shoebox, an early speech recognition device that could recognize spoken digits—it was thought that future phones would use voice recognition instead of either a dial or button touchpad.) In the 1960s TouchTone phones became available to consumers in various areas, at a premium cost. Dial service continued to be available throughout the century.

TouchTone phones and electronic exchanges also permitted entirely new services, such as call waiting and call forwarding. One of these services was voicemail, which allowed callers to leave a recorded voice message. However, most residential customers relied on **telephone answering machines** for this function.

The use of tones to control the switching network also led to the rise of "phone phreaks," who built small electronic tone generators ("blue boxes") to control the telephone network and thereby permit illegal no-cost long-distance calls—theft of service. This unintended consequence of tone-controlled switching became an increasingly large problem in the 1970s. It diminished in significance after a long antitrust court battle resulted in the breakup of AT&T and its long-distance monopoly on January 1, 1984, and the subsequent substantial decline in the cost of long-distance service.

PICTUREPHONES

The story of telephony in the twentieth century is largely the story of one successful innovation after another. A notable exception was the Picturephone. The first test system was built at AT&T in 1956; the low-bandwidth telephone connections restricted it to one small image every two seconds. The 1964 successor system became a fixture at Disneyland, in demonstrations that connected it to a Picturephone at the New York World's Fair. Commercial service debuted in Pittsburgh in 1970. AT&T confidently predicted that by 1980 a million Picturephone sets would see service. They were wrong.

There was no great consumer enthusiasm for being seen by callers. The cost remained high, demand never came close to AT&T projections, and all in all, the service was a failure. Whatever interest there was in a two-way video connections was later satisfied by computer-based communication over the Internet, with small "webcams" digitizing images for transmission to remote users (see **Digital Telecommunications**).

MODEMS

The phone system was based on sound; computers are digital. Connecting computers to the phone system required a conversion device—a modulator/demodulator, or modem. A modem takes a digital signal and converts it to sound, and vice versa, allowing digital computers to be linked by audio signals sent over the ordinary telephone system. This innovation made it possible to link personal computer users to the Internet and thus to each other.

The technology story is familiar: the first modems were large and bulky devices, and transmitted at a rate of up to 300 baud (about 300 characters per second). These modems did not connect directly to the phone network—only phones could do that. They used an "acoustic coupler"—the modem had a special cradle with a microphone and speaker, in which the telephone handset was placed. By the 1980s, in a move accelerated by the breakup of the Bell System, a variety of manufacturers produced modems at speeds of 1,200 and soon 2,400 baud. In 1981, Hayes Microcomputers introduced the Hayes Smartmodem. This modem used a set of commands to allow the computer to control the modem; these became industry-wide standards. By the end of the decade, modems (costing nearly $2,000 each) had reached 9,600 baud.

In the 1990s, modems used a range of complicated data-handling techniques to reach their maximum speeds of near 56,000 baud, and prices dropped well below $100. However, by this time alternative ways of connecting home computers to the Internet had been introduced. Cable television wires and direct satellite links provided higher-speed connections. By the end of the century, many computer users had a choice of ways to connect to the Internet: ordinary telephone connection using modem, digital subscriber link (DSL) using higher-band-

A "cordless" phone. These phones are two-way radios; a base unit in the home is connected to the wires leading to the telephone exchange. Such phones have operated at various frequencies allowed by the FCC. The range of cordless phones is limited to a few hundred feet. The battery of the handset must be frequently recharged by returning it to the base. (Courtesy of Corbis)

width signals over telephone lines, cable-television-based Internet service, and satellite link.

CELLULAR TELEPHONES

While radio had been used for long-distance telephony in the 1920s, the vast majority of individual phones remained connected by a fixed wire to the central office. Early phones were permanently attached to junction boxes at the wall. The Bell Company began with the practice of leasing all telephones to users—and no customer was permitted to use a telephone that he or she owned on the Bell System. This arrangement resulted in enormous profits—the lease charges for a telephone could exceed $1,000 over the life of the phone. With customers legally forbidden to use their own phones, the Bell companies gradually made it easier for them to move their phones from one location to another. First, large four-prong plugs were introduced, then much smaller (and less expensive) "modular" plugs. But these were hardly mobile phones.

A portable cellular telephone. This model folds in half to become very compact. The telephone service area is divided into "cells," each with a short-range radio transceiver. The system uses computers to switch the phone call from one transceiver to another as the user leaves one cell and enters another. Using short-range radio signals and many cells allows the same radio frequency to be shared by users in remote cells, allowing efficient use of the crowded radio spectrum. (Courtesy of Corbis)

Cordless phones, for short-range use inside the home, did not become feasible until the 1980s, when integrated circuits became common. Cordless phones are two-way radios (transceivers). Over the years they have operated at ever-higher frequencies, including 49 mhz, 900 mhz, and most recently, 2.4 gigahertz. Higher frequencies use smaller antennae. Digital cordless phones, which convert the audio signal to digital data, appeared in the late 1990s.

The first mobile phones were typically installed in automobiles. They were very expensive, and in addition, since each telephone call tied up a radio communication frequency, there was very limited capacity in an urban area for mobile telephone calls. The first commercial radio-telephone service was established in St. Louis in 1946. The Federal Communications Commission (FCC) allocated few radio channels to mobile phone use, and many cities could handle only 12 simultaneous mobile calls in the entire city! Nevertheless, demand was high and by 1976 there were 545 Bell mobile phone subscribers in a city as large as New York—with 3,700 names on a 5–10-year waiting list. This situation could be corrected only by electronic switching and a new system.

The original mobile phones communicated with a central tall and expensive radio tower that served the entire urban area. The conceptual breakthrough was to divide the service area into much smaller "cells," served by low-wattage transceivers. Computers could monitor signal strength and automatically switch a call from one cell's transceiver to the next, and to a new frequency, as the telephone moved through the area. Now many callers in different cells could use the same signal frequency. This system was introduced in the United States in 1983.

At the same time, microelectronics—integrated circuits—allowed the mobile telephone to shrink in size. From a large box in the trunk of a car, it became possible to have a mobile phone small enough to be mounted in a brief case. Finally, integrated circuits and advanced battery design permitted the small handheld phones that became ubiquitous by the end of the twentieth century.

The future is expected to see evolution of the cellular phone. Cell phone systems were originally analog; they were increasingly digital by the end of the century. Some phones began to incorporate the features of personal digital assistants—address books, personal schedules, along with e-mail and even Internet browsers (see **Digital Telecommunications**). Thus telephones were evolving in the direction of handheld computers, with full text, image, and voice communication abilities. Some also expect that users will have telephone numbers for life, much like Social Security numbers. The more distant future may hold phones that are worn, like clothing, and so cannot be misplaced.

REFERENCES

Brooks, John. *Telephone: The First Hundred Years.* New York: Harper & Row, 1975.

Farley, Tom. "TelecomWriting.com's Telephone History Series." 2001. http://www.privateline.com/TelephoneHistory/History1.htm

Riordan, Michael, and Lillian Hoddeson. *Crystal Fire: The Invention of the Transistor and the Birth of the Information Age* (Sloan Technology Series). New York: W.W. Norton Company, 1998.

Rippey, James C. *Goodbye Central; Hello World: A Centennial History of Northwestern Bell.* Omaha, NE: Published for Telphone Pioneers of America by Northwestern Bell Telephone Company, 1975.

Seybold, Andrew, and Mel Samples. *Cellular Mobile Telephone Guide.* Indianapolis, IN: Howard Sams and Company, 1986.

Stern, Ellen, and Emily Gwathmey. *Once upon a Telephone: An Illustrated Social History.* New York: Harcourt Brace & Company, 1994.

Television

The basic problem of television is how to convert a two-dimensional scene to a one-dimensional electrical signal, transmit the signal over a distance, and then convert it back to a two-dimensional image. The basic idea of television then becomes fairly obvious: scan the image as a series of lines, thereby converting the two-dimensional image into a single stream of voltage varying with the brightness levels in the lines of the image. *How* to do this is not so obvious, and the history of television is in part a history of two quite different solutions to the problem, only one of which ultimately emerged as victorious.

The possibility of television was appreciated very early. "Victor Appleton" makes the idea of wired television the center of the plot in *Tom Swift and His Photo Telephone* (New York: Grosset & Dunlap, 1914)—very soon after his adventure with radio in 1911's *Tom Swift and His Wireless Message*. Television is again the topic of a 1933 Tom Swift book, *Tom Swift and His Television Detector* (New York: Grosset & Dunlap, 1933). Television often appears in the matinee movie serial *Flash Gordon* in the 1930s.

The basic idea of scanning that will make television possible is an idea common to both fax and television. In both cases, an image-to-electrical-signal converter scans the image, the now serial signal is transmitted to a receiver, and the receiver produces a narrow beam of light that exactly retraces the original image scan. It is clear that the transmitter and the remote receiver must be kept perfectly in synchronization for the image produced by the receiver to be a faithful reproduction of the image before the transmitter. Thus there must be an agreed-upon standard for the signal, and in practice there must also be transmitted synchronization signals that lock the receiver to the transmitter. Fax transmits at a slow rate, need not create a nonflickering illusion of motion, is single recipient, and is two-way (the receiver can acknowledge receipt, or request retransfer of garbled data). Television is much faster, in real time, and is one way to a mass audience. The transmission technology is that developed for **radios** using a wider slice of the electromagnetic spectrum than is required by an audio signal.

BAIRD'S MECHANICAL TELEVISION

The development of workable television occurs in the 1920s and is the story of the competition between two rival approaches to solving the scanning of the image. A twenty-three-year-old German, Paul Nipkow, had received a German patent for a mechanical "electric telescope" in 1883, although apparently he did not build a working system. The brute force electromechanical scanning method invented by Nipkow was developed in the 1920s by the Scottish inventor John Logie Baird (1888–1946). Baird used a camera containing an opaque scanning disc rotated by a synchronous electric motor. The disc had a spiral of holes punched in it. Behind one half of the disk was a light-sensitive photodiode that detected the changing level of light coming through the holes in the spinning disc. As a hole in the disc moved, it scanned a line of the scene, converting it into a spot of varying brightness depending on the light reflected from the scene in front of the camera. Then the next hole in the spiral came by, a bit closer to the right edge of the scene (Baird used a vertical scan). With a single spiral of holes, one revolution of the disc produced a complete scan of the scene, and the number of holes in the disc determined how many lines the image was divided into. Baird demonstrated a thirty-line television in late 1925. American Charles Jenkins also demonstrated a mechanical television in the same year. General Electric developed a mechanical receiver in 1928, the Octagon.

Baird's receiver was also simple: a duplicate of the original disc turned at exactly the same speed. A neon lamp (invented in 1917 by D.M. Moore in the United States) behind the disc resulted in the original image being reproduced as a series of lines of (neon orange) light. An incandescent lamp could not be used because the hot filament could not change brightness levels fast enough to reproduce an image.

ELECTRONIC TELEVISION

The competing alternative method of scanning and reproducing was purely electronic, and more sophisticated. Just before the turn of the century, prolific German inventor Karl Ferdinand Braun had invented the cathode ray tube (CRT) with a movable focused electron beam that could produce a controlled pattern of light on a fluorescent screen (1897). An electronic camera took longer to develop. Young twenty-year-old Utah farmboy inventor Philo Farnsworth (1906–1971) convinced Crocker Bank of San Francisco to bankroll his idea of a purely electronic television. Farnsworth submitted his patent application on January 7, 1927, and by September of that year Farnsworth finally had a prototype that could transmit a simple image. Farnsworth spent the next 10 years perfecting television, and received over 100 patents.

During roughly the same period RCA was also working on electronic television; the primary television inventor at RCA was Russian-born Vladimir

Zworykin (1889–1982; sometimes spelled "Zworkin"). Like Farnsworth, Zworykin worked on the image and display tubes, and RCA became an important factor in television. Zworykin applied for a patent in 1923. It is not clear that it was for a viable system—but RCA had one by 1932. The key to these all-electronic television systems was special scanning vacuum tubes based on the work of Farnsworth and Zworykin, including RCA's Image Iconoscope for the camera. The image-displaying tube in the receiver is the ubiquitous CRT, or Kinescope as RCA called them—or "television picture tube" as they are generally known.

Experimental broadcasts (for mechanical sets) were made in the United States in 1928, and by RCA broadcasting Felix the Cat cartoons from an antenna atop the Empire State Building in 1931. A "chicken-and-egg problem" plagues new media: consumers won't buy receivers/players unless there is programming, but there is no incentive to produce content unless there are consumers equipped with receivers/players. David Sarnoff (1891–1971), head of RCA, had solved the problem by setting up NBC (the National Broadcasting Company) as a broadcasting division of RCA, and so he could provide programming to drive sales of his company's receivers. In London, the BBC broadcast for the Baird mechanical sets from 1929 to 1931. Germany had regular broadcasts by 1935.

Meanwhile Allen B. Dumont (1901–1965) resigned as chief engineer of De Forest Laboratories in 1931 to work on the development of electronic television. Dumont's first set, with a 14-inch picture tube, was released in 1938, the first commercial television set in America. Dumont also produced programming. A few months later RCA introduced a 12-inch set. Early RCA sets had around 30 vacuum tubes and cost the equivalent of several thousand current dollars. RCA put on a major promotion at the 1939 World's Fair, including the first presidential television address. The FCC did not finalize standards until 1941. Television sales took off after World War II, and sets flowed into living rooms in the 1950s. The most distinctive sets were the Philco Predicta sets. Introduced in 1958, these sets had the electronics enclosed in a small case at the bottom above which the picture tube was mounted in a frame that could swivel and rotate, or even be detached from the electronics console altogether.

COLOR TELEVISION

In this same period, the 1950s, color television was developed by RCA. On January 1, 1954, NBC provided the first nationwide colorcast, of the Tournament of Roses Parade from California. Color television required separating the red, green, and blue image signals, while using a signal compatible with existing monochrome sets. Color sets were built around a complex picture tube with three electron guns, a shadow mask, and a much more complex surface on the front of the tube containing an array of tiny dots of three different types of phosphor emitting red, green, and blue light when struck by the streams of electrons from the three electron guns. Only in 1969 did Sony produce a workable one-gun color picture tube, the Trinitron. Both types of picture tube are also used in color monitors for computers.

The television camera contains a vacuum tube that must produce a varying electrical signal as the image is scanned. The image is focused on a surface coated with a mosaic of spots of photosensitive material at one end of the tube. This surface is insulated from a very thin metal plate just behind it. As the light image falls on the front it forms positive charges in the cells of photosensitive material. From the rear of the tube, a scanning electron beam moves across the cells, passing through the plate. As the electron beam discharges the cells, a small voltage is induced in the metal plate just behind the cells. This small voltage varies, depending on how many electrons each cell of the matrix absorbs, which in turn depends on how much light has fallen on the cell since the last scan. In this way, the cells store charge proportional to the total light falling on them between scans, making this tube more sensitive to light than non-storing systems such as the mechanical television systems of Baird and others. The small voltage from the plate is then amplified, and combined with synchronization and audio signals to form the broadcast television signal. A color television camera splits the incoming light and uses three imaging tubes, one each for red, green, and blue.

In the receiver, a tuner selects from all the incoming signals a specific frequency of signal for further processing. The FM audio signal is separated out and sent to a separate audio circuit. The video signal is separated into its component color signals and these are amplified and sent to the three electron guns of the conventional picture tube. To produce an image, the picture tube also requires two other circuits: deflection circuits to scan the image by moving the electronic beam. A rapid horizontal deflection circuit sweeps the beam from side to side, while a slower vertical deflection circuit moves the beam down the image (60 vertical sweeps a second in the United States and Japan). The deflection of the electron beam can be achieved electrostatically (plates inside the tube have varying high-voltage charges) or magnetically (coils wrapped around the neck of the picture tube produce a varying magnetic field that deflect the beam)—the latter is most common. To reduce flicker, each image is scanned twice. Every other line of the image is scanned on the first pass, then the intervening lines are scanned—an "interlaced" scan system. Thus, though the scanning beam in both camera and receiver moves from top to bottom 60 times a second, the result is 30 complete images a second (Europe uses an interlaced vertical scan rate of 50, giving 25 frames a second).

In addition to deflection signals to produce scanning, the picture tube requires a very high positive voltage at the "plate," an element inside the tube near the front that attracts the electrons to the front surface of the picture tube. It is this high voltage, over 10,000 volts, that makes working inside television sets dangerous.

The inside front surface of the glass picture tube is coated with phosphors, materials that emit light when struck by electrons. For a monochrome tube, this phosphor coating can be uniform. For color, the coating must divided into triads of tiny dots of phosphor. In addition, in a three-gun color CRT a "shadow mask" punched with holes must be hung across the tube to make sure the electron beam from each electron gun reaches only the phosphor dots it should (the others are masked off). The shadow mask gets hot, and work has been done to find materials that do not expand and distort from the heat (Invar is a current favorite). In addition, the development of color television involved finding phosphors that would emit enough light of each color—finding good red phosphors was especially difficult.

Tuners originally had a continuous slide dial, like those on many radios. Soon the turret tuner was introduced on American sets (see **Remote Controls**). American television provided for 12 VHF channels. European countries usually had government control of all television broadcasting and many fewer possible channels. In the United States, reception of 70 UHF channels was mandated by the FCC on all television sets sold after April 30, 1964. Converter boxes were sold for earlier sets. In 1972, Home Box Office (HBO) introduced a pay-for-movies cable television channel (by 1987 half of all U.S. homes with television would have cable). In the 1980s solid-state tuners replaced turret tuners and made possible flexible remote controls.

In the 1950s and 1960s, neighborhood convenience stores had tube testers and a stock of common tube types. In the early 1960s, Sony introduced an all-transistor television with a 5-inch screen. It cost about a third more than a tube-type "portable" with a 16-inch picture—but it was much lighter weight (8 pounds), and could run on batteries, using a 10-pound battery pack! It was difficult to develop transistors to handle the high voltages required by large television picture tubes, but as the cost of transistors came down, all television manufacturers converted to solid state over the next 15 years. By the late 1970s, the only tube left in a television set was the picture tube.

HIGH-DEFINITION (HDTV) AND FLAT-SCREEN TELEVISION

High-definition television (HDTV) has been a gleam in the eye of some television fans during the last decade of the twentieth century. HDTV provides an image with greater detail—high fidelity for video. It is uncertain how much consumers value higher video fidelity—Betamax provided better image quality than VHS, but lost in the marketplace; the S-VHS format provides greater image quality than VHS, but has a tiny share of the market; video discs also provide higher image quality than the tape used in VCRs (see **Home Video**). When consumers have had a choice, they have not generally placed a high value on greater image quality. HDTV also makes possible a wider image, more like those that movies are created in, and so will provide more of the original movie image (standard television broadcast usually cuts off the sides of movie images).

The cathode ray tube was a wonderful invention, but its days are numbered. Flat-panel solid-state television displays have been available for some time, but only in very small handheld, portable televisions with around 2-inch screens. In the 1990s color flat-panel displays became common in portable "laptop" computers, but they remained very expensive and gradually increased in size to around 14-inch diagonal display. Research continues to create larger flat-panel displays—and most important, attempts to bring costs down to levels that will permit home television application. Alternatives to LED technology include improved LCD displays, mirrored integrated circuits, and plasma displays.

And so it is expected that the one remaining tube, the most expensive part of the television set, will be replaced by flat panels, most likely composed of LEDs. Alternatives are being worked on as well, including plasma displays. Projection television should come down in cost until it is competitive, for larger displays. 3D television is possible, but demand is uncertain and there is little, if any, programming content. Holographic projection is possible, but remains in the distant future.

Television is also likely to integrate increasingly with the Internet. "Convergence" may mean that a single appliance will combine television, computer, and telephone (see **Digital Telecommunications**). Some degree of increased interactivity is certain, as the obvious value to consumers of on-screen display of television programming content, and the value to advertisers of enabling consumers to link to additional product and sales information, will lead to provision of these services as costs fall.

REFERENCES

Brinkley, Joel. *Defining Vision: The Battle for the Future of Television.* New York: Harcourt Brace, 1997.

Fisher, David E., and Marshall Jon Fisher. *Tube: The Invention of Television.* New York: Harvest Books, 1997.

"The Media History Project." *http://www.mediahistory.com*

"MZTV Virtual Museum of Television." *http://www.mztv.com*

Schatzkin, Paul W. "The Farnsworth Chronicles." *http://www.songs.com/philo/index.html*

Vacuum Cleaners

Vacuum cleaners are electrically powered cleaning machines that remove dirt and debris by means of suction that is produced by a fan, depositing the dirt temporarily in a bag or canister for later disposal. Although there are many industrial, medical, and other specialized applications of vacuum cleaners, the household flooring cleaner is most familiar. A nineteenth-century invention, broadloom, spurred the invention of vacuum cleaners, but it was early twentieth-century development of small ("fractional horsepower") electric motors that made these popular domestic appliances viable.

Before power looms for weaving carpets were invented (by Scotsman James Templeton in 1839 and American Erastus Bigelow in 1840), large carpets were rare and very expensive, being handwoven or hand-knotted by skilled workers in the Middle East and China. Templeton's invention copied these Asiatic patterns. Bigelow (1814–1879) had already patented looms for laces and ginghams, but his broadlooms made it possible to produce carpets in popular Brussels and Wilton patterns as well as many others. During most of the century, the looms were limited to 27 inches in width, although these strips could be sewn together for room-sized floor coverings. As stylish mass-produced rugs and carpets became available, the usual wood, stone, and brick floors, which were "easily" swept and scrubbed (cleaning floors is never an easy task!), were replaced by fabric coverings that became embedded with tracked-in soil and soot and small ashes from fireplaces and coal stoves. Cleaning these presented a new problem for housewives and servants, and with the scientific discovery that disease-causing microorganisms were found in dust, household hygiene became a middle-class obsession. Two muscular cleaning methods were used: manufactured brooms made of special broom-corn straw were first produced by Ebenezer Howard of Fort Hunter, New York, in 1859. Much superior to homemade brooms made of bundles of twigs, these were produced in the millions by the 1890s. Vigorous brooming loosened the dirt and dust, which largely resettled around the room. Dampening the broom helped, as did bringing in fresh snow to catch the dust. The other method, an annual ritual of "spring cleaning," was to take the rugs outside, lay them upside down on grass, and pound them with a wood or wire carpet beater.

A number of mechanical carpet sweepers were invented, but none was so famous or long-lasting as those of Melville and Anna Bissell of Grand Rapids, Michigan, first patented in 1876. Cylindrical brushes were enclosed in a flat case at the end of a long handle. The case moved on casters, the motion rotated the brushes, and dirt and fluff was rubbed off the brushes and deposited in the case, which could be opened to dispose of the debris. There were many imitators (these are still produced for between-vacuuming cleanups) but the Bissell's products were so popular that they produced a new verb—"Bisselling" rugs.

EARLY VACUUM CLEANERS

Carpet sweepers remove surface dirt, but not that which is embedded in the carpet's pile. Herbert Booth of England is generally credited with the idea of using suction. The story is that he got the idea while sitting in a restaurant and immediately tested the idea by placing his mouth against the upholstery on the back of his chair, and sucking in. The experiment worked (and, like Benjamin Franklin's flying a kite in a thunderstorm, is not recommended for repeating). In 1901 Booth patented a vacuum cleaner, powered by a gasoline piston engine. This device took two men to operate and was obviously too bulky to bring into a house. So Booth mounted his vacuum cleaner on a wagon (later a truck), with a long, flexible hose that could be passed into houses through doors and windows. Thus equipped, he was able to establish a house-cleaning business.

In the same year, David E. Kenney, a New Jersey plumber, applied for a patent for another large vacuum cleaner system. This had its vacuum pump installed in the house basement with pipes reaching to various wall inlets. His patent (granted in 1907) also included features that became essential to all the attachments of later vacuums: a flexible hose that fitted into the wall inlet, a metal tube handle, and a nozzle about twelve inches wide. Until his patents expired, almost all vacuum cleaners had to be manufactured under the Kenney license. Kenney used a rotary suction motor. Meanwhile, other schemes for portable cleaners were devised. Some used the principle of a bellows, operated either by foot or by arm power; others had a piston like that in a hand water pump. Neither was very successful. But about the same time as Booth's and Kenney's inventions, a Savannah, Georgia, woman, Corinne Dufour, developed ideas for what would become the typical "upright" portable vacuum. Instead of bellows, piston, or rotary suction, she used a fan, and like the Bissell carpet sweeper, her vacuum had revolving brushes. As an "electric sweeper and dust gatherer," her vacuum drew on the traditional method of broom wielders to capture the dust: the fan blew the dust that had been loosened by the brushes against a damp sponge, which could be periodically wrung out.

HOOVERING THE HOME

Like the word "Bisselling," *Hoovering* derives from the name of a manufacturer. However, William Hoover was not the inventor of the most famous

These 1922 Montgomery Ward vacuums reflect the transition to home electrification. The Thuro's cord screws into a lamp socket and its motor can operate on either AC or DC electricity. Cities supplied by Thomas Edison's power company used direct current at this time. For farms, there is another Thuro with a 32-volt motor for current supplied by a home generator. For homes without electricity, there is the vacuum cleaner whose fan runs on mother's arm power.

portable electric vacuum cleaner. The credit must go to his wife's cousin, Murray Spangler of Canton, Ohio. Spangler, a not too successful inventor, worked as a night janitor in a department store, operating a large carpet sweeper on endless expanses of aisle rugs. He first adapted a motor from an electric fan to rotate the brushes on the sweeper and propel it forward. This eased the muscle power, but stirred up more dust to irritate his already congested lungs. Spangler experimented further, using a fan to draw the dust into a pillowcase. The department store's floors became a "laboratory" for continued improvements, finally leading to a 1908 patent and the establishment of a manufacturing company.

Sales were poor, but when Spangler demonstrated his electric suction sweeper to his cousin, the Hoovers decided to buy the company, with Spangler as plant superintendent. There were two keys to the success of the Hoover company: one was the beating action of the rotating brushes, the other was door-to-door marketing. These appliances were expensive, and housewives refused to buy one without a demonstration in their homes. In-home sales became a standard practice in the industry, as well as buying on weekly or monthly payments. Although the term "Hoovering" became current mainly in England, the Hoover was the first dominant vacuum cleaner in the United States. A 1909 full-page advertisement in the *Saturday Evening Post* touted an upright model for seventy dollars with an additional fifteen dollars for Kenney-style hose attachments for cleaning drapes and walls. "Simply attach the wire to an electric light socket," the ad said, "turn on the current and run the machine over the carpet as you would an ordinary carpet sweeper." Well, possibly, but the early Hoover weighed forty pounds, most of the weight being the motor.

There were many rival firms, and a huge variety of designs. The most successful departure from the upright on wheels was a tank or canister model, the Swedish "Electrolux," introduced to Americans in 1924. The Electrolux had a flexible hose, and the tank could be pulled from one location to another on smooth skids. As more homes became electrified and the vacuum cleaner more commonplace, home demonstrations declined, though it wasn't until after World War II that most sales were made in stores. Almost all models came with attachments for cleaning furniture and drapes and hard-to-reach corners.

There are many reasons for the many competing models. Partly, of course, there is the potential for high profits. But also there have been many nagging problems that vacuum cleaner designers have tried to address. One problem was emptying the debris from the container into a trash can. This messy and dirty task was solved by using disposable paper bags. The problem of electrical cords getting in the way (or being too short) was addressed by Black & Decker's cordless "Dustbuster" in 1979. Some plug-in models featured spring-wound cord retractors. Creating high suction was solved early with faster and stronger motors, but this resulted in other problems as powerful vacuums caught up edges of rugs, either burning out drive belts and motors, or raveling decorative fringes. This problem has not been adequately solved. Another irritation is that long pet hair, string, yarn, and thread wind on the revolving brushes, causing overheating and lowering brush efficiency. Brushless vacuums partly solve this, but at the cost of

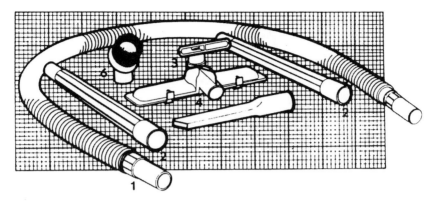

Upright vacuum cleaners were designed for cleaning floors. Most manufacturers offered kits with hose and wand attachments for walls, ceilings, crevices, and drapes. In this Kenmore model from the early 1990s, the cleaner had to be turned over to attach part no. 4 to deflect the airflow from the floor to the end of the hose. (This is reprinted by arrangement with Sears, Roebuck and Co. and is protected under copyright. No duplication is permitted.)

the loss of the beater effect for embedded particles. In the 1950s high-pile carpeting became popular, but most housekeepers also wanted to vacuum wood and linoleum floors. Manufacturers came out with adjustable heights and multiple-speed machines, again without universal success. Weight and noise continue to be problems. Cleaning carpeted stairs or automobile interiors requires handheld vacuums or the bother of converting an upright vacuum to a hose by attachments. Big cleanups for garages and workshops brought various "shop-vacs" to the market, including some "wet-dry" models that could suck up basement flooding and other liquid spills. Many homeowners find that there is no universal household vacuum, and buy two or more machines for different tasks.

Two trends at the end of the twentieth century reach back to the very earliest practices. One trend is to hire commercial cleaners with high-powered machines with the suction unit on a truck. A second trend is to build homes with a central suction unit and wall inlets for moving hoses from room to room. For portability, cordless machines will probably replace all long cords, while robotic vacuum cleaners that were experimental gadgets in the 1980s and 1990s came out in 2000 as commercial machines that may do much to end some of the drudgery of house cleaning.

REFERENCE

Lifshey, Earl. *The Housewares Story.* Chicago: National Housewares Manufacturers Association, 1973.

Vending Machines

Vending machines dispense various products, services, and entertainments in exchange for currency in the form of coins, paper bills, tokens, or electronic credit. Some of the most common products are soft drinks and packaged snacks. Services include such things as coin-operated automatic **washing machines, copiers,** and coin and bill changers. Entertainment vending is found in **juke-boxes, video game** arcades, and gambling devices (see also **Motion Pictures** for a discussion of the nickelodeon). The commercial idea behind vending machines is to facilitate sales without having to provide a sales attendant, although repairs, regular maintenance, and collecting the revenue are essential. The trade-off for customers is primarily convenience, and a key to commercial success is the placement of vending machines where large numbers of people pass by but do not linger, such as in lobbies, corridors, subway platforms, and gas stations. The products are usually cheap, so high volume is needed.

This "silent salesman" who cheerfully took in pennies from the passing parade was a natural commercial invention. The essential underlying technology was the production of coins of consistent size and weight, not fully achieved until the Industrial Revolution of the late eighteenth century. The basic physics underlying most product-vending machines is gravity. A coin is dropped via a slot or slide into a secure till box, and on the way triggers a mechanical lever or electrical contact to release the product into a delivery bin or cup. The actual release may be automatic or may require that the customer pull a lever.

GUM BALL MACHINES

The simplest form of vendor is entirely mechanical and can still be found in small vending machines dispensing peanuts or gum balls. The product is visible; a coin inserted in a slot allows the customer to turn a handle that opens and closes a door, allowing a premeasured amount to drop into a bin. The customer opens the bin and the product drops into his or her hand. Invented by H.S. Mills and introduced to the public in 1901 at the Pan American Exposition in Buffalo, these machines are often used to collect small change for charity, under the sponsorship of various service clubs. Surprisingly, this charitable practice is virtually as old as the invention of coin-operated vending machines. The first vending machines in France were introduced in 1889 by the Society of the Stores for the Blind, dispensing chocolates and bonbons in railway stations along the route from Paris to Marseilles. They were instantly popular. Several patents in that decade for vending machines were issued in Europe and America; the first success that established the industry in the United States was in 1888 when Thomas Adams installed machines at stations of the New York elevated trains to sell his "tutti-frutti" chewing gum. Adams' name continued to appear on a number of gum flavors (especially clove and licorice-flavored Black Jack) through most of the twentieth century as brands of the American Chicle Company. His great rival was William Wrigley, whose Spearmint, Doublemint, and Juicy Fruit were some of the most heavily advertised commodities of the century. Candy and gum continue to be mainstays of the vending business, rivaled later only by soft drinks.

BEVERAGE DISPENSERS

France also led in the dispensing of beverages. In the 1890s "fountains" for wine, beer, and coffee were popular in several French cities. America's pioneers were the brothers H.S. and Bert Mills of Chicago, who around 1906 introduced a ten-selection soda pop dispenser. Ten five-gallon bottles were mounted in a row. The operator put cracked ice on top of the bottles each morning, but by afternoon the pop was lukewarm. Glasses were provided, and reused—water tanks were provided to rinse the glass before drawing a premeasured drink from a tube. Sanitation was an issue, and this led to the invention of disposable cups in 1908, first as a penny-a-cup drink of water. A few years later, vending of empty cups for use with pop machines was introduced; the company was destined to become the Dixie Cup Company. Early machines were limited to a single product, so the 1926 Sodamat at Coney Island had a bank of separate machines for each flavor and for cups. In 1934 Leslie Arnett introduced his "self-contained" soda machine to include both beverage and cup. The problem of refrigeration in soda machines was not solved until the 1940s (about the same time that heaters were installed for hot drinks).

SLUGS AND STAMPS

Other challenges faced the industry, especially slugs (counterfeit coins). In 1908 the U.S. Post Office tested two dozen postage stamp vendors (already common in Great Britain), but rejected most as unreliable, and ultimately rejected all of them for not being slugproof. The solution should have been fairly simple as U.S. coins contain no iron and slugs could be drawn off by magnets. However, practical slug rejectors appear not to have been installed until the 1930s. Slugs were declared illegal by federal law in 1944.

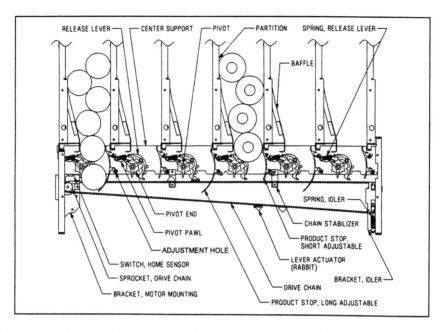

RELEASE LEVER — CENTER SUPPORT — PIVOT — PARTITION   SPRING, RELEASE LEVER

BAFFLE

PIVOT END

PIVOT PAWL

ADJUSTMENT HOLE

SWITCH, HOME SENSOR

SPROCKET, DRIVE CHAIN

BRACKET, MOTOR MOUNTING

SPRING, IDLER

CHAIN STABILIZER

PRODUCT STOP,
SHORT ADJUSTABLE

LEVER ACTUATOR
(RABBIT)

BRACKET, IDLER

DRIVE CHAIN

PRODUCT STOP, LONG ADJUSTABLE

Soda pop vending machines are complex electronic systems. This 2001 Royal Vendors model includes features to compare the credit (such as coins or bills) with the price of the items in each column; prevent people from using the dispenser as a change-maker; frustrate vandals; maintain even refrigeration; communicate sales messages in different languages, including Portuguese and Slovenian; and communicate errors in its own operation to owners. This diagram shows how the delivery system is basically mechanical as a drive chain carries a "rabbit" that triggers a spring lever to release a can or bottle by old-fashioned gravity. (Courtesy Royal Vendors)

Nevertheless, vending machine manufacturers pursued the postage market. The first practical postage stamp machine was invented by Joseph J. Schermack of Freeport, Illinois. His was also the first to be used for profit. A nickel would deliver either four one-cent or two two-cent stamps, and thus the vending machine owners could pocket a 20 percent profit. This was too good to pass on, so in 1926 Schermack set up a company to install and service stamp vendors. Two years later he merged with several other vending machine firms, the new Consolidated Automatic Merchandising Corporation boasted 36,000 penny weighing machines, 30,000 stamp machines, and 25,000 nut vendors. The company also moved into cigarette vending machines, in 1929 introducing "talking" machines that thanked each purchaser.

Sanitary drinking cups and counterfeit coins were not the only controversies. When cigarette vending machines first came out in 1925 the issue was money. One of several inventors, William Rowe of Los Angeles, proposed to sell the cigarettes at fifteen cents a pack. Operators objected. Not only was this four or five cents more than smokers paid at a store counter, but it was the first departure from penny and nickel vending. Rowe argued that convenience would justify the higher price to consumers. He was right, and by mid-century, cigarettes joined gum, candy, and soda as the big moneymakers in vending. In the last two decades of the century, however, the easy accessibility of the machines to underage smokers led to local, state, and federal restrictions that put a virtual end to these coin machines in the United States.

A similar health issue of the 1990s affected soda and candy machines. School boards and administrators had found that installing vending machines in school buildings was highly profitable, and if they played off one vendor against another in selling them exclusive rights (for example, Coca-Cola and Pepsi-Cola), the profits were even more attractive. One Ohio school district in 1999 negotiated a 10-year contract with Pepsi-Cola for $700,000. Over 20,000 school districts in the late 1990s generated $750 million annually for the vending companies. The health issue is that sodas and chips have little or no nutritional value, and students were bypassing wholesome cafeteria fare for junk food and drink. Federal, state, and local regulations attempt to control the trend, but not very successfully. Technology comes into play as well, with some schools installing timers to shut off the machines during lunch hours. (This has also been done to curfew beer machines in Europe.)

Another socioeconomic trend of the century that spurred inventions is inflation. Pennies and nickels could purchase a good deal through the 1940s: not just the major vending products, but parking meters, jukeboxes, pinball machines, pay phones, and locks to public toilets (patented in 1909 as Nik-O-Lok by Dr. Emil Luden). But monetary inflation was soon to make dimes, then quarters, the necessary coins. By 1960 machines that could change a paper dollar into quarters were in laundromats and near other vending machines. By 1990 vending machines that took dollar bills directly became common. From 1971 to 1981 dollar coins were minted, very much because of the vending machine industry. Neither the Eisenhower nor Susan B. Anthony coin took the public's fancy and the U.S. Treasury didn't reintroduce dollar coins until 2000.

The technology of coin-operated vending machines has kept pace with advances in electronics, primarily striving for trouble-free performance. From the earliest times, customers have been moved to frustrated rage with vendors that don't deliver the goods, and machines have had to be sturdy enough to withstand angry fists and feet—at some peril, as there have been fatalities from angered customers being crushed by top-heavy soda machines. Having to cart away a heavy machine for repairs means a total loss in revenue, so now machines are made with easily replaceable components. Greater choice among products has produced such marvels as beverage machines that dispense coffee and tea, with buttons to select hot or iced, decaffeinated or regular coffee, the strength of the brew, the amount of sweetener, whitener, or lemon.

Since the 1980s one popular cafeteria-style vending machine has an array of vertically stacked carousels of individual compartments, each compartment containing an apple, yogurt, slice of pie, microwavable sandwiches or soup, etc. The proper coinage activates a button that activates a motor that advances the appropriate carousel forward to expose the product to an accessible door. The machine is all automated, but otherwise resembles the famous Horn & Hardart Automat that opened in Philadelphia in 1902 (patterned after German models). These restaurants had a wall of cupboards with coin-activated locks on the doors. Live attendants were behind the scenes to restock immediately. (The last Automat, in Manhattan, closed in 1991.) In 2000, frozen-food entrepreneur Jeno Paulucci brought out a vending machine for office buildings that dispenses prepared frozen dinners for workers to take home and microwave for a "home-cooked" meal, having been saved the trouble of stopping at a deli, convenience store, or supermarket.

The sheer variety of vending products and services at the dawn of the twenty-first century probably is as sure a guide to the future as any. Casino gamblers do not have to drop a coin in a slot machine; they simply insert a plastic "stored value" card. This same device has eliminated coin slots at subway turnstiles (see **Barcodes and Magnetic Stripes**). Credit-card-operated pumps dispense gasoline at self-service fuel stations. Blue jeans have been dispensed by vending machines in France (with a belt to measure the customer's girth). Sunkist peeled citrus fruits come from a machine that reads a barcode to reject products with expired dates. Some Japanese vending machines are solar-powered. Denmark, Germany, and France provide vendors of syringes and needles for drug addicts. And in 1993 the "Gumball Gizmo" was introduced in Salt Lake City, initiating a whole new twist on the oldest of vending products in America, with "entertainment vending" machines that send a gum ball into a psychedelic frenzy of chutes and rides before the gum comes home to roost.

REFERENCES

How to Start a Coin-Operated Vending Business. Entrepreneur Business Guide #1375. Irvine, CA, 1993.

Schreiber, G.R. "A Concise History of Vending in America." *Vend* (Magazine of the Vending Industry), 1961.

Vail, Kathleen. "Insert Coins in a Slot; School Vending Machines Generate Funds—and Controversy." *American School Board Journal*, February 1999, 28–31.

Zorn, Robert L. "The Great Cola Wars; How One District Profits from the Competition for Vending Machines." *American School Board Journal*, February 1999, 31–33.

Video Games and Computer Games

Video games and computers have an intertwined history and are based on the same basic enabling technology, the microprocessor. However, they entered homes through quite different routes—the home video game system came in from video arcades (previously home of pinball machines), while for many the computer came into the home from school or the office.

PINBALL ARCADES

The most familiar electrified arcade game for much of the twentieth century was the pinball machine. This electromechanical machine dates from the 1930s, replacing mechanical machines that go all the way back to eighteenth-century France. An arcade pinball machine was a coin-operated entertainment machine, so no attendant was required. When pinball was electrified, steel balls replaced marbles. In a typical machine, the player pulls back on a plunger to launch a ball up an inclined playing field (sealed under glass). The ball then rolls down the field, hitting various bumpers and scoring devices as it descends. The player can operate at least two paddles near the bottom of the field, launching the ball back up the field. If the player misses, the ball disappears into a hole at the bottom of the field. A running score is automatically tabulated by the game machine. If the player achieves a sufficiently high score, free additional game play is awarded— more balls are released. In the 1940s more lights and bells were added, not to mention electrically operated flippers, and the machine became a noisy interactive game environment, involving tense excitement.

VIDEO GAMES

Compared with the very real progress of a steel ball down a field in their pinball machine ancestors, video and computer games produce virtual realities—electronically produced images of a scene or situation. Video games require a video display—and so depend upon the display technology developed for

television. The first simple computer games did not require video displays—they could be played on a teletype machine. Examples of very early computer games include "Moo," "Hunt the Wumpus," and "Colossal Cave Adventure"—the first text-based adventure game. One of the first computers to use a cathode ray tube display for the control console was the DEC PDP-1. In 1962, MIT student Steve Russell and friends created Spacewar, a space battle game played on the mainframe computer. By the 1970s, video terminals became widely used with computers, and computer-based games with a graphic display became much more widely available. Still, these games required access to a large and expensive (around $100,000 and up) computer—access that very few people had.

The first game to use a video display is attributed to pinball enthusiast William A. Higinbotham, who used an oscilloscope and analog circuits to make "Tennis for Two" for display at an open house at Brookhaven National Laboratories in 1958. Then in 1966–1967 engineer Ralph Baer became interested in using a television as the basis for interactive game play. He designed a game that used movable lines ("paddles") and a square "ball," played something like tennis. Baer and associates filed for the first videogame patent in 1968. By 1971 Baer's technology was sold to Magnavox Corporation, which began work on the first home video game system, the Magnavox Odyssey.

Also in 1971, one of the best-known pioneers of the video game industry, Nolan Bushnell (1943–), just three years out of college, began building an arcade machine to adapt the game Spacewar that he had seen while he was a student using the computer at the University of Utah. Bushnell left Ampex corporation (see **Audio Recording**) to develop his "Computer Space" machine at Nutting Associates. Soon he formed his own company, which he named Atari, after a board configuration in the ancient Chinese and Japanese game Go. Atari's better-known next product was Pong. Pong machines were produced in several forms, including a glass-topped-cocktail-table version for use in bars (the video display faced up to be visible through the tinted-glass-tabletop).

Early home video machines connected to a TV and played Pong or a few minor variants, selected by a switch. Graphics were extremely simple, formed from blocky square shapes. In 1976, the Fairchild Camera and Instrument Company, an early producer of integrated circuits, released the first home game machine to put the games on removable cartridges, the Fairchild F system. This machine was followed in 1977 by the Atari VCS (later 2600), an enormously popular cartridge-based home video machine. The Atari VCS had joystick controllers and paddle controllers connected to the console with cables. Games were in plastic cartridges that housed a read only memory (ROM) integrated circuit chip on a small circuit board. Popular games of this time were Space Invaders (Taito 1978, Midway importer) and Lunar Lander, the first vector graphics game (1979).

Video games were enormously popular in the late 1970s and early 1980s. In 1981 Nintendo introduced Donkey Kong (the character Mario was named after a landlord of some of the designers), and the U.S. video arcade industry reached peak revenues. Many game producers were attracted to the booming business and a glut

Video game systems brought the arcade into the home in the 1980s. (Courtesy of Corbis)

of low-quality games followed. The video game industry suffered a collapse in 1983–1984. Toy makers Mattel and Coleco abandoned their game machines.

At this time (July 1983), a Japanese playing-card maker founded in 1889, Nintendo, introduced its "Famcom" ("family computer") in Japan. Soon, despite reluctant retailers, it was successfully marketed in the United States and by 1986 Nintendo was outselling its video game competitors 10 to 1.

The machines produced in this period used 8-bit processors. Second-generation machines, such as the Super Nintendo and Sega Genesis, used 16-bit processors; 64-bit processors were introduced in the mid-1990s. By the end of the century, the home video game industry was dominated by the Nintendo 64 (cartridge based) and the Sony Playstation (CD-ROM based), with the Sega Saturn a very distant third. The systems cost less than $150. The handheld, battery-operated video game was dominated by the Nintendo Gameboy, which finally got a color LCD display in 1998. Tiger Electronics made a host of dedicated handheld game machines.

COMPUTER GAMES

Computer games developed in complexity along with the evolution of computer technology, especially storage devices, processor speed, and display. Some early home computers used a television set for display, severely limiting resolution. Early successful computer games were the series of text-based adventure games descended from Colossal Cave Adventure (especially Zork and other game series from Infocom), platform games such as Lode Runner, and arcade adaptations such as Frogger. In addition, there were role playing games, such as the Ultima series. As computer graphics displays improved, adventures moved from text to graphics—a leading producer was Sierra On-Line, with its Kings Quest series. A shareware game, Wolfenstein 3-D, introduced the "first-person perspective" to a shoot-'em-up game. This game play was greatly refined in the enormously influential follow-up, Doom. By the end of the millennium, many computer games fell into several main categories, including: successors of Doom, flight and racing-action simulations, world-building simulations (e.g., Simcity, Civilization, Age of Empires), hand-to-hand combat games, graphic adventure games (many from LucasArts), simulations of card games and board games (e.g., Monopoly), and simulations of sports, including team sports and hunting.

Video game systems are special-purpose computers. They share their main functional parts with computers, with differences that reflect their purposes:

Input. The most popular input devices for video game systems are handheld plastic control pads with a few easily accessed buttons. Some controllers include small joysticks and tactile feedback ("rumble packs"). Light guns have had limited use. By contrast, computer input devices are usually a full keyboard resting on the desktop, and a mouse for moving a cursor or pointer around on the screen. Game pads are available for computers as well, to play computer games.

Processor. A computer chip that controls the game, using information from the player's controllers, the processor also requires fast short-term memory (RAM) in which to store the data it processes. Processors run at "clock" speed; the faster the clock speed, the more operations per second the processor can perform, and so the more complex can be the game it runs. Processors are also described in terms of how many bits they can process at a time, and this increased from the first 8-bit to century's-end 64-bit systems. Video game systems typically have much less RAM (up to a few megs) than do personal computers (10 times as much, or even more).

Game data storage. The two most popular storage media have been CD-ROM (e.g., Sony Playstation) and cartridge (Nintendo) systems. The CD-ROM has the advantage of lower production cost and greater storage capacity. But CD-ROMs can be copied more easily than cartridges, and are slower to load data into the processor's memory (resulting in pauses during the game).

Video output. Both videogame systems and computers need special circuitry to produce the image, whether it is displayed on a television or a computer monitor. Early video games connected to the antenna input on a TV. More recent video games use more direct input ("composite video") for a more detailed (higher-resolution) image. By contrast, to display small text clearly, computers have used a much higher resolution signal that keeps the red, green, and blue (RGB) color signals separate, and special "computer monitors." Current televisions are poorly suited for display of fine text, but work well for video games designed for them.

On the other hand, computer displays work very well as game displays, but typically have a smaller viewing area and are more expensive than televisions. Video game systems, like most computers, also have separate sound output circuitry, and may contain an electronic music synthesizer (see **Electronic Musical Instruments**). While video game systems control only a television set used as a video display, home computers typically connect to a variety of peripherals, including printers, modems, and scanners.

Data Storage. An important difference between video game systems and home computers lies in data storage. Computers have devices for recording large amounts of data (e.g., floppy drives, hard drives, CD recorders). These add significantly to the system cost. Twentieth-century video game systems lacked these but most used small-capacity "memory cards" to store game positions ("saved games").

Finally, computer systems are often built to be expandable, using a large case into which additional components can be installed, and a large power supply with a cooling fan. Again, these increase the cost difference between computers and video game systems.

Game Design

In a sense, all video and computer games are simulations. But the games come in a few main types or genres:

Platform games (e.g., Mario). Players manipulate a character through a scrolling scene, leaping over hazards, dealing with bad guys. By the end of the century these games were largely replaced by 3D role-playing games.

Simulations (of some specific activity, such as flying and driving, even sailing, business, stock market transactions).

Sports and board games, a subcategory of simulation of sports and games, such as football, chess, solitaire, Monopoly. An important subcategory of the simulation games are the fighting games, where players manipulate characters in hand-to-hand combat (e.g., the Street Fighter series).

Adventure games, which evolved from the early text-based computer games into graphic adventures. These have a complicated story line, exploration of a large virtual world, emphasis on puzzle solving rather than on fighting and precise timing.

Role playing and 3D "shooters," which are similar to graphic adventures in their emphasis on a quest through an elaborate virtual world, except the focus is on fighting (often monsters), not puzzle solving. Timing and dexterity are important game elements.

Strategy games, including war games. Players control multiple characters on a map, often in a top-down view. These games are often multiplayer; the goal is typically to control territory.

Of course, every possible hybrid of these basic types has been explored. In their software design, computer and video games typically share these core elements: a program (determining game play), art, and music and sound. The art includes the background scenery, usually scrollable (it appears to continue beyond the current screen view). Animated characters move against this background. Games with complex worlds have maps linking one scene with another. Computer-controlled characters require scripts, subprograms that determine how the character, a monster say, will behave. 3D games are the most complex, as both the background scenery and the characters must allow being viewed from many possible positions. The computer must then generate this image, rather than just use a prerecorded background image. In this case, characters are no longer simple 2D "sprites," but are programmed as a complex polygonal skeleton (the computer calculates how that shape should appear at any time from the player's perspective), covered with a skin, a textured surface that fills in and conceals the underlying polygonal structure.

INTERNET AND 3D GAMES

An exciting late-twentieth-century development in gaming was networked games, where players were each at their own computer, and the computers were linked to each other by a local network or the Internet. Players then controlled characters that appeared in each other's rendering of the shared virtual world. In addition, genuine 3D was introduced into computer games using goggles with LCD shutters—these goggles could display one screen to the player's left eye, then block vision in that eye while the right eye viewed the scene; in that way, slightly different views were presented to the player's two eyes, creating a true depth effect. In addition, surround sound, using front and rear speakers, has been used to make video games more immersive.

In general, game research has concentrated on improved graphics, with more detail and lighting effects. These are made possible by 3D graphics accelerator chips and ever larger amounts of high-speed RAM memory dedicated to video. At the end of the twentieth century, the highly specialized graphics chip companies, such as 3dfx and Nvidia, were introducing two generations of chip a year. Game play enhancements, in addition to the crucial Internet connectivity, included better artificial intelligence for the computer-generated characters.

New generations of video game systems are introduced every few years. Each new generation brings increased processing power and video display capability. Most likely future video game improvements include a move from CD-ROM to DVD as a storage medium. As television sets convert to digital, video game systems will be able to take advantage of the much needed higher-resolution images that will be possible. The difference between TV and computer monitor will disappear. Nintendo introduced a 3D system, VirtualBoy, in 1995; it had several limitations (a reddish monochrome display, single player's head confined to looking into a goggle-like display), and the system was not a commercial success. However, if limitations can be overcome at reasonable cost, 3D gaming may be part of the future of home video gaming.

Game content has centered on 3D action shoot-'em-ups (descendents of Doom), road racing and flight simulations, and hand-to-hand fighting games. Many of these share core content with other entertainment media, such as movies. But many popular movie and book content areas have not been as popular in video games: romance and mysteries are two examples. This may well change in the future as more women become involved in microprocessor-based gaming.

REFERENCES

Hayes, Michael. *Games War: Video Games—A Business Review.* London: Bowerdean Publishing Co., 1996.

Herman, Leonard. *Phoenix: The Fall & Rise of Home Videogames.* Springfield, NJ: Rolenta Press, 1997.

Herz, J.C. *Joystick Nation: How Videogames Ate Our Quarters, Won Our Hearts, and Rewired Our Minds.* Boston: Little, Brown & Company, 1997.

Katz, Arnie, and Laurie Yatges. *Inside Electronic Game Design.* Roseville, CA: Prima Publishing, 1995.

Levy, Stephen. *Insanely Great: The Life and Times of Macintosh, the Computer That Changed Everything.* New York: Penguin Books, 1995.

Veit, Stan, ed. *Stan Veit's History of the Personal Computer.* Alexander, NC: Worldcomm Press, 1993.

Washing Machines and Dryers

Washing clothing and linens has long been done by hand—and it has been long, hard work, since most cloth items require agitation in water, which must be fetched and heated, and cloth often requires scrubbing, wringing, and pounding. Alternatively, cloth could be boiled and stirred in a washtub on a wood stove. Soap, made from animal fat, aided in removal of oily dirt. Utensils such as washboards have been around a long time, but hand-operated mechanical washing machines, wooden bins with crank-driven paddles to move the cloth around, did not appear until the mid-nineteenth century. And even with such devices, washing was still long, hard work.

MACHINES THAT WASH

Real change did not come until the twentieth century. The first innovation was to add an electric motor to handle the hardest parts of the work. The first electric washing machines were produced by Americans. Alva J. Fisher made an electric washer in 1906, and received the first electric washer patent on August 9, 1910. The resulting "Thor" electric washer was produced by the Hurley Machine Company of Chicago. A year later, in 1911, another electric machine was produced by Lou Upton and his uncle Emory. Lou had a patent on a manual washing machine, and Emory ran a machine shop. Their company was an ancestor of Whirlpool Corporation, now a major appliance manufacturer. Also in 1911, F.L. Maytag first produced an electric washing machine at his factory in Newton, Iowa (originally Maytag made farm machinery). In 1915 Maytag introduced the Multi-Motor, a gasoline-engine-powered washing machine for the many homes that did not yet have electricity.

Development was very rapid—by 1920 more than 1,300 companies were producing washing machines! Although many designs were tried, in the first half of the twentieth century washing machine design converged on wringer washers. In these machines, an electric motor provided power to agitate clothes in a tub. The operator could manually control the filling and emptying of the water in the tub. After the clothes were washed (and again after they were rinsed), a gear or clutch was shifted by the operator, and the motor now powered the wringer. The wringer

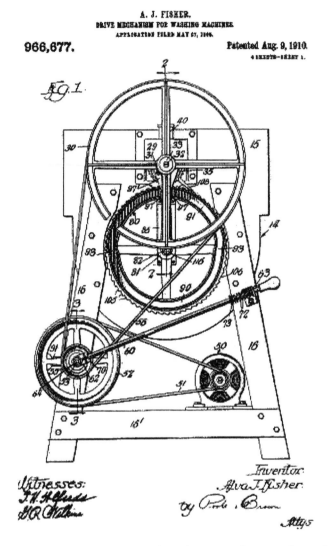

A. J. FISHER.
DRIVE MECHANISM FOR WASHING MACHINES.
APPLICATION FILED MAY 27, 1906.

966,677.   Patented Aug. 9, 1910.

Alva Fisher's 1906 patent drawing for the first electric washing machine, the Thor, made by Hurley Machine Company, Chicago. The next big breakthrough was the fully automatic washer, which was introduced by Bendix in 1937, but not widely available until after World War II.

was supported above the level of the washing tub, and consisted of two slowly turning rollers held against each other by powerful springs. The wash was fed by hand, one piece at a time, between the two rollers, which squeezed the water out. The process was repeated again for the rinse. Several loads of wash might be done using the same tubful of soapy water. It was standard to have a single day of the week set aside for laundry chores, often Monday. Although a motor did some of the work, doing laundry was still a long process.

AUTOMATIC WASHERS

The solution was to automate the process, and, as is often the case, the process had to be modified for that to be possible. Bendix introduced the first automatic washer in 1937 at the Louisiana State Fair. Westinghouse followed with its "Laundromat" in 1940. However, with washing machine production halted during World War II, it was not until the late 1940s that automated vertical-tub washing machines came to be produced on a large scale. (And even then, Maytag continued to produce nonautomatic wringer washers until 1983.) Whirlpool's automatic washer, sold through Sears, was introduced in 1947, and Maytag's in 1948. The automatic washer was a huge success. A Bendix ad in the 1938 *Saturday Evening Post* proclaimed: "The Successor to the Washing Machine. No Backache . . . No Wet Hands . . . No Muss."

Two innovations changed the electrically powered wringer washing machine into the automatic clothes washer. First, a timer, turned by a clock motor, was introduced to step the washer through a series of stages in the washing process (a "cycle"). In addition, the motor powering the washing machine was generally made reversible. Electric solenoids (a coil that becomes a powerful electromagnet when current is applied) were added to provide electric control of the transmission, pump, and water inlet valves of the washing machine.

Second, part of the process of washing was itself changed: the wringer method of extracting water from clothes was replaced by centrifugal extraction—an inner perforated tub that could be spun at (relatively) high speed was added just inside the water-holding washtub. (A nonautomatic machine with spin dry had been produced much earlier, by the Horton Manufacturing Company of Cleveland, Ohio; it featured a tall copper tub, and the operator pressed a foot pedal to lift and support the inner basket completely above the wash water for the spin dry.)

In the automatic washer from the 1940s on, as the wet wash was spun around in the perforated inner tub, centrifugal force pushed water out of the wash through the holes in the wall of the perforated inner tub, and from there onto the walls of the stationary outer tub. A pump sent the water down the drain. The wet wash was often unbalanced in the spinning drum, and to prevent the machine from "walking" across the floor, these early automatic washing machines needed to be bolted to the floor. Various flexible suspension systems were introduced, and eventually the problem of vibration from unbalanced spin was solved.

These two core innovations—spin dry and timer-controlled mechanisms— made possible an automated washer that could wash, rinse, and damp-dry cloth goods without the operator doing any work or even being present, after the machine was loaded and turned on.

A typical vertical-tub automatic washer from the 1950s on holds about 10–15 pounds (dry) of washing. The washer consists of an outer box-shaped sheet metal case. A hinged metal door in the top provides access to the inner washtub. A raised control panel sits on top of the machine at the back. Inside the case is an outer tub that is suspended to permit limited movement of the tub assembly from side to side as the wash is agitated and spun. This outer tub does not rotate. Immediately inside the outer tub is an inner perforated tub that can rotate. In the middle of the inner tub rises the agitator, a shaft with a few large fins. Beneath the outer tub are three main components: the motor (often one-half horsepower), the solenoid-operated transmission (with gears), and the pump. The other smaller components elsewhere in the case are the solenoid-operated water inlet valves (one for the hot-water line, one for the cold) and a fill switch that detects when the tub has filled with water to the selected level. The remaining components are the switches and timer inside the raised control panel atop the main case.

The typical automatic washing cycle includes the following phases: open fill valves until level detector shuts the water off; start motor, with transmission set to move the agitator back and forth slowly for duration of wash portion of cycle (about ten minutes); stop agitation and pump out water; spin inner tub to remove sudsy water from the contents of the tub; fill tub with water again for rinse portion of cycle; start motor again to power agitator; pump out; and finally, several minutes of spin to partly dry washing.

It is simplest and standard to provide three water temperatures: "hot" (only hot water valve opens), "cold" (only cold water valve opens), and "warm" (both water inlet valves open). Some automatic washers can add rinse additives ("fabric softener") during the rinse cycle. And some have multiple fill levels and a two-speed motor (allowing a "gentle" cycle). For a time, some manufacturers offered "suds saver" options that would pump the wash water out into a separate holding tub, and then back in again for reuse in a second wash load. Affluence largely killed suds saving.

Top-loading washers have been most common in the United States, but front-loading models are made as well. These are more popular outside the United States, but were gaining in popularity in the United States at the end of the twentieth century. Front loaders typically have a similar outer case, but with a front-mounted round door with a glass window. Washing is in a horizontal inner drum. The advantage of the front loader is that it uses less water and energy (the main cost of washing is the energy used to heat the wash water). The main disadvantages are that the capacity is typically smaller than that of a top loader, initial cost is higher, and one must stoop to load and unload. Some front loaders required special low-sudsing detergent.

Essential to modern washers are synthetic detergents (see also **Cleaning Products**). The first synthetic detergent in the United States was Dreft, introduced by soap (and, formerly, candle) maker Procter & Gamble in 1933. It took over ten years to develop a heavy-duty synthetic detergent, and immediately after World War II P&G introduced Tide. Synthetic detergents work better than soaps in hard water, and in lower water temperatures. They quickly displaced soap powder for laundry. In addition, chlorine bleach was a common laundry chemical. Some detergents added enzymes, but widespread concern about skin reactions caused enzyme use to be greatly reduced. In addition, ecological concern forced detergent manufacturers to reduce use of their main surfactants, which were phosphate based. By the end of the century satisfactory alternatives to phosphates had been developed.

A washer and dryer of the design popular in American homes after World War II. The top-loading automatic washer (left) contains a large round tub open at the top. A motor agitates the clothing in the water-filled tub, and can drive a pump to empty the tub. When the tub is empty, the motor spins the tub at high speed to extract water from the clothes. The dryer (right) is simpler internally. A fan blows air through an electric or gas heater and into a large drum. The clothes tumble through the hot air as the horizontal drum rotates. Each machine has a small timer to control its cycles. (Courtesy of Corbis)

DRYERS

Sun and fresh air have dried clothing (and the skin beneath it) since life began. The clothesline is a rope from which clothing could be suspended to dry, using clothespins. Even in tall buildings, lines could be run from one building to another, and using pulleys, a wash could be hung to dry from a fifth-floor balcony or window. At mid-century, clotheslines were a fixture in backyards across America.

Inside the house, drying on a small scale had been carried out near the sources of domestic heating—on a rack near the fireplace, kitchen stove, or furnace in the basement. In the first decades of the twentieth century, some large homes were built with drying rooms near the central heating boilers. These rooms had racks of pipes connected to the domestic heating source (steam or hot water) from which the wash could be hung to dry.

By the second half of the century, as incomes rose and women entered the workplace, dryer machines became common. Whirlpool introduced an automatic dryer in 1950, Maytag in 1953. These appliances are about the same size as automatic washers, and usually come in matching models from the same manufacturers. The standard design has a large rotating drum with a horizontal axis. As the drum rotates, the clothes tumble around inside, and heated air is blown through the drum. Access is through a door in the front of the cabinet (unlike the most common American washer, which is top loading).

A dryer is simpler than a washer, and usually costs less. The main internal parts of the dryer are a timer, the large metal drum inside which the clothes tumble, the motor, a blower (often mounted at the end of the motor shaft), a belt to transfer power to the drum (many use a long belt that goes around the outside of the drum), and a heater to heat the air going into the drum. The incoming air is heated by one of two methods: a simple electric heater consisting of coiled nichrome wire, or an electrically ignited gas flame. Gas dryers are more expensive initially, but cost significantly less to operate.

Dryers also have a simple screen lint filter. The moist exhaust air from dryers is usually vented outside. Since a dryer does only one thing—tumble clothes in heated air—basic controls are just a timer and a temperature selector. Some models have "automatic" settings. The simplest form cuts the dryer off when the temperature of the exhaust air rises above a certain point (it rises after sufficient moisture has been removed from the drying load). "Sensor" controls use moisture sensors to detect the moisture in the exhaust air. These sensing controls help prevent under- and overdrying (and resulting energy waste).

Combination front-loading washer-dryers were manufactured, partly to save space. But in the United States, unlike Europe, they were not very successful. Most American buyers opted for side-by-side separate washer and dryer, and for space-critical applications (such as mobile homes) combination units were displaced by stacking washer-dryers (a separate compact dryer is stacked above the washer).

LAUNDROMATS

The introduction of automatic washers and dryers led to the Laundromat, a commercial laundry that consisted entirely of coin-operated washers and dryers. The first Laundromat, a "Washateria," opened in Fort Worth, Texas, in April 1934. A Laundromat can operate long hours with minimal oversight. In addition, coin-operated washers and dryers appeared in apartment houses and dormitories. Laundromat washers are usually essentially the same as domestic models, though some have "commercial" dryers that are gas dryers that are substantially larger and faster than home dryers.

With the introduction of domestic automatic washers and dryers and the Laundromat, the commercial neighborhood laundry—and the laundress in domestic service—all but disappeared over the course of the twentieth century. On the face of it, the automatic washer and dryer save considerable time. But whether they have or not turns out to be controversial: sociologist Ruth Cowan, in her 1983 book *More Work for Mother: The Ironies of Household Technology from Open Hearth to Microwave*, has set out an interesting argument that domestic laundry equipment actually increased the time spent on housework. However, it appears that some of the data Cowan relied on (from the 1930s) reported use of appliances that were not automatic. The slogan of one early washing machine manufacturer, "Saving Women's Lives," may be warranted after all.

Washer design is interesting because there has been ongoing competition between the front- and top-loading approaches. But the basic technology (fill, agitate, pump out, spin) is the same in both designs. Controls are increasingly electronic, and various innovations appear possible, including washers that automatically detect how dirty clothes are and adjust the cycle and detergent use accordingly (similar control was available in some automatic dishwashers by the end of the twentieth century). It is also possible to have electronic fabric care tags on clothing that communicate directly with the washer (see **Barcodes and Magnetic Stripes** for a discussion of machine-readable codes). Other technologies that have been applied to cleaning include ultrasonic cleaners. These cleaners, used for small parts since the middle of the century, do not have a mechanical agitator but instead use an ultrasonic transducer to cause the cleaning solution to dislodge dirt. However, the predominant type of washer and dryer technology matured by the middle of the twentieth century and has seen small refinements since then.

REFERENCES

Brooke, Sheena. *Hearth and Home: A Short History of Domestic Equipment.* London: Mills & Boon, 1973.

Cohen, Daniel. *The Last Hundred Years: Household Technology.* New York: M. Evans, 1982.

Cowan, Ruth. *More Work for Mother: The Ironies of Household Technology from the Open Hearth to the Microwave.* New York: Basic Books, 1983.

De Haan, David. *Antique Household Gadgets and Appliances, c. 1860 to 1930.* Poole, England: Blandford Press, 1977.

Du Vall, Nell. *Domestic Technology.* Boston: G.K. Hall & Co., 1988.

Hardyment, Christina. *From Mangle to Microwave: The Mechanization of Household Work.* New York and Oxford: Blackwell Publishers, 1988.

————. *Home Comfort: A History of Domestic Arrangements.* Chicago: Academy Publishers, 1992.

Hoover, Robert, and John Hoover. *An American Quality Legend: How Maytag Saved Our Moms, Vexed the Competition, and Presaged America's Quality Revolution.* New York: McGraw-Hill, 1993.

Langley, Billy C. *Major Appliances: Operation, Maintenance, Troubleshooting and Repair.* Englewood Ciffs, NJ: Prentice-Hall, 1993.

Maxwell, Lee. "Olde Wash Site." *http://216.160.174.6/oldewash_docs/index.html* (Maxwell has a well-documented collection of over 700 washing machines.)

Sparke, Penny. *Electrical Appliances: Twentieth-Century Design.* New York: E.P. Dutton, 1987.

Strasser, Susan. *Never Done: A History of American Housework.* New York: Pantheon, 1982.

Time-Life Books Editors. *Major Appliances (How to Fix It, Vol. 2, No. 20)* New York: Time-Life Books, 1998.

Yarwood, Darleen. *Five Hundred Years of Technology in the Home.* London: B.T. Batsford, 1983.

Index

About the Authors

DAVID J. COLE is Head of the Department of Philosophy at the University of Minnesota, Duluth, where he teaches and writes articles on values and technology.

EVE BROWNING is Associate Professor of Philosophy at the University of Minnesota, Duluth.

FRED E.H. SCHROEDER is Professor Emeritus of Humanities at the University of Minnesota, Duluth. He specializes in popular culture topics.